NORDIC WARRIORS

*SS-Panzergrenadier-Regiment 24 Danmark,
Eastern Front, 1943-45*

RICHARD LANDWEHR
HOLGER THOR NIELSEN

Series Editor: J G Lewthwaite MA PhD (Cantab)
Editor: Robert A Ball BSc (Hons)

STAHLHELM SERIES 124

Published by SHELF BOOKS LTD,
HALIFAX, WEST YORKSHIRE, UK

SHELF BOOKS LTD ⓟ1999

16 Calderdale Business Park, Club Lane, Ovenden,
HALIFAX, West Yorkshire HX2 8DB
Tel: 01422 347766 Fax: 01422 347788
Email: enq@shelf.dircon.co.uk
Internet: http://www.shelf.dircon.co.uk

ISBN 1 899765 07 7
Printed in the UK

The cover art represents an SS-Sturmmann (Lance-Corporal) of the SS-Panzergrenadier Regiment 24 *Danmark* on the Eastern Front.

Front cover artwork and maps by Ramiro Bujeiro

> The Orders of Battle (Appendix C) and the section on Waffen-SS Ranks (Appendix D) were compiled by Robert Ball, who may be contacted through SHELF BOOKS LTD.

> All rights reserved. Apart from any fair dealing for the purpose of private study, research, criticism or review, as permitted under the Copyright Designs and Patents Act, 1988, no part of this publication may be reproduced, stored in a retrieval system, or transmitted in any form or by any means, electrical, chemical, mechanical, optical, photocopying, recording or otherwise, without prior permission of the copyright owner. Enquiries should be addressed to the publishers.

British Library Cataloging in Publication Data. A catalogue record for this book is available from the British Library.

SHELF BOOKS
<u>Stahlhelm Series: The History of the Armed Forces of the Third Reich</u>

Fifty years after the end of World War II in Europe, it is felt imperative that the English-speaking world comprehend the perspectives of those who fought on the other (losing) side, which to a great extent can only be appreciated by a familiarity with their unique experiences, particularly on the decisive Eastern Front.

Shelf Books therefore initiates <u>The Stahlhelm Series</u>, consisting of translations of primary sources - often eyewitness accounts by participants - and reprints of secondary literature, which have be come established as classics in their field.

Neither translations nor reprints have been edited in any way in order to bring the authors' perspectives and values into agreement with contemporary mainstream attitudes i.e. through deletion or euphemism. Each text is treated as an unique historical document redolent of its era. Given the temporal span between this and the date of publication, additional material has been added to assist the reader wherever it is felt necessary in such a way that it cannot be confused with the original text.

Publishing History

This volume is based on a previous work by the same author incorporating new information and a vastly expanded photographic section:

**Bibliophile Legion Books Inc
PO Box 612, Silver Spring
Maryland 20901-0612, USA**

Published 1990
ISBN 0 918184 02 9

The copyright has since reverted to the author:

© **Richard Landwehr
PO Box 6718, Brookings
OREGON 97415, USA**

This book is respectfully dedicated to the memory of

SS-Unterscharführer Holger Thor Nielsen

*7 Kompanie, II Bataillon
SS-Panzergrenadier-Regiment 24 Danmark*

***SS-Obergruppenführer und General der Waffen-SS* Felix Steiner**

Commander III (Germanische) SS-Panzerkorps

Contents

CONTENTS

Prelims		I-V
Preface		5
Chapters		
I	Activation of the III (Germanische) SS-Panzerkorps	7
II	The First Months	11
III	Croatia 1943	43
IV	The Oranienbaum Cauldron	63
	The Soviet Offensive	65
	Counterattack	66
	Withdrawal	68
V	The Retreat to Narva	76
VI	The Battle for Narva	86
VII	The Battle for the Tannenberg Positions	101
VIII	Defence of the Tannenberg Line	104
IX	Fighting for Destiny	109
X	Relocation to Latvia	117
XI	Kurland	123
	On the Kurland Front	123
	The Second Battle of Kurland	125
	Purmsāti	127
	The Third Battle of Kurland	129
	The Fourth Battle of Kurland	130
XII	Battles in Pomerania	138
	Attack on the Arnswalde Salient	139
	The Red Storm Breaks	141
	The Altdamm Bridgehead	145
XIII	Berlin	147
	To the East of Berlin	147
	The Final Cataclysm	150
	Last Battles	152

Appendices
- A   Awards and Decorations 161
  - Knight's Cross with Oakleaves (*Ritterkreuz mit Eichenlaub*) 161
  - Knight's Cross (*Ritterkreuz*) 161
  - German Cross in Gold (*Deutsches Kreuz in Gold*) 161
  - Honour Roll Clasp (*Ehrenblattspange*) 161
- B   Command Roster 162
- C   Orders of Battle 167
  - 11 SS-Freiwillige-Panzergrenadier-Division *Nordland* 167
  - SS-Panzergrenadier-Regiment 24 *Danmark* 169
- D   Waffen-SS Ranks 170
- E   Badges and Insignia 171
  - The National Emblem (*Hoheitsabzeichen*) 171
  - Cuff-Titles 171
  - Arm-shield 172
  - Collar Patches 172
  - Formation Signs 173
- F   Shelf Books General Translation Policy 174
- G   Estonian Pronunciation Guide 176
- H   Latvian Pronunciation Guide 178
- I   Gazetteer 181
- J   Glossary 182

Bibliography 184
Publisher's Acknowledgements 185
Index 186

Preface 5

PREFACE

As a young man in post-war Denmark, the schools taught me the 'official' story about Denmark's participation in the World War II. I was told how this peace-loving little nation was brutally attacked by Nazi Germany and how the Resistance - the so-called 'freedom fighters' - fought against the occupation during the five dark years, so that Denmark could at last win the war alongside her allies: Great Britain, the United States and the Soviet Union. The bad side was comprised of the evil Germans and a few Danish traitors who joined a criminal force known as the *Freikorps Danmark*. This official story was fully backed up by movies, narratives, comic books, etc., etc.

Few can imagine what a shock it was for me, when one day I was told that not only my own father and his whole family, but also all of the acquaintances of my parents had been on this 'bad' side. I could not understand it. All of them, not the least my father, seemed rather intelligent to me and not at all 'criminal'.

So I began my own research into the matter. And what started out over ten years ago as a hobby to learn more about my own family, has today become an obsession to me. I have visited a lot of the old men from the 'bad' side, I have listened, I have read unofficial documents, I have collected photos and insignia and I have learned.

I have learned that the 'brutal attack' on Denmark was in reality a very smooth occupation carried out in accordance with long established plans. Denmark was only occupied by the Germans to prevent an English take-over, and was therefore, at first, treated with extraordinary leniency.

I have learned, that the 'few traitors' were really several thousand volunteers, who believed in their cause and in Denmark, and who were not only found in the *Freikorps Danmark* but in all 38 divisions of the first European Army in history called the Waffen-SS.

I have learned that their 'criminal' activity consisted of a fanatical struggle on the Eastern Front in a fight for Europe against Asia and the hated communists, who had already almost overrun their brothers in Nordic Finland. Here on the Eastern Front, these Danes fought with a spirit and determination that could match that of the best soldiers found in any army in the world. Many of them could be found in the ranks of the Waffen-SS from the summer of 1940 on to the last days in Berlin in May 1945. About 4,000 of them fell in action.

After their last defeat, they were sentenced to prison as criminals by the same politicians and King who had once sent them off with their blessings. This was all done through the medium of retroactive laws. Afterwards their stories were kept silent.

With the help of Mr Landwehr, a well-known historian, I am now able to tell a little bit of their story. It is what I would call part of the 'forgotten' Danish history. It is a great privilege for me to co-operate with Mr Landwehr on this project and I hope that my photos can match his professional text.

It is also my hope that this book can serve as a little brick in the rebuilding of the monument to the honour of the Danish Waffen-SS soldiers. This is for the fallen, the murdered, the dead, the condemned, the crippled and those few still alive with psychological scars. In 1992, in Århus, the second largest city in Denmark, at an 'official' exhibition, you could still find a photo of the swearing-in ceremony of the *Freikorps Danmark* in Langenhorn in 1941 with the text:

> "These are, of course, not Danish soldiers. It is only German propaganda".

It is against such stupidity that I want to continue to fight!

Holger Thor Nielsen
Kolding, Denmark
January 1993

CHAPTER I

Activation of the III (Germanische) SS-Panzerkorps

The III (Germanische) SS-Panzerkorps was established on 30th March 1943 on the orders of the Wehrmacht High Command. The first contingent of troops used to provide a cadre for the Corps staff came from the Ersatzbataillon of the SS-Panzergrenadier-Regiment 9 *Germania* of the 5 SS-Division *Wiking* which was transferred from Holland to the military training ground at Dębica, Poland. On 19th April 1943, the Corps officially began forming, as its first troop contingents began arriving at the Grafenwöhr Training Ground in Upper Franconia from the Dębica and Heidelager camps. The divisions chosen to make up the Corps were the 5 SS-Division *Wiking* and a new German-Scandinavian SS-Division to be based on the *Nordland* Regiment which already included many volunteers from Norway and Denmark, some of whom had joined the Waffen-SS as early as the summer of 1940. The Scandinavian volunteers for the new division did not only come from the national legions.

Original plans called for expanding *Nordland* into a division with the addition of a Dutch SS volunteer regiment. III (Germanische) SS-Panzerkorps would then consist of this division along with the SS-Division *Wiking* and, surprisingly, the SS-Division *Totenkopf*. However, it proved impossible for the latter two divisions to be withdrawn altogether from the Eastern Front, and they were in fact later grouped together in the IV SS-Panzerkorps. As for the new Germanic volunteer division, the Dutch SS volunteers were not particularly keen on serving in it; they wanted their own formation and they were backed up in this by the Dutch National-Socialist leadership in the Netherlands. Therefore new adjustments had to be made; the Dutchmen would be given their own brigade and the new Germanic divisions would be filled out with ethnic Germans from south-east Europe (primarily Romania).

The new Germanic volunteer division to serve in the Corps was named *Waraeger* in February 1943 by the *Reichsführer-SS*. This was a reference to the ancient Norse Varangian Guard which served in Byzantium. However, the title was considered a little too obscure and the division received the name *Nordland*, a carry over from the regiment of the same title, from Adolf Hitler on 17th March 1943. Combat experienced personnel from the *Legion Norwegen* and the *Freikorps Danmark* were to provide important cadres for the *Nordland* units.

In the spring of 1943 the III (Germanische) SS-Panzerkorps elements began to assemble; those from the 4 SS-Freiwilligen-Sturmbrigade *Nederland* in Sonneberg and those from the 11 SS-Freiwilligen-Panzergrenadier-Division *Nordland* at the Grafenwöhr training camp in Upper Franconia. At Grafenwöhr the *Nordland* Division began forming under the control of a headquarters staff set up by *SS-Sturmbannführer* Vollmer. The divisional commander, *SS-Brigadeführer und Generalmajor der Waffen-SS*

Fritz von Scholz, was not appointed until 1st May 1943. Von Scholz had been the original commander of the SS-Regiment *Nordland* and from 26th January 1943 had been in charge of the multinational SS-Infanterie-Brigade 2 (mot), which had controlled the four Germanic SS Legions (Dutch, Flemish, Danish and Norwegian).

Selected to command the III (Germanische) SS-Panzerkorps was *SS-Obergruppenführer* Felix Steiner who had led the *Wiking* Division since its inception. He was considered one of the most innovative and capable general officers in the Waffen-SS. The SS-Regiment *Nordland* arrived at Grafenwöhr on 10th May 1943 after almost two unrelenting years of heavy fighting on the southern part of the Eastern Front. After holding a last regimental parade and review before Steiner and von Scholz, the soldiers of the regiment were given a three week home leave before having to report back to their new division.

The two infantry or panzergrenadier regiments of the *Nordland* Division were initially entitled as follows: SS-Grenadier-Regiment 1 *Danmark* and SS-Grenadier-Regiment 2 *Norge*. The I Battalion of *Norge* was formed from some 600 surviving volunteers from the *Legion Norwegen*, while its II Battalion was based on a cadre from II/SS-Rgt. *Nordland* and its III Battalion was formed from the old I/SS-Rgt. *Nordland*. The regimental staff was formed to a large extent from Norwegians who had been serving in the SS-Regiment *Nordland*. *Norge* would add an amphibious VW *Schwimmwagen* section to its III Battalion while also forming three specialised companies:

13 (Infanteriegeschütz) Kompanie	13th (close support artillery) Company
14 (Flak) Kompanie	14th (anti-aircraft) Company
16 (Pionier) Kompanie	16th (combat engineers) Company
15 (Kradschützen) Kompanie	15th (motorcycle) Company - added later on

The formation of the SS-Panzergrenadier-Regiment 24 *Danmark* did not go quite as smoothly. Denmark was still functioning as an 'independent' state (its government did not have time to flee the advancing Germans in April 1940) and the Danish leadership was apprehensive about incorporating a Danish volunteer unit into a nominally German SS formation. In addition a German, *SS-Obersturmbannführer* Graf von Westphalen had been given command of the SS-Panzergrenadier-Regiment 24 *Danmark*, a decision that was not appreciated by many Danes. Nonetheless, the new SS Regiment was officially established on 6th May 1943, although it would not fully take shape until 20th May 1943 when the *Freikorps Danmark* was dissolved and many of its soldiers were voluntarily incorporated into *Danmark*. It should be noted that the Danish volunteers from the *Nordland* were considered 'fully-fledged' SS men, so the question of their joining a 'German' SS formation was already moot; they had already been doing that!

At the same time, the other key elements of the *Nordland* Division, including SS-Panzer-Abteilung 11 (Tank Detachment), SS-Artillerie-Regiment 11 (Artillery Regiment), SS-Panzerjäger-Abteilung 11 (Anti-Tank Detachment) and SS-Panzer-Aufklärungs-Abteilung 11 (Armoured Reconnaissance Detachment), all began forming at Grafenwöhr. SS-Nachrichten-Abteilung 11 (Signals Detachment) was developed at Nürnberg, while the combat engineers of SS-Pionier-Bataillon 11 (Engineer Battalion) were given special instruction at the SS Pionier training camps at Dresden and Hradischko, Bohemia. Additionally, SS-Wirtschaft-Bataillon 11 (Vehicle Maintenance Detachment) was assembled at Schwabach, using as its nucleus the 1st Platoon of the *Wiking* Division maintenance section. *Nordland*'s anti-aircraft unit, SS-Fla-Abteilung

Activation of the III (Germanische) SS-Panzerkorps

11, began forming at the troop training ground at Arys, East Prussia, while the division's reinforcement unit, SS-Feldersatz-Bataillon 11 (Field Replacement Battalion) composed to a large extent of Scandinavian volunteers, was stationed at the Sennheim Germanic volunteer training camp at Alsace under *SS-Sturmbannführer* Franz Lang.

SS-Panzer-Abteilung 11 was commanded by a former *Wiking* officer, *SS-Sturmbannführer* Paul-Albert Kausch, but the responsibility for its training was given to *SS-Obersturmbannführer* Johannes-Rudolf Mühlenkamp, who had been the commander of the *Wiking* Panzer Regiment. Members of the Panzer-Abteilung received special training from the Army's Panzer-Lehr-Abteilung at Erlangen and schooling in vehicle maintenance from the tank construction factory in Nürnberg. Other members of the abteilung attended instructional courses at Panzertruppenschule *Wünsdorf* and *Putlos*. Marksmanship and tank 'shooting' were taught at the latter facility. Under the guidance of *SS-Obersturmbannführer* Mühlenkamp, the abteilung was built up with older model Panzer IIIs and IVs. Map orientation and radio sections also had to be trained and developed.

By the early part of August 1943, *Nordland*'s training and formation activities had largely been completed, although the combat engineer elements were still not ready for deployment. There would be three engineer battalions assigned to III (Germanische) SS-Panzerkorps; one each to the Corps Staff, the *Nordland* Division and the *Nederland* Brigade. Each of the four Panzergrenadier regiments in the Corps also would have an engineer company, designated as the regimental 16th Company. In mid-August 1943. the Corps' engineers were still hard at training at Hradischko and Beneschau near Prague. There was adequate room at those facilities to practice river crossing activities including bridge building and ferrying operations.

The construction of 4 SS-Freiwilligen-Sturmbrigade *Nederland* in Thuringia with the SS-Panzergrenadier-Regiment 48 *General Seyffardt* and SS-Panzergrenadier-Regiment 49 *De Ruyter*, closely paralleled that of the *Nordland* Division in Bavaria, and by August all that was needed was the attachment of an artillery regiment to complete the job. In the meantime, the Corps troops had been trained and formed under the supervision of the former Army officer, *Oberst* Joachim Ziegler, who now became a Waffen-SS *Standartenführer*. In only three months he had been able to have the Corps elements certified ready for duty.

It was intended that III (Germanische) SS-Panzerkorps should receive some 'hands-on' field duty before being committed to front-line action and apparently a proposal had been made to send the Corps to the Atlantic coast on security duty. This notion was opposed by *SS-Obergruppenführer* Steiner, who did not want the various European volunteers to be exposed to possible combat duty against the Western Allies. He also preferred to have his troops placed in an area where some live firing conditions existed; thus at the end of August 1943, a decision was made to send the Corps to Croatia for security deployment against the active communist partisans led by Tito.

For the rest of this text the emphasis will be on the SS-Panzergrenadier-Regiment 24 *Danmark*, and we will attempt to follow its deployment and combat activities in a chronological order.

A signed, commemorative photo issued by *SS-Obersturmbannführer* Graf von Westphalen to former members of the *Freikorps Danmark* who joined Regiment *Danmark*. This was given to *SS-Unterscharführer* Holger Thor Nielsen despite having never served in the *Freikorps* but coming instead from the *Wiking* Division!

CHAPTER II

The First Months

On 20th March 1943 the Danish SS Legion (*Freikorps Danmark*) was detached from the SS-Infanterie-Brigade 1 (mot) in Russia and over the next several days would be transported back to Germany. By the 31st March 1943 the *Freikorps Danmark*, under the leadership of *SS-Sturmbannführer* Neergard-Jacobsen, reached the Grafenwöhr training camp in Upper Franconia, about 30kms to the south-east of Bayreuth. The official commander was still *SS-Obersturmbannführer* Knud Borge Martinsen, who would return from Denmark to lead the *Freikorps* in its final parade on 20th May 1943. The unit strength was about 900 men; it would be joined by 250 men from the unit's reserve company that had been stationed in Babruisk under *SS-Hauptsturmführer* K I Hansen, on 1st May 1943.

The SS-Grenadier-Regiment 1 *Danmark* of 11 SS-Freiwilligen-Panzergrenadier-Division *Nordland*, was officially established at Grafenwöhr on 6th May 1943, but it did not have the full approval of the Danish Government. The regiment would not receive its final numerical designation (24) until 29th November 1943, when the Waffen-SS adopted a chronological numbering scheme for its grenadier regiments.

On 20th May 1943, the *Freikorps Danmark* was officially dissolved at Grafenwöhr and a final parade and inspection was held before the III (Germanische) SS-Panzerkorps commander, *SS-Obergruppenführer* Steiner and the *Danmark* Regimental commander, *SS-Obersturmbannführer* Graf von Westphalen. The vast majority of the *Freikorps Danmark* men, along with some Danes from the *Wiking* Division and other Waffen-SS units, including many Danes who were serving with the SS-Regiment *Nordland* before the summer of 1943, now entered the ranks of the Regiment *Danmark*. At the end of the month, Regiment *Danmark* had roughly the following nationality breakdown: 1,280 Danes, 1,120 Romanian ethnic Germans and 800 'Reich' Germans for a total of 3,200 troops assigned. The actual fighting strength of the regiment was far smaller. The officer corps was almost exactly divided between Danes and Germans. Other Danes of course served throughout the Division *Nordland*, and by the time the unit was deployed on the Eastern Front in December 1943, there were 1,357 Danes on duty with the division as a whole.

The Regiment *Danmark* was visited by the Danish emissary to Germany, Ambassador Mohr, on 28th July 1943, who along with *SS-Obergruppenführer* Steiner, inspected the unit. Mohr was favourably impressed and, during lunch with Steiner at Schloß Plassenburg in Kulmbach, gave his government's approval for the regiment, with the stipulation that it would remain a Danish 'national' formation. This was agreed. However, *SS-Obersturmbannführer* K B Martinsen decided to leave the regiment when he realised that he would not become the commander (a move that could have helped his political career in Denmark). He returned to Denmark to take a more politically active role and build up the Schalburg-Korps, the Danish branch of the Germanic SS. The post-war Danish Government would later execute Martinsen for his activities with the Schalburg-Korps.

Ambassador Mohr made a short speech to the men of Regiment *Danmark*, acknowledging their brave struggle against the Bolsheviks and assuring them of the support of the 'entire Fatherland' until the final victory took place. This talk was encouraging to the troops, and many volunteers stayed on because of it. They felt that they had the full sanction of their government. But in the hypocritical political arena many things change, and the post-war ruling clique in Denmark did not stand by the earlier government support, treating the Danish volunteers instead as 'criminals'; executing some of them and imprisoning all of the rest for varying lengths of time. Some of the *Freikorps Danmark* veterans did leave the Waffen-SS in the summer of 1943, mainly because they had only wanted to serve in an all-Danish formation. Many of them later joined the Schalburg-Korps in Denmark, which at the time was being planned as the nucleus for the future Danish Army. The few veterans who left for Denmark when the *Freikorps Danmark* was disbanded and did not join any other pro-German forces later, were not in fact punished after May 1945. But in most cases the post-war 'democratic' government managed to 'find' a suitable crime to charge them with.

Finally, on 28th August 1943, after several hard weeks of training and formation exercises at Grafenwöhr, the Regiment *Danmark* accompanied the rest of III (Germanische) SS-Panzerkorps on its journey to Croatia for field security duty.

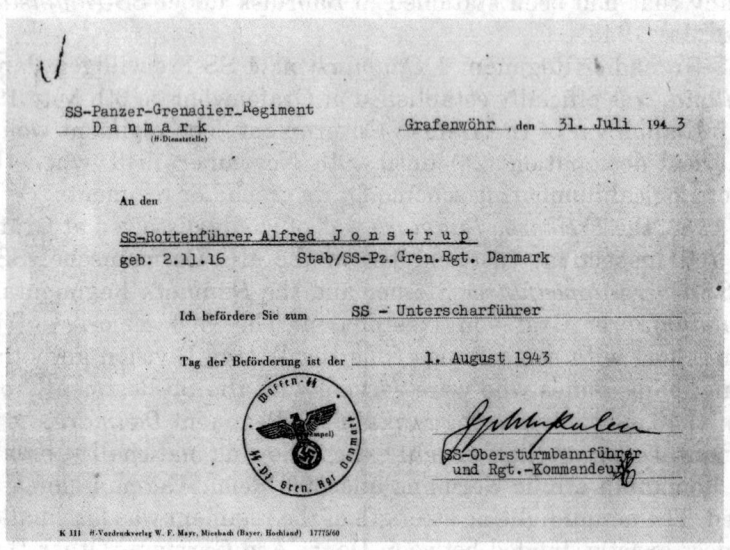

Document authorising the promotion of *SS-Rottenführer* Alfred Jonstrup from the Staff of Rgt.*Danmark* to the rank of *SS-Unterscharführer* signed by the regimental CO, *SS-Obersturmbannführer* Graf von Westphalen

Initial Command Roster (age of officers in brackets)

Commander	*SS-Obersturmbannführer* Graf von Westphalen (34)
Regimental Adjutant	*SS-Obersturmführer* Walter Seebach (Dutch, age 24)
Orderly Officer	*SS-Untersturmführer* Freiherr Eggers (30)
Administrative Officers	*SS-Hauptsturmführer* Kogelgruber and
	SS-Untersturmführer Hecht (34)
Ib (Supply Officer)	*SS-Obersturmführer* Hein (33)
Staff Company Officers	*SS-Untersturmführer* Erik Brørup (25)[1]
	(later with 9/SS-Pz.Gren.Rgt.24 *Danmark*)
	SS-Untersturmführer Salskov (25)

I Battalion

Commander	*SS-Obersturmbannführer* K B Martinsen (37)
Adjutant	*SS-Obersturmführer* Rott (25)
Orderly Officer	*SS-Untersturmführer* Freiherr Gyldenkrone (32)
Medical Officer	*SS-Obersturmführer* Dr Konrad Lotze (28)
Motor Transport Officer	*SS-Obersturmführer* Wolf (38)
Administrative Officer	*SS-Untersturmführer* Jens Wilhelm Petersen
1st Company Commander	*SS-Hauptsturmführer* Per Sørensen (29)
1st Company Officer	*SS-Untersturmführer* Hazal (21)
2nd Company Commander	*SS-Untersturmführer* H Larsen (35)
2nd Company Officer	*SS-Untersturmführer* H P Jensen
3rd Company Officer	*SS-Obersturmführer* H Hennecke (30)
3rd Company Officer	*SS-Untersturmführer* Schröder (45)
4th Company Commander	*SS-Obersturmführer* Stenger (26)

II Battalion

Commander	*SS-Hauptsturmführer* K Walther
Adjutant	*SS-Obersturmführer* Knud Thorgils
Orderly Officer	*SS-Untersturmführer* Szwerinski (23)
Motor Transport Officer	*SS-Untersturmführer* Gerls (33)
Administrative Officer	*SS-Obersturmführer* Schäfer (32)
5th Company Commander	*SS-Obersturmführer* Poulsen (30)
6th Company Commander	*SS-Obersturmführer* Rudolf Ternedde
7th Company Commander	*SS-Obersturmführer* Heinz Hämel (29)
7th Company Officer	*SS-Untersturmführer* Jørgensen (26)
8th Company Commander	*SS-Untersturmführer* O P Kure (25)

III Battalion

Commander	*SS-Sturmbannführer* P Neergard-Jacobsen (42)
Adjutant	*SS-Untersturmführer* Landmesser (26)
Orderly Officer	*SS-Untersturmführer* V E Largen (25)
Administrative Officer	*SS-Obersturmführer* Schramm (32)
9th Company Commander	*SS-Obersturmführer* Meyer (31)
10th Company Commander	*SS-Untersturmführer* E Fenger
11th Company Commander	*SS-Obersturmführer* Worsoe Larsen (30)
11th Company Officer	*SS-Untersturmführer* F Bünte (32)
12th Company Officer	*SS-Obersturmführer* Thorius (23)

---

[1] *SS-Untersturmführer* Brørup had been serving with the SS Cavalry Division prior to his posting to Regiment *Danmark*.

SS-Sturmbannführer Knud Borge Martinsen. He was the last official commander of the *Freikorps Danmark*. He is seen here in summer 1942 at Lake Ilmen.

SS-Hauptsturmführer K I Hansen. He had commanded the Ersatzkompanie of the *Freikorps Danmark* at Babruisk. The photo dates from January 1944 when he was an officer cadet at the *SS-Junkerschule* Bad Tölz, hence the NCO rank insignia.

On the right is *SS-Hauptsturmführer* (here *SS-Obersturmführer*) Willi Roßmann, who was the transport officer of Regiment *Danmark*

SS-*Untersturmführer* Erik Brørup, who served with the Staff Company of Regiment *Danmark*

SS-*Untersturmführer* Hecht, the supply officer of Regiment *Danmark*

SS-*Hauptsturmführer* P Neergaard-Jacobsen. As a *Sturmbannführer* he was in command of *Freikorps Danmark* for a time and later served as the first commander of III/SS-Pz.Gren.Rgt.24 *Danmark*

SS-Hauptsturmführer Per Sørensen. Considered "the best of the best" of the Danish SS volunteers. He was the only commander of 1/*Freikorps Danmark*, then led I/SS-Pz.Gren.Rgt.24 *Danmark* and II/SS-Pz.Gren.Rgt.24 *Danmark*. As a *Sturmbannführer* he received the command of Regiment *Danmark* on 20th April 1945. He was killed in action during the fighting for Berlin on 24th April 1945. Sørensen was awarded the German Cross in Gold on 14th October 1944 and the Honour Roll Clasp on 17th December 1944.

SS-Untersturmführer Egil Poulsen. Poulsen was a veteran of the *Freikorps Danmark* and was the first commander of 5/SS-Pz.Gren.Rgt.24 *Danmark* with the rank of *Obersturmführer*. He was the last commander of the SS-Vagtbataillon Sjaelland (SS Guard Battalion Zeeland) in Denmark. This unit was the former Schalburg-Korps

SS-Obersturmführer Walter Seebach (born in Holland), succeeded Egil Poulsen as CO of 5/SS-Pz.Gren.Rgt.24 *Danmark*. Seebach won the Knight's Cross as commander of this company on 12th March 1944. He later transferred to the SS-Panzer-Abteilung 11 *Hermann von Salza* of the *Nordland* Division

SS-Untersturmführer Ole Peter Kure. Also a veteran of the *Freikorps Danmark*, Kure went on to lead 8/SS-Pz.Gren.Rgt.24 *Danmark* with the rank of *Obersturmführer*.

SS-Hauptsturmführer Rudi Ternedde

SS-Obersturmführer Bent Worsoe Larsen. Another veteran of the *Freikorps Danmark*, he was commander of II/SS-Pz.Gren.Rgt.24 *Danmark* until he was killed on 1st February 1944 in Yamburg

SS-Brigadeführer Fritz von Scholz, the legendary commander of the *Nordland* Division until his death in Estonia in July 1944

SS-Hauptsturmführer Heinz Hämel as commander of II/SS-Pz.Gren.Rgt.24 *Danmark*

SS-Obersturmführer Dr Konrad Lotze, medical officer with I/SS-Pz.Gren.Rgt.24 *Danmark* from July 1943. He was later declared missing-in-action

SS-Unterscharführer Petersen from 5/SS-Pz.Gren.Rgt.24 *Danmark*. He fell at Riga, Latvia in 1944

SS-Unterscharführer Erik Westergaard. He was a well-known political activist in pre-war *Denmark*. He served as *Der Spieß* for 1/SS-Pz.Gren.Rgt.24 *Danmark*. In the photo he wears the Danish flag collar patch belonging to the *Freikorps* reserve company

Four officer cadets from the 9th Waffen-SS Officer's Training Class at *SS-Junkerschule* Bad Tölz, seen here at St Anton, Austria in early 1943. They are, left to right: Peter Köppen, Georg Erichsen, Olav Clausen and Christian Dall. Olav Clausen was a Dane from Copenhagen and the other three were Nordschleswigers, ethnic Germans from North Schleswig in Denmark. Georg Erichsen finished as first in his class and was promoted directly to *Untersturmführer* upon graduation. The others had to serve first as *SS-Standartenoberjunker* (officer designates). Georg Erichsen fell in action in Kurland in 1945 as an *SS-Obersturmführer* while serving as an adjutant to *Sturmbannführer* Rudolf Saalbach the commander of SS-Panzer-Aufklärungs-Abteilung 11. Peter Köppen became an *Untersturmführer* and served as an adjutant with I/SS-Pz.Gren.Rgt.24 *Danmark*. He fell in action in October 1944. Christian Dall became an *Obersturmführer* and served for a time as commander of 13/SS-Pz.Gren.Rgt.23 *Norge*. Olav Clausen became an Untersturmführer and served with the *Wiking* Division

The First Months

The last parade of the *Freikorps Danmark* at Grafenwöhr on 20th May 1943. The staff officers are shown. In the lead is *Obersturmbannführer* K B Martinsen; third from the left is *Sturmbannführer* P Neergaard-Jacobsen

Staff officers, colour guard and main body of the *Freikorps* on parade, 20th May 1943.

Obergruppenführer Felix Steiner, III (Germanische) SS-Panzerkorps commander, awaits the approach of the *Freikorps*

Obersturmbannführer K B Martinsen (right) reporting to *Obergruppenführer* Felix Steiner (centre)

The *Freikorps* staff officers saluting *Obergruppenführer* Steiner

The Musik-Korps lead the way

The First Months

Another photo of the head of the *Freikorps* column

The men of the *Freikorps Danmark* pass by

Colour guard carrying the Dannebrog (Danish flag). On the left is *Untersturmführer* O P Kure and on the right is *Untersturmführer* Frederiksen

1/*Freikorps Danmark*, being led by its commander, *Haupsturmführer* Per Sørensen

The *Freikorps* drawn up for its final inspection. Steiner and Martinsen are in the foreground

Musik-Korps, staff officers and colour guard at the final inspection

Standing in his command car, the first commander of SS-Pz.Gren.Rgt.24 *Danmark*, *Obersturmbannführer* Hermenegild Graf von Westphalen. In the back seat on the right is his adjutant, Dutch-born *Obersturmführer* Walter Seebach

Officers of the new Regiment *Danmark*. From left to right Hein, Stenger, Poulsen, Riedler, Neergaard-Jacobsen, Worsoe Larsen, von Westphalen (white jacket) and Thorius

After the parade:

Untersturmführer Frederiksen (left) and *Untersturmführer* O P Kure

Danish officers after the parade

The First Months

Decorations are presented to the Danish volunteers. Third from the left is *Obersturmführer* Walter Seebach; *Obersturmführer* Stenger is in the centre (right)

The *Freikorps* Danish volunteers being decorated by *Obersturmbannführer* von Westphalen, *Obersturmführer* Seebach and *Obersturmbannführer* Martinsen

SS-Obergruppenführer Felix Steiner arriving to inspect the Regiment Danmark at Grafenwöhr, Upper Franconia, 1943

SS-Obergruppenführer Felix Steiner, holder of the Knight's Cross with Oakleaves, greeting his Danish soldiers

The First Months

Obergruppenführer **Steiner and his aide-de-camp**

Obergruppenführer **Steiner meeting Danish SS volunteers**

Obergruppenführer Steiner shaking hands with *Sturmbannführer* Per Neergaard-Jacobsen. The *Danmark* regimental adjutant, *Obersturmführer* Walter Seebach is just to the right of the two

Obergruppenführer Steiner shaking hands with a Danish *SS-Unterscharführer*. On the right is the *Danmark* commander, *Obersturmbannführer* Graf von Westphalen

The First Months

Ambassador Mohr arriving at Grafenwöhr to convince the *Freikorps Danmark* veterans to stay on with the Regiment *Danmark*. Left to right: *Untersturmführer* Frederiksen, *Obergruppenführer* Steiner, Ambassador Mohr and unknown

Ambassador Mohr with *Obersturmbannführer* Graf von Westphalen

Mohr talking to *Obersturmführer* Knud Thorgils (left) and *Obersturmbannführer* von Westphalen

Ambassador Mohr with *Danmark* officers. From left: Thorgils, Mohr, Westphalen. In the far right foreground: *Untersturmführer* Jørgen Salskov

Obergruppenführer Steiner inspecting his men from the Regiment *Danmark*

Steiner again in conversation with Danish SS men. An SS Panzer officer is on the left

Freikorps volunteers that Ambassador Mohr was not able to convince to stay with the Regiment *Danmark*. They would return home and most would join other organisations such as the Schalburg-Korps, HIPO, ET, Naval Volunteer Corps, Sommer-Korps, etc. The sign over the railway station reads: "Victory or Bolshevik chaos! Wheels must roll for the victory!"

An unknown Danish *SS-Sturmmann* at Grafenwöhr in 1943. He wears the *Freikorps Danmark* cuff title and an old-style Danish arm shield

1/SS-Pz.Gren.Rgt.24 *Danmark*

2/SS-Pz.Gren.Rgt.24 *Danmark*

Soldiers from 2/SS-Pz.Gren.Rgt.24 *Danmark*

The First Months

3/SS-Pz.Gren.Rgt.24
Danmark

4/SS-Pz.Gren.Rgt.24
Danmark

5/SS-Pz.Gren.Rgt.24
Danmark

6/SS-Pz.Gren.Rgt.24 *Danmark*

6/SS-Pz.Gren.Rgt.24 *Danmark* **being inspected by** *Untersturmführer* **Bünte**

(Above and below) 7/SS-Pz.Gren.Rgt.24 *Danmark*

Two Danish NCOs from 7/SS-Pz.Gren.Rgt.24 *Danmark* (note sign). On the right is *Unterscharführer* Holger Thor Nielsen

On the right: *Sturmbannführer* Per Neergaard-Jacobsen as CO of III/SS-Pz.Gren.Rgt.24 *Danmark* conversing with *Obersturmbannführer* Graf von Westphalen the first regimental commander. *Sturmbannführer* Neergaard-Jacobsen is wearing both the cuff-titles of the *Freikorps Danmark* and that of Regiment *Danmark* (against regulations!). Von Westphalen's daughter is in the left foreground

The First Months

```
11./SS-Pz.Gren.Rgt.Danmark,Grafenwöhr.

        Urlaubsschein Nr. 28.

          Soldbuch Nr. 41.

Inhaber dieses Ausweises hat Nachtur-
laub bis 2.oo Uhr nach Grafenwöhr
vom 1.Juni bis 30.Juni 1943.

              Bent Worsoe Larsen
      SS-Obersturmführer u. Kp.-Fhr.
```

```
SS-Unterscharführer
Aage  D a h l , geb.8.12.10
Stabskp./SS-Pz.Gren.Rgt.Danmark 24
              (dän.Nr.1)
```

Leave pass for *SS-Unterscharführer* Aage Dahl from 11/SS-Pz.Gren.Rgt.24 *Danmark* signed by the company commander, *SS-Obersturmführer* Bent Worsoe Larsen

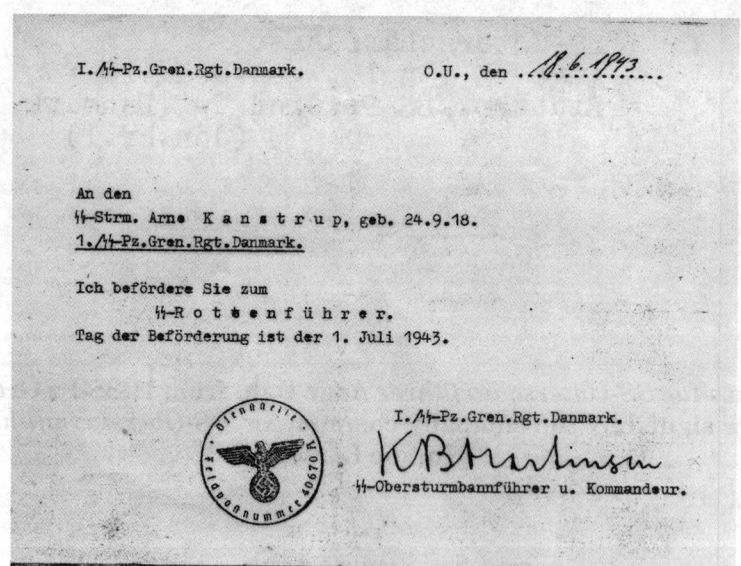

3rd Class railway warrant for Waffen-SS personnel, signed by the *Danmark* company commander, *Obersturmführer* Rudolf Ternedde

Certificate promoting *SS-Sturmmann* Arne Kanstrup from I/SS-Pz.Gren.Rgt.24 *Danmark* to the rank of *SS-Rottenführer*. It is signed by the CO of I/SS-Pz.Gren.Rgt.24 *Danmark*, *SS-Obersturmbannführer* K B Martinsen

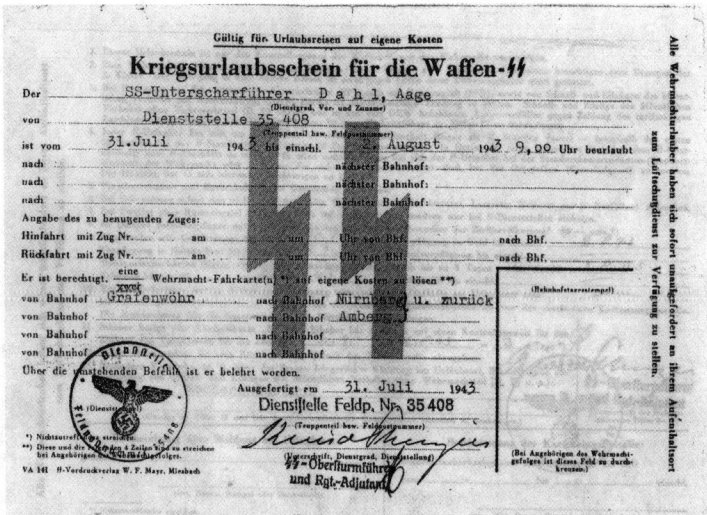

Leave travel authorisation issued to *SS-Unterscharführer* Aage Dahl by the *Danmark* regimental adjutant

Travel pass allowing *Unterscharführer* Aage Dahl to go to Nuremberg from Grafenwöhr and back again signed by the *Danmark* regimental adjutant, *Obersturmführer* Walter Seebach

CHAPTER III

Croatia 1943

From early to mid-September 1943, troops from the SS-Panzer-Abteilung 11 along with soldiers 'on temporary loan' from the *Wiking* Panzer Regiment and III/SS-Rgt.9 *Germania*, were engaged in disarming and rounding up demoralised Italian Army troops in the Samobor and Karlovac areas. The Italian troops had, of course, ceased to be German allies as a result of the overthrow of the Mussolini government and the subsequent attempted surrender to the Western Allies by the new Italian leadership.

The SS Division *Nordland* was now deployed around Sisak, Glina, and the Bosanski Novi region, with its headquarters in Sisak, about 50kms south-east of Zagreb. It was not long before the divisional grenadier regiments were caught up in serious fighting with Tito's partisans. SS-Grenadier-Regiment 2 *Norge* operated out of Bosanski Novi and for several weeks was engaged in an effort to relieve a trapped garrison of troops from the SS-Polizei Regiment 14 in Ogulin, 90kms to the west of Sisak. The regiment's efforts, in conjunction with troops and tanks from Panzer-Abteilung 11, were eventually successful but not until after many short, violent battles and the loss of several officers.

Meanwhile, the units of SS-Grenadier-Regiment 1 *Danmark* were stationed at Petrinja (10kms to the west of Sisak) and Glina (30kms to the west of Sisak). Daily routine consisted of training exercises combined with security duties. A special detached company was always kept in readiness to go into action at any time if the need arose, and the various companies in the regiment rotated with one another for this assignment. In spite of the dangers of the ubiquitous, but difficult to find, partisans, the *Danmark* soldiers were quartered in small units in the various towns and villages.

The small town of Glina, which was occupied by I/SS-Pz.Gren.Rgt.24 *Danmark*, was at considerable risk from the partisans since it had only one access route: a winding, mountain road leading to Petrinja. From early in the battalion's stay in Glina, Tito's bandits made themselves felt with repeated hit-and-run attacks on the town. This made the *Danmark* troops more vigilant, but still some of them were taken prisoner by the communists whilst travelling on the Petrinja road. With the help of some of the local residents, I/SS-Pz.Gren.Rgt.24 *Danmark* was able to arrange a prisoner exchange with the Red Army partisans near Glina on 26th September 1943; it was to be the battalion's last friendly contact with the partisans. Almost immediately afterwards, the battalion found itself confronted by more violent enemy attacks.

On 12th November 1943, SS-Grenadier-Regiment 1 *Danmark* was retitled SS-Panzergrenadier-Regiment 24 *Danmark*, whilst SS-Grenadier-Regiment 2 *Norge* became SS-Panzergrenadier-Regiment 23 *Norge*. Since all Waffen-SS grenadier regiments were now being renumbered in order of their formation, *Norge* slipped ahead

A 'small' travel warrant issued to *Rottenführer* Arne Kanstrup enabling him to rejoin his unit in Croatia from his home leave in Denmark. Signed by *Obersturmführer* O R H Norreen

Croatia 1943

of *Danmark* in the numbering scheme. The formation of Regiment *Danmark* had been held up for some time by the bickering Danish Government.

Between 20th-25th November 1943, after several weeks of small, nasty cut-throat actions, Tito's partisans launched a massive assault on the I/SS-Pz.Gren.Rgt.24 *Danmark* positions in Glina. Fully 5,000 of the communist irregulars attacked the town. Against this force, I/SS-Pz.Gren.Rgt.24 *Danmark* could deploy 300 front-line troops and another 150 in reserve. For two days and nights, bloody, violent fighting raged for the town. Glina was almost lost to the partisans on 21st November, but the Danish volunteers grimly hung on. By 22nd November the battle had slackened off somewhat, and the battalion commander, *SS-Sturmbannführer* Fischer (who had replaced *SS-Obersturmbannführer* K B Martinsen) decided to attempt a phased withdrawal to Petrinja. Leading the retreat was the 1st Platoon of 1/SS-Pz.Gren.Rgt.24 *Danmark*, but part way down the Petrinja road it was caught in an ambush, and only a few of the troops were able to make it safely back to Glina. An assault troop was sent out to try and clear the way but it too was turned back with heavy casualties: 3 killed and another 8 wounded.

At 1600 hours on 23rd November, a strong partisan force led by 3 tanks launched a savage attack on Glina. Almost immediately two of the tanks were destroyed by anti-tank guns assigned to 4/SS-Pz.Gren.Rgt.24 *Danmark*, while the third was driven off in damaged condition. This was followed by more biter, close combat in Glina on 24th and 25th November. The situation finally improved when Stuka dive bombers were called in to blast the enemy positions; this forced the partisans to withdraw to the high mountains. Therefore, finally, the battalion was successfully able to defend the town, with assistance from the Luftwaffe. The Danish *SS-Obersturmführer* Octavious Righardt Holger Norreen, who had been commanding 1st Company during the fighting, was afterwards made the battalion orderly officer. Later in the war he received the War Merit Cross 2nd Class for his duties as commander of the HIPO (pro-German Danish auxiliary police) in Denmark.

Meanwhile the *Danmark* regimental headquarters had been considerably distressed by the encirclement of I Battalion at Glina, and on 22nd November 1943, the commander, *SS-Obersturmbannführer* Graf von Westphalen, decided to launch a relief attempt. II and III/SS-Pz.Gren.Rgt.24 *Danmark*, less their 5th and 10th Companies which were being left behind for security purposes, were to mount the relief effort. However, once the operation got underway, it was learned that 5/SS-Pz.Gren.Rgt.24 *Danmark* had become surrounded by the partisans at Hrastovica. III/SS-Pz.Gren.Rgt.24 *Danmark*, led by *SS-Sturmbannführer* Neergard-Jacobsen, accompanied by two Russian Cossack companies, was ordered to rescue 5th Company.

On 24th November, the lead element of III/SS-Pz.Gren.Rgt.24 *Danmark*, *SS-Hauptsturmführer* Heinz Hämel's 7th Company, broke through to Hrastovica and found it to be largely deserted; the partisans had vanished into the hills and the civilians also were gone. Seventeen survivors from 5th Company had so far turned up, but the rest were missing. What had happened to the others? They did not have to wait long for the answer. The mutilated bodies of 15 Danish volunteers were found on display in the town square; they had apparently been tortured to death. After further investigation it was learned that the rest of the company had apparently also been massacred by the partisans. It was a face of warfare that most of the *Danmark* soldiers had not previously encountered. However, the inhumanity displayed by Tito's bandits did not alter the glowing praise and support they continued to receive from the Western Allies!

Whilst *Danmark* had been kept busy in the Petrinja-Glina area, the rest of III (Germanische) SS-Panzerkorps had been similarly engaged elsewhere in Croatia. Units such as Nordland's Panzer-Abteilung 11 and SS-Panzer-Aufklärungs-Abteilung 11 now received their final allotment of vehicles (SS-Panzer-Abteilung 11 had been utilising a number of 'booty' Italian tanks!) and continued alternate training and anti-partisan operations. But change was in the offing; towards the end of November 1943, the military authorities felt the time had come to shift the entire Corps to a combat zone on the Eastern Front. The destination would be the very weak Oranienbaum pocket defensive perimeter to the west of Leningrad.

In all, I/SS-Pz.Gren.Rgt.24 *Danmark* suffered the following losses during its three months in Croatia: 41 killed, 38 wounded and 2 missing-in-action. Of the 41 dead, 16 were Danish volunteers.

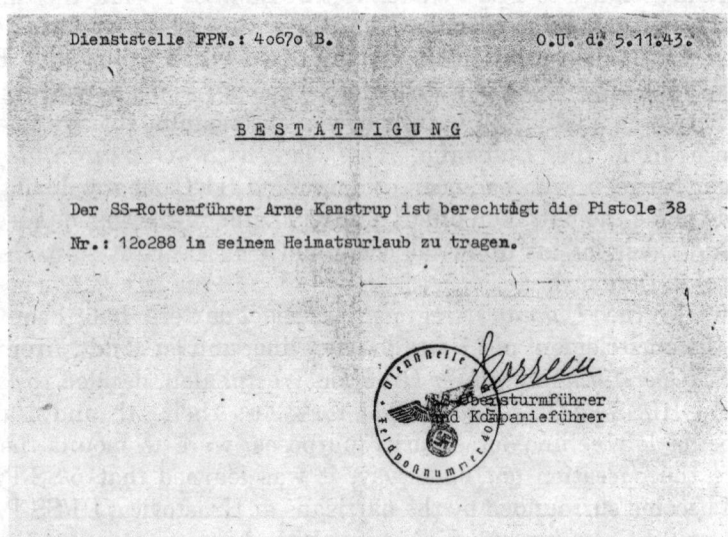

Authorisation for *SS-Rottenführer* Arne Kanstrup to carry a sidearm (P38 pistol) during his home leave, signed by his company commander, *SS-Obersturmführer* O R H Norreen

Croatia 1943

K B Martinsen as an *SS-Obersturmbannführer* at Grafenwöhr, Upper Franconia. He was the first commander of I/SS-Pz.Gren.Rgt.24 *Danmark* before he left for Denmark to lead the Schalburg-Korps

SS-Obersturmführer Octavious Righardt Holger Norreen. He commanded 1/SS-Pz.Gren.Rgt.24 *Danmark* for a short time in Croatia. He later transferred to III/SS-Pz.Gren.Rgt.24 *Danmark* as an orderly officer before eventually joining the HIPO (Auxiliary Police) in Denmark. He is seen here at the time of his capture by the Danish 'resistance' in Copenhagen. He is wearing the uniform of the leader of the ET (Intelligence Service)

SS-Unterscharführer Holger Thor Nielsen who transferred from 5/Rgt. *Germania* of the *Wiking* Division to 7/SS-Pz.Gren.Rgt.24 *Danmark*. Nielsen was murdered by the communist resistance in his home town of Odense, Denmark in November 1943

(Above and left) *SS-Sturmmann* Carl Nielsen. A veteran of the *Freikorps Danmark*, he later served with 6/SS-Pz.Gren.Rgt.24 *Danmark*. In the above photograph, taken at the Marienbad military hospital in 1943, he is wearing two cuff titles - one for the *Freikorps* and one for Regiment *Danmark*. This was a not uncommon practice amongst *Freikorps* veterans

Post-dated citation for the Winter War Medal 1941/42 issued to *SS-Unterscharführer* Holger Thor Nielsen of 7/SS-Pz.Gren.Rgt.24 *Danmark*. It is signed by *SS-Hauptsturmführer* Fechner, the head of the SS-Ersatzkommando in Denmark

On the rails they went off to Croatia. The Dannebrog (Danish flag) was always with them

By rail to Croatia. Note the Dannebrog on the mudguard

SS-Untersturmführer Egil Poulsen, the commander of 5/SS-Pz.Gren.Rgt.24 *Danmark*, on his way to Croatia in an open rail car

Croatia 1943

Two unknown Danish *Rottenführers* in Petrinja

Two Danish SS officers in Petrinja, Croatia. On the left is *Obersturmführer* Poul Victor Broberg and on the right is *Untersturmführer* Jørgen Salskov

A group of unidentified Danish volunteers in Petrinja, Croatia

Part of the *Danmark* regimental vehicle transport column in Petrinja. Note the flag Insignia on the fender of the foremost truck

Funeral service for fallen volunteers in Croatia. The flag in the background is the old *Freikorps* banner so this is probably I/SS-Pz.Gren.Rgt.24 *Danmark*

Graves of the fallen *Danmark* volunteers in Croatia

Croatia 1943

In Feldbach, Austria at the border to the former Yugoslavia, many of the Danes from reserve units were asked to return to Denmark to join the Schalburg-Korps or other pro-German units to help maintain civil order in Denmark. Here are four Danes with a German NCO (centre) who refused to go back, preferring to serve at the front. On the far right is Stensen, who later fell at Narva and second from the right is Ernst Cristiansen

Two NCOs from SS-Ersatzbataillon *Germania* at Graz-Wetzelsdorf who transferred into the *Nordland* Division. On the right is *Unterscharführer* Fritz Ihle, a volksdeutsche from North Schleswig in Denmark, who came from 15/SS-Rgt. *Nordland* of the *Wiking* Division and served for a time with 2/SS-Pz.Gren.Rgt.24 *Danmark* before going on to serve in 2/SS-Pz.Aufkl.Abt.11. On the left is *Unterscharführer* Holger Thor Nielsen, a veteran of 5/SS-Rgt. *Germania* of the *Wiking* Division who went to 7/SS-Pz.Gren.Rgt.24 *Danmark*. Sadly, he was murdered during a home leave in Denmark in November 1943

On the left is *Sturmbannführer* Per Neergaard-Jacobsen with officers of III/SS-Pz.Gren.Rgt.24 *Danmark* at Petrinja, Croatia, 1943. In the centre with his back to the camera is *Obertsturmführer* Meyer, the CO of 9/SS-Pz.Gren.Rgt.24 *Danmark*

The same group of officers. Neergaard-Jacobsen is now in the centre; Meyer is still turned away from the camera

Obergruppenführer Steiner as Commanding General of III (Germanische) SS-Panzerkorps, arriving by Fieseler-Storch light aircraft to visit the Regiment *Danmark* in Petrinja, Croatia, 1943

The III/SS-Pz.Gren.Rgt.24 *Danmark* drawn up for inspection by *Obergruppenführer* Felix Steiner in Petrinja, Croatia, 1943

Obergruppenführer Steiner shaking hands with a member of III/SS-Pz.Gren.Rgt.24 *Danmark* at Petrinja, Croatia

Obergruppenführer Steiner talking to *Danmark* officers. Directly to his left is *Obersturmbannführer* Graf von Westphalen. On the far right is *Obersturmführer* Seebach

Obergruppenführer Steiner conversing with *Brigadeführer* Fritz von Scholz, the commander of the *Nordland* Division and a Panzer officer. Behind Steiner are *Obersturmführer* Seebach and *Obersturmbannführer* Graf von Westphalen

Obergruppenführer Steiner and *Obersturmbannführer* Graf von Westphalen

Croatia 1943

Steiner visits the graves of the fallen Danes at Petrinja. To his right is *Obersturmführer* Seebach

Obergruppenführer Steiner chatting with *Danmark* soldiers who had been training with an Infanteriegeschütz

Obergruppenführer Steiner with one of his soldiers from Regiment *Danmark*

Obergruppenführer **Steiner with his men from Regiment *Danmark***

Obersturmbannführer Graf von Westphalen inspects a *Danmark* company in Croatia

SS-Sturmmann Tage Knudsen. He was another *Freikorps* veteran who went to the staff of Regiment *Danmark*

On the right is Andreas Mortensen, a *Freikorps* veteran who was promoted from *Sturmmann* to *Rottenführer* in Croatia

Rottenführer Mortensen trying on the local costume

Unterscharführer Alfred Jonstrup as the postmaster of Regiment *Danmark*. He had previously served on the staff of the *Freikorps Danmark*

Croatia 1943

SS-Untersturmführer **Robert Hansen riding on the front of a Schwimmwagen in Croatia. *Untersturmführer* Hansen was a platoon leader in 7/SS-Pz.Gren.Rgt.24 *Danmark***

Danmark **motorcyclists in Croatia**

Danmark **grenadiers moving into a Croatian village**

Danmark soldiers at rest in Croatia

A Danish *Unterscharführer* in Copenhagen during a home leave

(Above) *Untersturmführer* Kaj Bertramsen with his wife whilst on leave in Denmark

(Right) *SS-Obersturmbannführer* K B Martinsen on leave in Copenhagen, summer 1943

CHAPTER IV

The Oranienbaum Cauldron

III (Germanische) SS-Panzerkorps departed for the Eastern Front from Croatia in stages beginning on 25th November 1943 with the departure of III/SS-Pz.Gren.Rgt.23 *Norge* from Karlovac and ending on 22nd December 1943, when the SS-Panzer-Abteilung 11 and part of the SS-Panzer-Aufklärungs-Abteilung 11 finally left Croatia. These troops had been fighting partisans in and around Samobor right up to their final night in the area!

Troops from SS-Panzergrenadier-Regiment 24 *Danmark* left Petrinja by rail for the Oranienbaum Cauldron between 25th November and 7th December 1943. The *Danmark* combat engineer company (16th) along with its sister company from *Norge* had never reached Croatia but instead would leave directly from Beneschau, Bohemia to actually arrive before their parent regiments on the Eastern Front.

Upon arrival on the Oranienbaum sector, III (Germanische) SS-Panzerkorps came under the command of *Generaloberst* Lindemann's 18 Armee situated to the west of Leningrad, covering a wide swath of territory from the Gulf of Finland to the northern shore of Lake Ilmen. For a year this had been a quiet and undermanned sector, but this calm was being threatened by a massive Soviet troop build-up in the Oranienbaum salient and in and around Leningrad itself. It was becoming increasingly evident that an effort to finally break the siege of Leningrad would begin shortly.

The staff of III (Germanische) SS-Panzerkorps reached the terminus of its journey from Croatia at the railway station at Volosovo on 4th December 1943. Here, a link-up was made with the Luftwaffe III Feldkorps, made up of the airmen of the 9 Feld-Division and 10 Feld-Division. This Corps, along with III (Germanische) SS-Panzerkorps was given the task of containing the Oranienbaum Pocket which began near the town of Peterhof[2] only some 25kms to the west-south-west of Leningrad. The pocket stretched for almost 75kms along a protrusion that extended into the Gulf of Finland and at its deepest points probably reached a depth of around 50kms. Manned by the ever-expanding Soviet 2nd Storm Army, this was a formidable front-line sector for the undermanned German-European volunteer side to defend.

On 5th December 1943, III (Germanische) SS-Panzerkorps HQ was established at Klopitsy, about 24kms to the south of the Oranienbaum Pocket. The engineers from *Danmark* and *Norge* arrived on 6th December, marching on foot from the railhead at Volosovo. Within two days they would be hard at work with their comrades from the Luftwaffe 10 Feld-Division in laying minefields and preparing defensive positions for the *Nordland* grenadier regiments.

---

[2] The Russian spelling is Pyetyergof as Russian has no 'H' sound.

The process of integrating the III (Germanische) SS-Panzerkorps units as they arrived into the Oranienbaum defensive perimeter was carried out very carefully and methodically under the codename Operation *Lützow*. 18 Armee made the decision to concentrate the SS troops on the western sector of the Oranienbaum Front, while the Luftwaffe soldiers would remain on the eastern section. Thus the SS-Panzergrenadier-Regiment 24 *Danmark* was routed to the railway terminal at Kotly, almost 50kms to the west-north-west of Corps HQ at Klopitsy. The *Nordland* Division was given the lion's share of the Oranienbaum Front to defend: a 30km stretch running along the west-central sector of the cauldron and taking in the towns of Gorbovitsy, Globitsy, Voronino, Dolgaya Niva and Lopukhinka. The SS-Panzergrenadier-Regiment 24 *Danmark* was given the western part of the front line beginning at Gorbovitsy and ending halfway through the divisional front where the lines were taken over by the SS-Panzergrenadier-Regiment 23 *Norge* to the town of Lopukhinka in the east. From there the lines were taken over by the Luftwaffe 9 Feld-Division and 10 Feld-Division for a distance of some 30kms to the Gulf of Finland. The *Nordland* headquarters was placed just behind the centre of the divisional lines at Kirovo.

By 10th December 1943, the *Danmark* and *Norge* battalions had taken up their assigned positions on the Oranienbaum Front and at midnight on 13th December, the whole Corps was officially activated for combat duty. The 15km north-west sector of the pocket was taken over by the 4 SS-Freiwilligen-Panzergrenadier-Brigade *Nederland*, which relieved the Kampfgruppe of 4 SS-Polizei-Panzergrenadier-Division which had been manning the area in conjunction with Estonian police troops, coastal artillery batteries and assorted odds and ends (convalescent troops and even veterinary companies). While the SS-Division *Polizei* troops soon departed, the 'odds and ends' remained and were incorporated into the Kampfgruppe *Küste* under the control of III (Germanische) SS-Panzerkorps.

Kampfgruppe *Küste* defended the seacoast from the mouth of the River Narva at Narva-Jõesuu (Hungerburg) in Estonia to the north-western terminus of the Oranienbaum Front at Kyernovo. This 9,000-man task force was drawn from almost every source of manpower imaginable and included an Estonian police battalion, several coastal artillery batteries, 4 convalescent companies, 3 veterinary companies, a Naval infantry regiment and two more battalions of the same, a disinfection company, an engineer battalion, three divisional replacement battalions, a mobile artillery abteilung and the students from a defunct NCO training school. The command for this unusual assembly was placed with the highest ranking Danish volunteer, *SS-Brigadeführer* Christian Poul Kryssing. Kryssing was the first CO of the *Freikorps Danmark*, a position for which he was found unsuitable. He had subsequently served as an artillery officer in the SS Divisions *Totenkopf* and *Wiking*. His chief-of-staff with Kampfgruppe *Küste* was the highly efficient Danish *Sturmbannführer* P Rantzau-Engelhardt.

On 30th December 1943, the troop strength for the *Nordland* Division stood at 11,393 (304 officers, 1,734 NCOs and 9,355 other ranks). Out of this, 1,357 were Danish volunteers (41 officers, 193 NCOs, 1,123 other ranks). The Danes therefore constituted 13.49% of the officers, 11.13% of the NCOs and 12.00% of the men. This meant that almost 12% of *Nordland*'s troops were Danish volunteers. At the same time there were 797 Norwegian volunteers in the division (29 officers, 63 NCOs and 705 other ranks). Many other nationalities were also represented in *Nordland* including some 25 Flemings, 274 Dutchmen, 39 Swedes and unknown numbers of Swiss, Estonians and others from all parts of Europe. The 'Reichsdeutsche' contingent only totalled 4,131 in all (232 officers, 1,496 NCOs, 2,403 other ranks), considerably less than half of the divisional strength. Most of the remainder were volksdeutsche from the Balkans, who made up about 40% of the total *Nordland* personnel.

By 14th December, SS-Panzergrenadier-Regiment 24 *Danmark* was fully deployed in the western part of the *Nordland* sector. The regimental command post was located in a complex of some 20 bunkers built into small hills, just north of the town of Zaozyorye. Just behind the *Danmark* HQ was a swamp and a 'corduroy' log road running south to the Koporye-Ropsha sector, near the headquarters of SS-Artillerie-Regiment 11.

In the regimental lines, III/SS-Pz.Gren.Rgt.24 *Danmark* was positioned farthest to the west and maintained contact with the *Nederland* Brigade. The battalion's positions extended for about three kilometres of the line between the villages of Gorbovitsy and Pyetrovichy, with the battalion command post being located 1½kms behind the lines at Kastivskoye. I/SS-Pz.Gren.Rgt.24 *Danmark* held a line running from Pyetrovichy to Voronino, from where the front was taken over by SS-Pz.Gren.Rgt. 23 *Norge*.

By the end of December, the Corps was engaged in building up secondary defensive positions near the Estonian border, known as the 'Panther Positions,' as it was expected that the Soviets would make a breakout from the Oranienbaum Pocket in the immediate future. SS-Panzer-Abteilung 11 was held back near Narva-Jõesuu and then at Yamburg to help constitute a mobile emergency reserve, if and when the Red Army offensive broke out. The month of December ended quite peacefully for the *Danmark* soldiers, who so far had seen limited activity in their sector. However 16 (Pi)/SS-Pz.Gren.Rgt.24 *Danmark* reported that the Soviets had made an appearance during the night of 31st December 1943/1st January 1944, but only to deliver propaganda leaflets to the Danish positions. The culprits were not seen, but in the morning numerous leaflets and posters were seen hanging from trees in the immediate vicinity of the *Danmark* lines! III/SS-Pz.Gren.Rgt.24 *Danmark* listed a strength of 12 officers, 57 NCOs and 435 men; somewhat less than the ideal. In fact most of the *Nordland* units were reporting manpower and ammunition shortages.

On 9th January 1944, *Danmark*'s commander *SS-Obersturmbannführer* Graf von Westphalen, ordered a raid to bring in prisoners for intelligence purposes. Westphalen selected *SS-Oberscharführer* Hvenekilde to lead the party. The operation proved to be a dismal failure; neither Hvenekilde nor his men ever returned to the *Nordland* lines; they ended up in Soviet hands.

Between 10th-13th January 1944, all indications pointed to an early, massive Soviet offensive on the Oranienbaum Front. The III (Germanische) SS-Panzerkorps positions were being bombed on a daily basis and Soviet reinforcements were observed pouring into the cauldron via Kronstadt[3] in the Gulf of Finland. *SS-Obergruppenführer* Steiner felt that the only realistic course of action would be to exercise an immediate tactical withdrawal of the German-European soldiers deployed in this sector. However, that was not to be permitted - the hand of fate would be allowed to take its course on the battlefield with near disastrous results!

The Soviet Offensive

Early in the morning of 14th January 1944, the great Soviet offensive began on the Oranienbaum and Leningrad Fronts to the accompaniment of a massive artillery bombardment. No-one on the German side knew just how strong the Red Army were, but they soon found out! Under the aegis of the so-called '2nd Baltic Front' with six full

---

[3] The Russian spelling is Kronshtadt

armies that outnumbered the Germans by a ratio of 4:1 in personnel, the Soviets made rapid breakthroughs over a large area.

On the Oranienbaum Front, the 2nd Storm Army with two Corps, nine Guards Divisions, three Tank Brigades and a Coastal Brigade, concentrated its attack on the eastern perimeter of the 'pocket' held by the weak Luftwaffe 9 Feld-Division. The division promptly crumbled under the massive artillery barrage and tank-supported infantry onslaught and a permanent enemy breakthrough in force was made. Within a few hours of the initial attack, the northern wing of the German 18 Armee was in hopeless disarray and *Generalfeldmarschall* von Küchler ordered an immediate withdrawal further to the south to the River Luga line. This hasty decision had the immediate effect of rendering the III (Germanische) SS-Panzerkorps positions untenable and placing the troops in very serious jeopardy. Von Küchler was immediately dismissed by the Führer and replaced by the very competent *Generaloberst* Model. But the damage had been done!

The *Nordland* units that had been deployed in the vicinity of the Luftwaffe Feld-Divisionen suffered most on the first day of the offensive. This was particularly true for the SS-Pionier-Bataillon 11, which had been engaged in building up defensive positions between the Luftwaffe 9 Feld-Division and 10 Feld-Division. Parts of the battalion absorbed the full force of the initial Soviet attack, but they held on to their positions in vicious hand-to-hand fighting against tank-supported infantry. The cost, however, was terrible: 2/SS-Pi.Btl.11 lost 100 men killed and wounded alone on 14th January. Despite this, the Waffen-SS troops held on doggedly by themselves even as the inexperienced neighbouring Luftwaffe troops fell back rapidly - often in near panic.

Elsewhere, I/SS-Pz.Gren.Rgt.23 *Norge*, which had been held in reserve near Lopukhinka was ordered to counterattack the enemy breakthrough force with the assistance of SS-Panzerjäger-Abteilung 11 and SS-Artillerie-Regiment 11. It would be joined by 1/SS-Pi.Btl.11, which had been participating in a joint training exercise with combat engineers from the Regiment *Danmark*.

Counterattack

On 15th January 1944 the counterattack spearheaded by I/SS-Pz.Gren.Rgt.23 *Norge* failed after a valiant effort to halt the enemy advance forces, but the following day, in heavy fighting, the *Nordland* sector held firm; with enemy attacks on the SS-Panzergrenadier-Regiment 23 *Norge* being repulsed. By 17th January, the *Nordland* troops in the breakthrough area began retreating amongst furious fighting. SS-Panzer-Aufklärungs-Abteilung 11 and SS-Pionier Battalion 11 had to struggle desperately to avoid being trapped in a Soviet encirclement. A relocation of all III (Germanische) SS-Panzerkorps troops from the west-east defensive lines on the Oranienbaum front now began in earnest to a north-south line, in an effort to halt the Red Army drive to the west. For the next few days, the *Nordland* front stabilised - to an extent - even though the enemy pressure was extreme.

On the night of 21st/22nd January 1944, II/SS-Pz.Gren.Rgt.24 *Danmark*, which had been in reserve, joined I/SS-Pz.Gren.Rgt.24 *Danmark* and the SS-Panzer-Aufklärungs-Abteilung 11 in front-line positions near Dyatlitsy in the breakthrough sector. Elsewhere 8/SS-Pz.Gren.Rgt.24 *Danmark* and a battery from SS-Artillerie-Regiment 11 assumed new defensive positions at Dolgaya Niva, a town in the old Oranienbaum defensive perimeter which was now being threatened from the east. In the course of 22nd January the Red Army broke through to the main highway east of Vitino where they were stopped by troops from the *Nederland* Brigade who had been rushed to the area south-east of Dyatlitsy. In an epic struggle, I/SS-Pz.Gren.Rgt.48 *General*

The Oranienbaum Cauldron

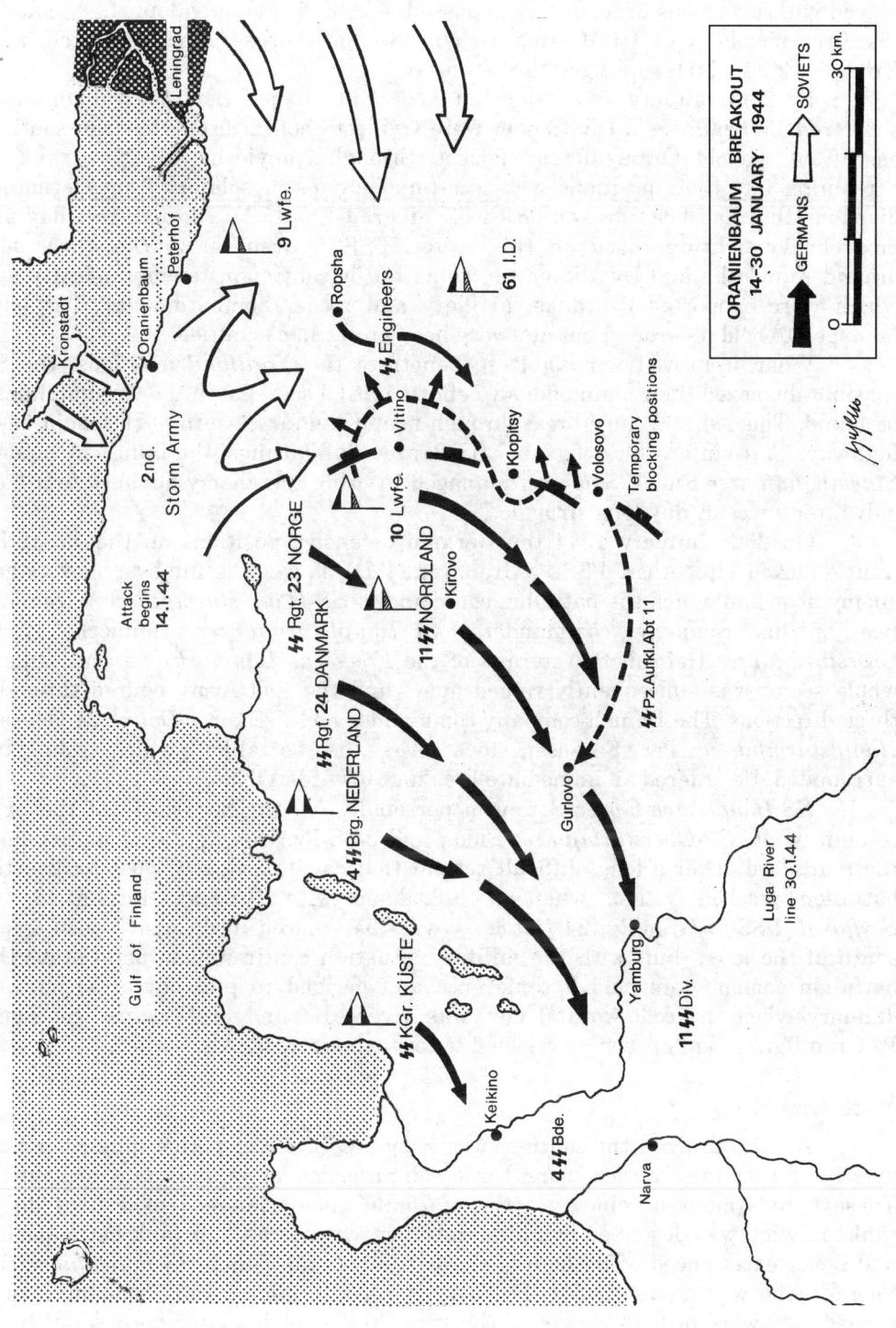

Seyffardt successfully withstood repeated, violent attacks on Vitino, and the battalion commander, *SS-Hauptsturmführer* Hans-Joachim Rühle von Lilienstern personally led some 17 close-combat counterattacks. Even though badly wounded, von Lilienstern stayed with his troops until the crisis passed. For his personal valour, he became one of the first members of III (Germanische) SS-Panzerkorps to be decorated with the Knight's Cross whilst serving with the Corps.

By 23rd January, *Nordland* and *Nederland* troops, along with remnants of the shattered Luftwaffe Feld-Divisionen, were trying to hold a front that ran south-southeast from the old Oranienbaum 'Pocket' through Kapylosha, Dyatlitsy and Vitino. Streaming into their positions were scattered groups of soldiers from German Army divisions that had been broken on the Leningrad Front. All through this day and the next, heavy fighting raged on this sector. I/SS-Pz.Gren.Rgt.24 *Danmark*, deployed around Kapylosha and Dyatlitsy, was being hit by continuous enemy infantry assaults which were supported by tanks, artillery and rocket bombardments. The battalion managed to hold its ground but at a very heavy price in casualties.

When it proved impossible to penetrate the *Nordland* positions, the Soviets continually moved their main offensive efforts until a soft spot in the German lines could be found. This led to a huge breakthrough near Khulduzy, south of the main east-west highway. A counterattack by the SS-Panzer-Aufklärungs-Abteilung 11 under *SS-Sturmbannführer* Rudolf Saalbach managed to bring the enemy advance to a halt, but only after a vicious day-long struggle.

On 25th January 1944 the German defensive positions on the 'breakthrough front' cracked altogether. I/SS-Pz.Gren.Rgt.24 *Danmark* was hit by an overwhelming enemy attack in which the battalion commander, *SS-Hauptsturmführer* Wichmann and two of his company commanders, *SS-Hauptsturmführer* Hennecke and *SS-Obersturmführer* Hein (both veterans of the *Freikorps Danmark*) were all killed. The whole sector was subsequently ripped apart and the Red Army poured through from three directions. The Danish company commander and *Freikorps Danmark* veteran, *SS-Hauptsturmführer* Per Sørensen took over the battalion, which was virtually surrounded. He ordered an immediate breakout towards Vitino.

SS-Hauptsturmführer Sørensen personally led the spearhead of the breakout column, while *SS-Obersturmführer* Sidon and 3/SS-Pz.Gren.Rgt.24 *Danmark* made up the rearguard. After a long, difficult retreat that came perilously close to disaster, the battalion reached Vitino, where it linked up with II/SS-Pz.Gren.Rgt.48 *General Seyffardt*. I/SS-Pz.Gren.Rgt.24 *Danmark* was then placed in defensive positions to the south of the town, but, with the military situation continuing to deteriorate the two battalion commanders held a conference and decided to pull out of Vitino on 27th January when the code-word 'Thaw' was given. 1st and 3rd Companies from I/SS-Pz.Gren.Rgt.24 *Danmark* were selected to cover the retreat.

Withdrawal

At Gubanitsy to the south-east of Klopitsy, SS-Panzer-Abteilung 11 repulsed a massive Soviet tank attack using three self-propelled guns and eight armoured cars. These light armoured vehicles, carrying 75mm guns, managed to destroy 48 enemy tanks in what was described by an unknown eyewitness as "...a tank battle such as we had never experienced". The hero of the battle was the Dutch *SS-Rottenführer* Kasper Sporck, who was credited with 11 Soviet tank kills alone. This brought Sporck the immediate award of both classes of the Iron Cross. For his later heroics on the Narva Front, Sporck would be awarded the Knight's Cross. He did not survive the war.

The Oranienbaum Cauldron

After the successful defence of Gubanitsy, the vehicles from SS-Panzer-Aufklärungs-Abteilung 11 were shipped by rail to Narva, Estonia. Kampfgruppe *Küste* and the rest of the *Nederland* Brigade, which so far had not been involved in the fighting, were also notified on 26th January to begin withdrawing to the west. By 27th January 1944 the whole III (Germanische) SS-Panzerkorps was engaged in the general retreat to Narva. SS-Panzergrenadier-Regiment 23 *Norge* helped cover the main *Nordland* withdrawal. *SS-Brigadeführer* von Scholz kept his divisional headquarters in place as long as possible to supervise the retreat. In fact he stayed too long and the *Nordland* HQ troops were cut off by a strong enemy force! Only through a quick counterattack by an assault troop from 7/SS-Pz.Gren.Rgt.23 *Norge* was the divisional headquarters rescued from disaster.

The other *Danmark* battalions were able to successfully disengage and join the withdrawal. III/SS-Pz.Gren.Rgt.24 *Danmark* left its positions and marched over 30kms on foot to Kyerstovo, while II/SS-Pz.Gren.Rgt.24 *Danmark* accompanied SS-Panzergrenadier-Regiment 23 *Norge* through Gorbovitsy to Kirovo and then to Byegunitsy. The *Danmark* regimental headquarters troops made their way to Zaozyorye. The retreat of these battalions was covered by 16 (Pi)/SS-Pz.Gren.Rgt.24 *Danmark* - the combat engineers - who slowly followed at the rear and on the flanks. This company linked up with the regimental HQ after nightfall on the 27th. The engineers were then sent to guard the bridge at Lamokha.

To say the least, the march through the snow-covered woods and swamps had been exhausting, although horse-drawn sleighs were used to transport supplies and the wounded. For the first time SS-Panzer-Abteilung 11, now titled *Hermann von Salza*, also went into action to provide cover for the withdrawing troops. It was quickly embroiled in a tank battle at Koporye, during which a direct hit from an enemy tank killed *SS-Hauptsturmführer* Holtkamp, the 1st Company commander, and one of his platoon leaders, *SS-Untersturmführer* Schmidichen, along with an NCO.

On the morning of 28th January, Kampfgruppe *Küste* and the 4 SS-Freiwilligen-Panzergrenadier-Brigade *Nederland* began readying to retreat, having first sending their heavy weapons and equipment ahead by rail. *SS-Brigadeführer* Kryssing first ordered the fortified positions erected by his command destroyed and then prepared to move out with the bulk of his troops. However, a message arrived directly from the Führer's Headquarters telling him to stay in place. Obviously this would hardly be a feasible proposition with all of the equipment gone and the positions demolished, so Kryssing appealed against the order to III (Germanische) SS-Panzerkorps HQ, which again gave the go-ahead to fall back. This was contradicted *again* by the Führer's HQ and the 'struggle' as to what to do went on for sometime, until Kryssing made the effort to radio supreme command directly and get the final word on what to do. When contact could not be made, Kryssing commenced the retreat from Vyelikino to Ostrov. Two days earlier, Kampfgruppe *Küste* had dispatched three convalescent companies with five 20mm Flak guns under the Norwegian engineer, *SS-Hauptsturmführer* Hoel, to guard the key bridge across the River Luga from the Gulf of Finland to the town of Yamburg. Its possession was critical to the withdrawal effort.

In the course of 28th January, SS-Artillerie-Regiment 11 reassembled at Rachino while the *Nordland* grenadier regiments came together around Gomontovo and Byegunitsy. The artillery regiment now kept up a steady fire on enemy forces farther to the east, both to hold back the Russians and to expend excess ammunition, so that it would not have to be transported or otherwise destroyed. In the afternoon of the 28th the retreat continued in the direction of Keikino and Yamburg on the Luga. *SS-*

Brigadeführer von Scholz personally led the column from I/SS-Pz.Gren.Rgt.23 *Norge* on its route through the woods to the south of the Yamburg highway.

To the north of the main *Nordland* body, III/SS-Pz.Gren.Rgt.24 *Danmark* found its way to the west blocked by a Soviet advance force near Kyerstovo. At the time the battalion commander, *SS-Sturmbannführer* Neergard-Jacobsen was with his 9th Company at Syergovitsy about 2kms to the east. He sent out his orderly officer, *SS-Untersturmführer* Herlov-Nielsen towards Kyerstovo to examine the situation, but he never returned - he had been captured by the Red Army. The decision was then made to veer to the south and try and find a clear route to the west.

Meanwhile SS-Artillerie-Regiment 11 had begun moving from Rachino to Gurlovo. *SS-Obersturmführer* Lärum's battery from III/SS-Art.Rgt.11 was caught in a Soviet ambush and lost most of its trucks and guns, as the vehicles towing the battery's howitzers were forced off into roadside ditches. However, the batteries following were far enough behind to avoid the entrapment, but even they had to abandon some of their heavy guns to make their way to safety.

By the evening of 28th January, the *Nordland* units were concentrated in an area running from Kyerstovo in the north to Opolye in the south. There were no 'front lines' *per se*, as Soviet forces probed and penetrated at will between the various Waffen-SS elements. The situation took a serious turn for the worse in the late afternoon when Gurlovo was seized by the Red Army before many of the *Nordland* troops *en route* to that town from the east had arrived. Gurlovo had to be recaptured immediately so that the withdrawal route from the east could be reopened.

At Litisno, *SS-Brigadeführer* von Scholz visited the command post of 7/SS-Pz.Gren.Rgt.24 *Danmark* and ordered the company CO, *SS-Hauptsturmführer* Heinz Hämel, to throw the Soviets back out of Gurlovo. Von Scholz and Hämel examined the terrain that would be covered in the attack from the low hills to the south-east of Litisno. After seizing Gurlovo, 7/SS-Pz.Gren.Rgt.24 *Danmark* would then have to keep the main highway open for as long as possible to enable everything to get through from the east that could. *SS-Hauptsturmführer* Heinz Hämel was a former NCO who had come up through the ranks (he was the first NCO of the *Wiking* Division to win the German Cross in Gold) and he had developed into a very reliable officer. In the coming night attack, 7/SS-Pz.Gren.Rgt.24 *Danmark* would be supported by a regimental motorcycle platoon led by *SS-Untersturmführer* Bertramsen and by two *sturmgeschütze* from SS-Panzerjäger-Abteilung 11.

Hämel started his attack at dusk along the road leading east to Gurlovo. The *sturmgeschütze* led the way, drawing heavy enemy fire in the process. This slowed them down and eventually stopped them altogether. When he saw this happen, Hämel was highly displeased and dashed over to the *sturmgeschütze* and ordered their commanders to proceed - in no uncertain terms! Once again they started up, guns blazing, and this time they did not stop. The *Danmark* grenadiers were right behind them. As Gurlovo burst into flames from the *sturmgeschütz* shells the Waffen-SS infantrymen surged forward. The Soviets attempted to retreat but they were too late; the men of 7/SS-Pz.Gren.Rgt.24 *Danmark* had closed in on them.

In two hours it was all over. The communist hold on Gurlovo has been broken in close combat. The main highway was reopened and a link-up was made with the beleaguered German troops to the east. The first unit to make contact with 7/SS-Pz.Gren.Rgt.24 *Danmark* was the SS-Artillerie-Regiment 11, which while advancing from the east helped to wipe out the last pockets of Soviet resistance around Gurlovo.

Also now free to continue on their way westwards were the main elements of SS-Panzergrenadier-Regiment 23 *Norge* and SS-Pionier-Bataillon 11. The next day, 29th

January 1944, saw heavy fighting around Opolye to the west of Gurlovo, where troops from *Norge* and the SS-Panzerjäger-Abteilung 11 spent most of the afternoon holding back advancing Red Army troops. In the fighting, the CO of SS-Panzerjäger-Abteilung 11, *SS-Hauptsturmführer* Roensch was killed standing alongside his command vehicle; he was replaced by the competent Army officer *Hauptmann* Dr Karl-Heinz Schulz-Streeck, who was later decorated with the Knight's Cross whilst serving with the Division *Nordland*.

By 30th January 1944, III (Germanische) SS-Panzerkorps troops finally reached positions around Yamburg on the River Luga, which was to be a temporary line of defence where, hopefully, all of the retreating elements could regroup. The first troops to reach Yamburg came from SS-Artillerie-Regiment 11 and they immediately took up firing positions. SS-Panzergrenadier-Regiment 23 *Norge* reassembled itself to the east of Yamburg and maintained a bridgehead across the Luga. To the north of Yamburg, the HQ of SS-Panzergrenadier-Regiment 24 *Danmark* was set up in the outskirts of Padoga with III Battalion in the nearby vicinity and II Battalion deployed along a railway line running north to Yukhkoma. I Battalion was not yet on the scene.

16 (Pi)/SS-Pz.Gren.Rgt.24 *Danmark* (combat engineers) had covered the regiment's withdrawal and had stayed for some time in positions to the rear of the railway line at Alyexyeyevka. After having lost contact with the rest of the regiment, the company CO, *SS-Untersturmführer* Aronious, ordered a retreat to the west, down the main highway. After travelling for more than a kilometre, the company ran into an approaching Russian column and a brief fire-fight ensued in which three of the *Danmark* engineers were killed and another four were wounded. When enemy heavy weapons began opening up on his troops, *SS-Untersturmführer* Aronious ordered a withdrawal 'on the run' to a forested area visible about a kilometre away to the south. The wounded were carried along but the dead had to be left behind. After reaching the woods the *Danmark* engineers were able to carry on their retreat without any further enemy interference. Later in the day the company linked up with II/SS-Pz.Gren.Rgt.24 *Danmark* to the north of Padoga.

From 28th January to 30th January 1944, SS-Kampfgruppe *Küste* and 4 SS-Freiwilligen-Panzergrenadier-Brigade *Nederland* made their way back to the Luga towards Keikino to the north of Padoga. Naturally the Soviets were in hot pursuit and time after time the Waffen-SS troops had to carry out emergency counterattacks to avoid being encircled. For a short time these units formed a bridgehead around Keikino on the east bank of the river, but by the evening of 30th January, all of the troops were pulled back across the Luga and the Keikino bridge was destroyed. During this time a convalescent company from SS-Kampfgruppe *Küste*, temporarily led by the Danish *SS-Sturmbannführer* Rantzau-Engelhardt was assigned to the SS-Panzergrenadier-Regiment 48 *General Seyffardt* of the *Nederland* Brigade.

Citation for the War Merit Cross 2nd Class to *Unterscharführer* Jørgen Johannsen from the Staff of II/SS-Pz.Gren.Rgt.24 *Danmark*. It is signed by the commander of the *Nordland* Division, *SS-Brigadeführer* Fritz von Scholz

SS-Untersturmführer Kaj A H Bertramsen. He was the first commander of 6/SS-Pz.Gren.Rgt.24 *Danmark* before taking over 11/SS-Pz.Gren.Rgt.24 *Danmark*. Bertramsen was killed in action in July 1944. In the photo he is wearing the Danish flag collar patch utilised by the Ersatzkompanie of the *Freikorps Danmark* at Babruisk

SS-Untersturmführer Leo Anton Madsen. Madsen was former NCO in the *Freikorps Danmark* who went on to command 7/SS-Pz.Gren.Rgt.24 *Danmark*

SS-Hauptsturmführer Erik Lärum, commander of 13/SS-Pz.Gren.Rgt.24 *Danmark*. Lärum was a former officer in the Royal Danish Army Air Force and wears his pilot's wings over his right pocket. Lärum was also leader of the NSU, the Danish National-Socialist Youth Movement

Erik Lärum as an *Untersturmführer* with the *Freikorps Danmark*

SS-Untersturmführer Robert Hansen. Hansen was a veteran of the Russo-Finnish Winter War and the Freikorps *Danmark*. He served for a brief time as a platoon leader in 7/SS-Pz.Gren.Rgt.24 *Danmark* before transferring over to the Panzer-Aufklärungs-Abteilung of the 5 SS-Panzer-Division *Wiking*

SS-Brigadeführer C P Kryssing, a Danish kampfgruppe commander with III (Germanische) SS-Panzerkorps

(Painting by Ramiro Bujeiro)

SS-*Untersturmführer* Robert Spahn who served with the staff of II/SS-Pz.Gren.Rgt.24 *Danmark*. He was missing-in-action in Kurland in January 1945

SS-*Oberscharführer* Oskar Kreutel, a German *Werkmeister* (Workshop Foreman) with 8/SS-Pz.Gren.Rgt.24 *Danmark*

Danmark officers with an unknown NCO. On the left is *Untersturmführer* Christian Ulrich Ditlev von Eggers; on the right, SS-*Obersturmführer* H Hennecke

CHAPTER V

The Retreat to Narva

The commander of Army Group North, *Generalfeldmarschall* Model, now intended to build up a new front behind the River Luga. Model gave III (Germanische) SS-Panzerkorps the task of defending the northern Luga and the bridgehead to the east of Yamburg. However, *SS-Obergruppenführer* Steiner argued that the Luga Line had already been compromised by breakthroughs by the Soviet 8th Army to the south. Instead, Steiner proposed a withdrawal to a permanent defensive line to the south and north of Lake Peipus on the Estonian frontier. He was overruled; III (Germanische) SS-Panzerkorps was ordered to stay put. The results would prove almost disastrous.

On 31st January 1944, the Red Army smashed through to Narva-Jõesuu on the coast of the Gulf of Finland; the Luga Line had now been broken in the north as well as in the south. The new breakthrough area, a road-less, swampy, forested region thought to be nearly impenetrable, had been defended only by an Army NCO training company subordinated to SS-Panzergrenadier-Regiment 48 *General Seyffardt*. The company lost all of its officers and half of its personnel trying to resist the Soviet advance. In the course of the day, small groups of the enemy were able to penetrate almost as far as the River Narva in Estonia.

At the same time, the Soviets launched a massive assault on the *Nordland* bridgehead positions from Yamburg to Padoga. II/SS-Pz.Gren.Rgt.24 *Danmark* and 16 (Pi)/SS-Pz.Gren.Rgt.24 *Danmark* were heavily engaged in defending a bridgehead without a bridge at Padoga; they were on the east bank of the Luga with no crossing points behind them. To get back across the river they would have to use the Yamburg bridge to the south; the northern Luga bridges had already been blown up.

After two hours of heavy fighting on 31st January, the entire *Danmark* sector began to weaken and the Red Army seemed on the verge of overrunning it. But once again, superhuman courage came to the fore to save the day. This time it was the spectacular performance of 5/SS-Pz.Gren.Rgt.24 *Danmark*, led by the former regimental adjutant, *SS-Obersturmführer* Walter Seebach, that carried out a desperate counterattack to hurl back the Soviet vanguard.

Following this success, 5th Company returned to the *Danmark* lines; it was then that *SS-Obersturmführer* Seebach discovered that seven of his wounded men had been left behind. Without hesitation he ordered his company back on the attack; their comrades would not be abandoned! In another raging fire-fight against strong opposition, 5/SS-Pz.Gren.Rgt.24 *Danmark* pushed its way back though the enemy positions and rescued all of the lost wounded from the first attack. In the forefront all the way was Walter Seebach. For his actions on this day, the Dutch-born Obersturmführer would be decorated with the Knight's Cross on 12th March 1944.

The Retreat to Narva

The Soviets renewed their strong assault on the *Danmark* sector on 1st February 1944. 9th and 10th Companies from III Battalion came under very heavy pressure and the lines began to buckle. I/SS-Pz.Gren.Rgt.24 *Danmark*, the regimental reserve, which had taken heavy losses during its retreat from the Oranienbaum sector (including the loss of its CO, *SS-Sturmbannführer* Fischer, who had been replaced by *SS-Hauptsturmführer* Wichart), was now placed on full alert. In addition the regiment's lightly wounded were gathered into a reserve company from *SS-Sturmbannführer* Neergard-Jacobsen's III/SS-Pz.Gren.Rgt.24 *Danmark*.

As the fighting raged on, 9/SS-Pz.Gren.Rgt.24 *Danmark* led by *SS-Untersturmführer* Darm, managed to throw back a Soviet spearhead force, while *SS-Obersturmführer* Worsoe Larsen was killed leading an unsuccessful counterattack. *SS-Sturmbannführer* Neergard-Jacobsen was wounded twice during the battle; as he was being evacuated following his second wounding, he ordered his battalion to fall back; the *Danmark* lines had been irrevocably broken.

Much of the regiment now retreated though Yamburg. On 1st February 1944, the town was abandoned and the bridge over the Luga destroyed. To the south of Yamburg, the Red Army had already made headway in a sector held by elements of SS-Panzergrenadier-Regiment 23 *Norge*. II/SS-Pz.Gren.Rgt.24 *Danmark* was now called into action in this to help block the enemy breakthrough. Somewhat farther to the south-east the *Danmark* engineers defended the Komarovka Road against enemy motorised forces until the evening of 1st February

On 30th January 1944, Kampfgruppe *Küste* was ordered to fall back to Narva-Jõesuu and organise defensive positions in the River Narva delta. *Nordland* and *Nederland* were still supposed to hold the Luga Line. At 1700 hours on 31st January 1944, III (Germanische) SS-Panzerkorps HQ sent out the following message to troops under its command "The Russians have broken through the Luga positions. Effective immediately, the River Narva is now the main line of defence".

The *Nordland* Division was instructed to occupy the city of Narva itself; the divisional retreat was to be covered by the battalions from *Norge* and *Danmark*, which were to 'leapfrog' each other on the way to the River Narva. The situation could get difficult as was exemplified by the plight of III/SS-Pz.Gren.Rgt.23 *Norge* and the *Norge* Regimental HQ, both of which were almost overrun by Soviet vanguard troops and had to be rescued by prompt counterattacks.

The strategic location of Narva was undeniable. The ancient, fortified city in north-eastern Estonia dominated a rather inhospitable terrain. To the north and south of the city were thick forests and near-impenetrable swamps. The city had evolved around the Narva Fortress on the west bank of the river, built by the Danish rulers of the area in the 13th Century. The old castle was eventually taken over by the German Teutonic-Livonian Order. In the early 16th Century the Germans added a 50m tall tower to the top of the castle known as the 'Long Herman'. From that time on the entire edifice was called *Hermannsburg*.

At the end of the 15th Century the Russians had begun to build their own fortress on the east bank of the river, directly opposite what would become the Hermannsburg. This castle was known as the Ivangorod. It was also modified in the 16th Century by Greek architects, to keep peace with the developments at the Hermannsburg. Both of these striking buildings still dominated the city of Narva in 1944, although they were now linked together by a bridge and the town had long since spread past the Ivangorod on the east bank of the river.

SS-Obergruppenführer Steiner immediately made the decision to set up an extensive bridgehead defensive position on the east bank of the River Narva taking in not only the Ivangorod but all of the eastern part of the city and its outskirts. Forward outposts were to be established around the defensive perimeter. All that remained was to get the troops back safely into the designated positions.

Fortunately the distance from the Luga to the Narva was not great and in the course of 1st February, most of III (Germanische) SS-Panzerkorps troops had managed to make their way back, under the protection of armoured cars from SS-Panzer-Aufklärungs-Abteilung 11. These vehicles stayed out as long as they could, seeking out the enemy and protecting stragglers. The last armoured car from 5/SS-Pz.Aufkl.Abt.11, under the Dutch *SS-Rottenführer* Kasper Sporck, returned to the Narva Bridgehead at dusk with the enemy right behind. Sporck would win the Knight's Cross while covering the next III (Germanische) SS-Panzerkorps withdrawal from Narva to the Tannenberg Positions in July 1944.

Initially, the *Nederland* Brigade took up positions in the central and northern sectors of the Narva Bridgehead and SS-Panzergrenadier-Regiment 23 *Norge* was placed in the south part of the bridgehead. *Norge* would gradually be replaced by SS-Panzergrenadier-Regiment 24 *Danmark*, and it would then fall back to the southern part of Narva on the west bank of the river. A number of Army and Police kampfgruppen were also brought in to reinforce the bridgehead defences. Over the next few days the 20 Waffen-Grenadier-Division der SS (*estnische Nr 1*)[4] would be brought up from the south to take up positions to the north of Narva on the west bank while at the same time maintaining outposts to the north of the eastern bank bridgehead.

The northern part of the Narva front was held by mixed troops from Kampfgruppe *Küste* and the *Nederland*'s SS-Pionier-Bataillon 54. The headquarters for Kampfgruppe *Küste* was established at Auga and positions were maintained along the Gulf of Finland to the west. The *Nordland* division command post was set up in two civilian busses which could move around the Narva Bridgehead as needed.

Helping to reinforce the bridgehead in early February was the Army's potent, Tiger-equipped, Schwere Panzer-Abteilung 502. It would soon be withdrawn however to help eliminate a Soviet incursion on the west bank of the Narva at Kudruküla midway between Narva-Jõesuu and Narva. With the help of some of the Tigers, reserve troops from Kampfgruppe *Küste* under the personal leadership of *SS-Brigadeführer* Kryssing flung the Red Army troops back across the Narva at Kudruküla in early February 1944.

Several more enemy penetrations were made and these had to be dealt with by other mobile elements by the *Nordland* Division. Since the River Narva was frozen solid at the time, it was fairly easy for the Red Army troops to make the crossing. On 12th February a particularly dangerous enemy inroad was made between Riigi and Siivertsi to the north of Narva. Here a strong Soviet force managed to breakthrough positions held by the *Nederland*'s SS-Pionier-Bataillon 54 and eventually reached the main road to Tallinn. The *sturmgeschütz* units from *Nederland* and *Nordland* had to be rushed from the outskirts of Narva to help stop the enemy advance. In the meantime the *Nederland* engineers, reinforced by the *Norge* and *Danmark* engineer companies had to do their best to block the foe from gaining any further ground.

An all-out battle for the sector around Siivertsi raged all day long on 13th February 1944. The first objective was to stop any further Red Army infantry from crossing the river. The III (Germanische) SS-Panzerkorps engineers, holding positions behind gravestones in the northern part of the Siivertsi cemetery, blazed away at the potential enemy reinforcements with everything they had and managed to prevent them from crossing the Narva. Afterwards, attention was paid to the Soviet troops who had already reached the west bank; the SS engineers managed to keep them pinned down in

---

[4] 20th SS Infantry Division (*Estonian No 1*), composed of Estonian volunteers

their own bridgehead perimeter. But once again the Red Army tried to cross the ice with additional soldiers. This time heavy weapons came into play and, fortunately, it the solid ice-field covering the Narva began to break up under the impact of the exploding shells! No more reinforcements could get through, but the battle continued through the rest of the month.

The Red Army were forced out of Siivertsi and eventually concentrated their west bank forces at Vepsküla. All efforts by the various III (Germanische) SS-Panzerkorps troops to expel them permanently seemed doom to fail. A kampfgruppe from SS-Panzergrenadier-Regiment 23 *Norge* supported by *Nederland* artillery and *sturmgeschütze*, Tigers and the *Norge* and *Danmark* engineers kept up the pressure but took heavy losses in savage fighting. In fact, 11/SS-Pz.Gren.Rgt.23 *Norge* virtually ceased to exist once all of its officers were lost; 20 of the survivors were incorporated as reinforcements in 16 (Pi)/SS-Pz.Gren.Rgt.24 *Danmark* while another 31 carried on under the leadership of an Army *Hauptmann*.

The fate of the Soviet bridgehead was not decided until 29th February 1944, when fresh Estonian SS troops from the 20 Waffen-Grenadier-Division der SS (*estnische Nr 1*) cleaned up the Red Army pocket in vicious close-combat. It was a heroic assault troop effort led by the Estonian *Waffen-Unterscharführer* Harald Nugiseks that finally succeeded in penetrating the enemy positions and eliminating them - a feat which would bring Nugiseks the award of the Knight's Cross.

SS-Unterscharführer Vagn Thor Nielsen, a veteran of the *Wiking* Division. Nielsen later graduated from the Motor Transport school of the Waffen-SS in Vienna in the summer of 1943 and he became the *Schirrmeister* (Foreman Mechanic) of II/SS-Pz.Gren.Rgt.24 *Danmark*

SS-Unterscharführer Svend Nielsen who served in 6/SS-Pz.Gren.Rgt.24 *Danmark* A veteran of the *Freikorps Danmark*, he was known as "Bette-Svend" (Little Svend)

SS-Rottenführer Helge Hansen, another veteran of the *Freikorps*, known as "Farmand" (Daddy). He served with the workshop (I-Staffel) of II/SS-Pz.Gren.Rgt.24 *Danmark*

SS-*Sturmmann* Erik Jacobsen, who was a *Schreiber* (typist-clerk) on the staff of II/SS-Pz.Gren.Rgt.24 *Danmark*

SS-*Rottenführer* Walter Strupp, a German who served as driver for the *Danmark* transport officer, *Hstuf* Willi Rossmann

SS-*Rottenführer* Aage Dahl as an *Unterführer-Anwärter* (NCO candidate). He first served with 11/SS-Pz.Gren.Rgt.24 *Danmark* but later was transferred to the Staff Company. Once again note the wearing of the two Danish cuff titles

Members of 12/SS-Pz.Gren.Rgt.24 *Danmark* with an Infanteriegeschütz.

From the left: *Obersturmführer* Grev Lercke and *Hauptsturmführer* Thorius

Two Danes with an *Osttruppe* (Eastern or Soviet volunteer) in the centre. On the right is *Unterscharführer* Aage Dahl

SS-Sturmmann Kurt Tebring, a Danish volunteer who served with a tank crew from SS-Panzer-Abteilung 11 *Hermann von Salza*

SS-Unterscharführer Hüscke with the Regiment *Danmark*

Danish volunteers: Aage Dahl (left) and J Olsen

SS-Rottenführer Borum with the Regiment *Danmark*

SS-Unterscharführer Aage Dahl with the Regiment *Danmark*

Danish volunteers: Aage Dahl (left), Alfred Jonstrup (centre) and J Olsen

The sign points to the Regimental Ferntross (rear echelon train). Note the Dannebrog on the sign post. On the right is *Rottenführer* Jens Peter Nielsen who was known as "Strom" (electric current). On the left is a Danish mechanic

(Left) Jens Peter Nielsen who came from 2/*Freikorps Danmark* to the workshop of II/SS-Pz.Gren.Rgt.24 *Danmark*

(Right and below) A Danish workshop mechanic. Many of the veterans knew him but none could remember his name

CHAPTER VI

The Battle for Narva

The night of 13th/14th February 1944 saw an ambitious Soviet attack launched from the Gulf of Finland directed at Mereküla behind the German Narva Front. After an initial surprise, the HQ staff of Kampfgruppe *Küste* began quickly to formulate a resistance. *SS-Sturmbannführer* Rantzau-Engelhardt, the kampfgruppe chief-of-staff, began to muster personally a relief force from the HQ staff and assorted other elements, while the CO, *SS-Brigadeführer* Kryssing alerted his reserves and called upon III (Germanische) SS-Panzerkorps for assistance. Help was soon on the way from the SS-Panzer-Aufklärungs-Abteilung 11.

Commencing at 0900 hours on the morning of 14th February, a combined unit attack utilising Army, Kriegsmarine and Waffen-SS personnel swept down on the Soviet force that had landed at Mereküla. With the support of Stukas and *sturmgeschütze* from 5/SS-Art.Abt.11, the attack was a complete success. *SS-Sturmbannführer* Rantzau-Engelhardt personally led a small troop of three tanks and thirty panzergrenadiere in the battle. In about an hour it was all over. Some 300 enemy soldiers were killed on the battlefield while another 50 or more had drowned trying to land earlier in the morning. Another 275 Red Army soldiers were captured. News of this defensive success was quickly radioed to III (Germanische) SS-Panzerkorps HQ. It had been the decisive leadership of the two senior Danish Waffen-SS officers that had helped settle the issue so swiftly.

The southern sector of the Narva Front also became threatened in late February 1944; here a heroic and successful defensive effort was carried out by the SS-Panzergrenadier-Regiment 23 *Norge* led by *SS-Obersturmbannführer* Arnold Stoffers (who would be killed leading a counterattack on 25th February). Within a month the grenadiers of *Norge* had not only halted the Soviet advance but had also regained much lost ground. This led to the tragic discovery of the mass murder of many Estonian civilians who had been forced into slave labour for the Red Army. For the SS soldiers it was just another example of the inhuman face of the enemy and only reinforced their further belief in the justice of their struggle against an uncivilised, barbaric foe!

During early March 1944, the Soviet ground offensive against the Narva Bridgehead ground to a halt and was replaced instead by massive air raids and artillery bombardments. The result was the near total destruction of the historic city of Narva. Most of the civilian population now fled to safety (to be replaced largely by Russians in the post-war era!) but the SS defenders simply dug in deeper. While personnel losses were not particularly heavy, material losses, including those suffered during the withdrawal from the Oranienbaum Pocket, were huge and not easily replaced. Regiment

Danmark alone reported a loss of 34 motor vehicles along with a third of its close support artillery and two-thirds of its Flak guns.

In the middle of March 1944, following days of constant bombardment of the bridgehead, the Red Army again launched a strong attack, first on the sector due east of the city of Narva which was defended by SS-Panzergrenadier-Regiment 48 *General Seyffardt* of the 4 SS-Freiwilligen-Panzergrenadier-Brigade *Nederland*. The regiment was stretched to its limit but managed to stop the new communist advance and then go over to the attack. The Soviets were thrown back, thanks to the valiant efforts of the Dutch and German SS volunteers. The SS-Panzergrenadier-Regiment 48 *General Seyffardt* commander, *SS-Obersturmbannführer* Wolfgang Jörchel, who led the operations from the front line, was awarded the Knight's Cross for his regiment's performance.

Following their failure against the SS-Panzergrenadier-Regiment 48 *General Seyffardt*, the Red Army began another heavy assault to the north-west of Narva, near Lilienbach. Here they ran into more troops from the *Nederland* Brigade; notably from *SS-Obersturmbannführer* Hans Collani's SS-Panzergrenadier-Regiment 49 *De Ruyter* and the SS-Pionier-Bataillon 54. After several days of very violent fighting and a necessary withdrawal from the foremost positions, the front lines in this area stabilised with the assistance of a kampfgruppe formed from 9/SS-Pz.Gren.Rgt.24 *Danmark* along with troops from SS-Panzergrenadier-Regiment 23 *Norge* and tanks from the SS-Panzer-Abteilung 11 *Hermann von Salza*. *SS-Oberscharführer* Philipp Wild, from 1/SS-Pz.Abt.11 *Hermann von Salza*, would receive the Knight's Cross for his deeds during this fighting.

The action at Lilienbach marked the end of the sustained combat that had begun with the Oranienbaum breakout. The Bolsheviks had finally run out of steam and an uneasy lull in the battle for Narva took over, but the 'war of the snipers' now began! For the next few months sniping, artillery shelling and small unit actions became the dominant features of the Narva bridgehead fighting. While the scope of the action was no longer intense, casualties still accumulated and the front lines remained extremely dangerous.

SS-Panzergrenadier-Regiment 24 *Danmark* now took over the defence of the entire south-eastern corner of the bridgehead; its positions stretched from the southern part of the main rail lines in the north where they joined those of SS-Panzergrenadier-Regiment 48 *General Seyffardt*, to a course bearing south-south-west along the whole southern perimeter of the Narva bridgehead ranging from the village of Dolgaya Niva in the south-east to fortified islands in the River Narva to the west. The *Danmark* HQ was established on the east bank of the river due east of the township of Kreenholm on the west bank. Initially, I/SS-Pz.Gren.Rgt.24 *Danmark* manned the north-east sector of the sector, with II/SS-Pz.Gren.Rgt.24 *Danmark* in the south-west to the River Narva and with III/SS-Pz.Gren.Rgt.24 *Danmark* in reserve to the north-east of the regimental headquarters. However I/SS-Pz.Gren.Rgt.24 *Danmark* would be removed from the front for refitting in April 1944 - never again to return to the Division *Nordland* - and III/SS-Pz.Gren.Rgt.24 *Danmark* would then assume its front line positions.

Opposite the *Danmark* positions to the south of Kreenholm on the west bank of the river was the SS-Panzergrenadier-Regiment 23 *Norge*, while Kreenholm itself housed the artillery and transport elements of the *Nordland* Division. The divisional headquarters were established in an old Estonian Army barracks to the north of Kreenholm. The *Danmark* sector was so large that elements from the SS-Pionier-Bataillon 11 were sent in to reinforce it. In effect, there simply were not enough soldiers to fully man the lines, particularly after the withdrawal of I/SS-Pz.Gren.Rgt.24

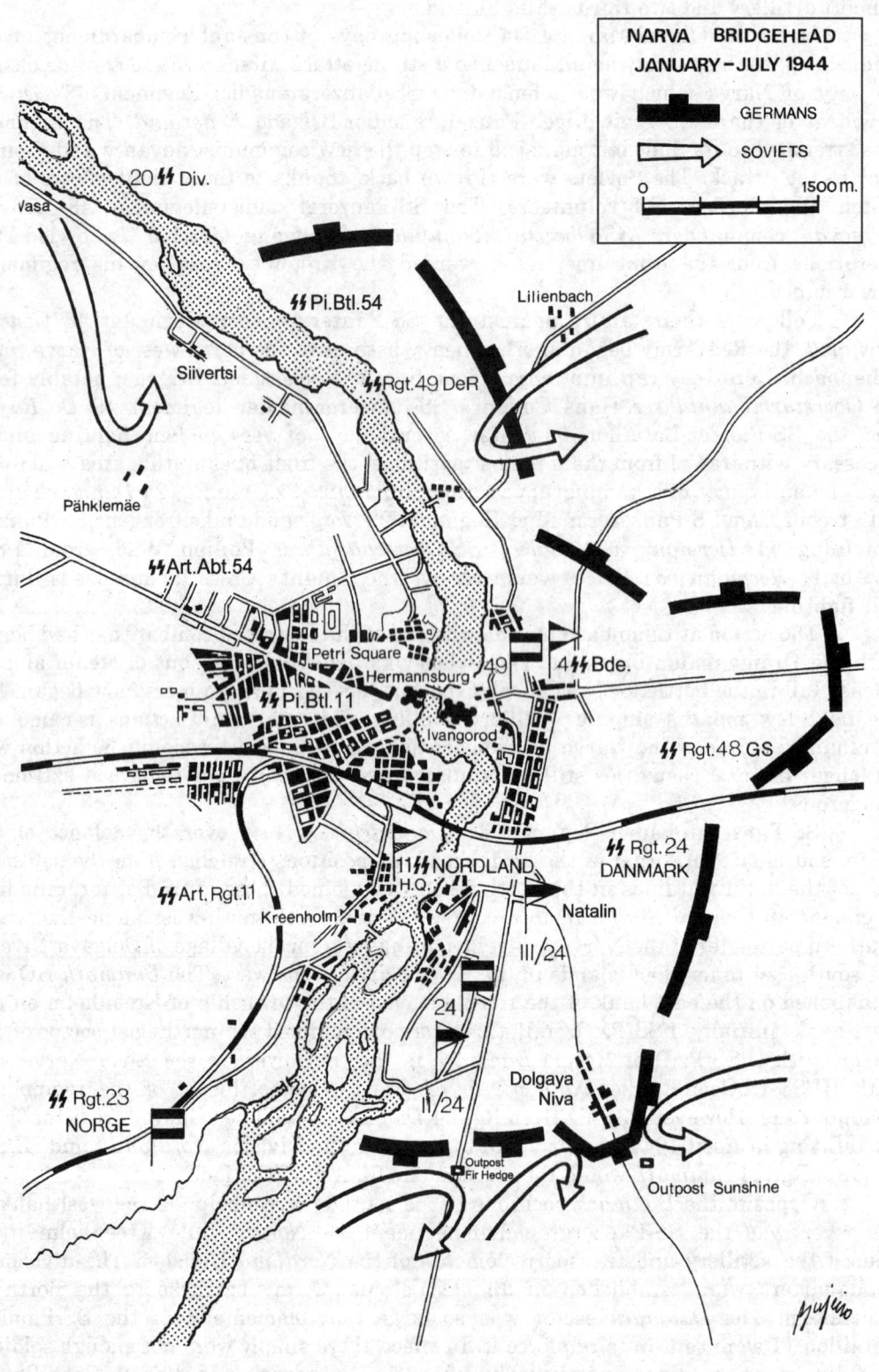

Danmark, so sections had to be guarded through the use of fortified outposts. This was a speciality of the combat engineers and it was where they were put to best use.

Near the village of Dolgaya Niva, which was the most south-easterly point on the Narva bridgehead front, 1/SS-Pi.Btl.11 constructed two forward outposts in 'no-man's land'. Named *Fir Hedge (Tannenhecke)* and *Sunshine (Sonnenschein)*, the two outposts were situated about ½km equidistant from both the German and Russian lines. They were designed to serve as jumping-off points for raiding parties and as early warning centres for any enemy offensive activities. Troops from II/SS-Pz.Gren.Rgt.24 *Danmark* along with some *Nordland* engineers manned the outposts, with 7/SS-Pz.Gren.Rgt.24 *Danmark* being placed in charge of Outpost *Sunshine*. These troops soon carried out a very successful raiding operation from *Sunshine* which bore the descriptive title of Operation *Stinkfisch (Smelly Fish)*!

During this period the I/SS-Pz.Gren.Rgt.24 *Danmark* positions received excellent protection from the guns of SS-Artillerie-Regiment 11, under *SS-Obersturmbannführer* Friedrich Karl, and from the heavy weapons of the SS-Panzergrenadier-Regiment 23 *Norge*, all of which were in place on the west bank of the River Narva, opposite the *Danmark* sector. The batteries of SS-Artillerie-Regiment 11 were so effective that they received the appellation "Our foot Stukas" from the front-line grenadiers!

In the meantime, the Waffen-SS high command took advantage of the relative calm to try and bolster some of the depleted units of III (Germanische) SS-Panzerkorps. As mentioned previously, it was decided to extract one battalion each from the *Danmark* and *Norge* regiments for complete refitting. Therefore, the two first battalions of each of the *Nordland* SS-Panzergrenadier-Regiments were pulled out of the front and sent back to Germany. All of the equipment and some of the personnel from the battalions were left behind to be used in stiffening the remaining two battalions in each of the regiments. No one would know it at the time, but neither I/SS-Pz.Gren.Rgt.24 *Danmark* nor I/SS-Pz.Gren.Rgt.23 *Norge* would ever return to the Division *Nordland*. After completing their reformation they would be sent to the 5 SS-Panzer-Division *Wiking* in December 1944 to participate in the Budapest relief attempts. Both battalions would then remain with *Wiking* as independent units until the end of the war. The detachment of I/SS-Pz.Gren.Rgt.24 *Danmark* cost the Regiment *Danmark* some 380 men while the similar fate of I/SS-Pz.Gren.Rgt.23 *Norge* took the overall *Norge* strength down by 369 troops.

On 9th April 1944, Regiment *Danmark* would suffer its greatest individual tragedy to date when the commander, *SS-Obersturmbannführer* Graf von Westphalen was mortally wounded by an enemy artillery shell fragment while crossing the Kreenholm bridge. Von Westphalen was evacuated to the III (Germanische) SS-Panzerkorps military hospital in Tallinn, Estonia, where he would eventually die on 28th May 1944. His replacement, named on 10th April 1944, was the very competent *SS-Sturmbannführer* Albrecht Krügel[5]. This highly decorated former officer of the *Wiking* Division had been awarded the Knight's Cross in March 1944 while leading II/SS-Pz.Gren.Rgt.23 *Norge*.

As of 25th May 1944, Danish SS volunteers constituted a little more than 10% of the net strength of the *Nordland* Division. At this time there were 1,109 Danes in total in the unit broken down as follows: 37 officers, 220 NCOs and 832 men. Despite heavy losses in the months to come, new replacements would help boost the number of Danes in the division to nearly 1,400 by September 1944. In comparison the total number of

---

[5] Born 22nd April 1913 - SS Number 11433

Norwegians in *Nordland* had slumped to 338 on 25th May 1944, increasing to 534 by September. Part of the reason for this disparity was that Norwegian volunteers were also being used to fill the purely Norwegian SS-Skijäger-Bataillon *Norge* (strength about 300 men) that served with the 6 SS-Gebirgs-Division *Nord* in Finland. Many of this battalion's soldiers probably would have otherwise ended up in the Division *Nordland*.

By early June 1944, enemy pressure on the outskirts of the *Danmark* positions began to increase and on 7th June the Soviets attempted to seize Outpost *Sunshine*. In the fierce fighting that ensued the Red Army was thrown back, but *SS-Untersturmführer* Berthelsen, the CO of 7/SS-Pz.Gren.Rgt.24 *Danmark* was killed. His replacement was *SS-Untersturmführer* Madsen, a veteran of the *Freikorps Danmark*. As it turned out this little action was just a prelude to things to come.

On 12th June the largest enemy bombardment of the *Danmark* sector to date began. Included in the barrage were smoke mortar shells directed at Dolgaya Niva where II/SS-Pz.Gren.Rgt.24 *Danmark* had its headquarters. The purpose was clearly to impede visibility and cause confusion amongst the Waffen-SS grenadiers. At Outpost *Sunshine* it became evident that an enemy attack was in the offing and *SS-Untersturmführer* Madsen fired off a signal flare directed towards the regimental HQ to give warning. As the afternoon of the 12th progressed the Red Army began to close in on the isolated outpost and a heavy skirmish began. Part of 7th Company fell back on the II/SS-Pz.Gren.Rgt.24 *Danmark* command post, but another element of the company took shelter in the high bush clumps that dotted no-man's land and began fighting back. A violent struggle now erupted near the northern part of Outpost *Sunshine* and two of 7/SS-Pz.Gren.Rgt.24 *Danmark*'s platoon leaders were killed in hand-to-hand combat.

The regimental headquarters reacted promptly to the signal flare from Outpost *Sunshine* and requested close artillery support for the threatened sector from SS-Artillerie-Regiment 11. The SS gunners directed an accurate fire on the Soviet forces advancing on Dolgaya Niva, disrupting their attack. Farther to the west an assault force of 120 Red Army troops had broken through the lines but they were soon targeted by the heavy weapons companies of Regiment *Danmark* situated near the regimental HQ. Standing in plain view on top of a ruined factory building, *SS-Hauptsturmführer* Lärum directed the fire of the *Danmark* guns by shouting directions down to the gun crews. Within a short time the enemy penetration force had been annihilated.

But now another critical situation developed at Dolgaya Niva: some 200 more Red Army troops had got through to the II/SS-Pz.Gren.Rgt.24 *Danmark* command post Everyone on the battalion staff was thrown into the fight under the personal leadership of the CO, *SS-Hauptsturmführer* Heinz Hämel. But again it was the accurate fire of SS artillery batteries that 'broke the back' of the communist attack; very few of the soldiers in the first Red Army assault wave would return alive to their own lines!

The situation at Outpost *Sunshine* was even more critical; the isolated position had largely been captured by the Soviets. Someone had to do something to prevent a total disaster from developing! Fortunately the initiative was taken by the Danish squad leader, *SS-Unterscharführer* Egon Christophersen. Gathering up other dispersed SS troops in no-man's land he personally led them in a swift counterattack against the Red Army-occupied positions in Outpost *Sunshine*. Storming forward, the *Danmark* troopers killed or drove back the communists and regained the old 7th Company lines. In savage close fighting all of the Red Army troops were driven out of Outpost *Sunshine* by Christophersen's small kampfgruppe and the threat to the Narva bridgehead was soon over. *SS-Hauptsturmführer* Hämel soon arrived at the regained positions and he immediately pinned the Iron Cross 1st Class on Christophersen's tunic. The valiant Danish NCO would also soon receive the Knight's Cross for his deeds.

The Battle for Narva

The war diary of II/SS-Pz.Gren.Rgt.24 *Danmark* recorded the following account of the events of 12th June 1944:

'After the deployment of heavy artillery fire and smoke mortars by the enemy against the battalion command post, the enemy troops worked their way to the battalion's positions, being stopped effectively at the positions of 7th Company. Afterwards, the enemy pressed into Dolgaya Niva, outflanking the forward post *Sunshine* and making Dolgaya Niva the focal point of the attack. The enemy was driven to cover and halted by our strongpoints. We had lost 25 men dead with 10 more missing; 2 others had fallen into shock. In our bunkers lay more corpses, identified by the battalion medical officer as belonging to the forward post *Sunshine*. It was assumed that the missing men had all perished in their burnt-out bunker, with perhaps 3 or 4 men being taken prisoner. The confused situation permitted little clear overview of what was transpiring. *SS-Hauptsturmführer* Hämel went into the foremost lines that had been cleared of the enemy in a counterattack by *SS-Unterscharführer* Christophersen and his group.

At the same time as the Soviet attack on Dolgaya Niva, groups of about 40 to 60 enemy soldiers assaulted Natalin and Usküla. These diversionary efforts were easily repulsed. With strong artillery assistance and the help of part of 7th Company, the regimental tank destruction platoon[6] and engineers supported by two *sturmgeschütze* and parts of 9th Company, Dolgaya Niva and outpost *Sunshine* remained in our hands. Our total losses amounted to 90 dead and wounded and 3 light machine guns destroyed. Enemy booty taken included one Pak [anti-tank] gun, 2 heavy machine guns and 4 light machine guns. *SS-Untersturmführer* Koopman, the commander of outpost *Sunshine*, was killed in the fighting".

---

[6] **Regiments-Panzer-Vernichtungs-Zug** Close combat infantry anti-tank platoon, equipped with panzerfaust, mines etc., rather than anti-tank guns.

SS-*Obersturmbannführer* Albrecht Krügel as CO of the Regiment *Danmark*. He was killed-in-action in 1945

Obersturmbannführer Krügel decorating soldiers of the Regiment *Danmark*. Behind him is *Hauptsturmführer* Rudi Ternedde

SS-Unterscharführer Egon Christophersen, a veteran of the Wiking Division who transferred into Regiment *Danmark*. He won the Knight's Cross on 11th July 1944 while serving with 7/SS-Pz.Gren.Rgt.24 *Danmark*. He had already been decorated with the Iron Cross 2nd (26.3.43) and 1st Class (28.5.44)

A ceremony in Hannover, Germany in July 1944 honouring Egon Christophersen. From left to right: *Gauleiter* Hartmann-Lauterbacher from Hannover, Christophersen, *Kreisleiter* Meier from Hannover, *SS-Hauptsturmführer* Otto Wojahn, the liaison officer for the Germanic SS volunteers and (concealed), *SS-Obersturmführer* Georg Langendorf, the CO of 5/SS-Pz.Abt.11 *Hermann von Salza*

SS-Sturmbannführer Heinz Hämel, CO of II/SS-Pz.Gren.Rgt.24 *Danmark* after receiving the Knight's Cross on 16th June 1944

Hauptsturmführer Hämel receiving the Knight's Cross from *Brigadeführer* von Scholz

Danish SS volunteers on the Narva Front

Danish SS men on the Narva Front

Two views of the Hermannsburg at Narva before the battle. Afterwards it was largely reduced to rubble

SS-Unterscharführer Vagn Thor Nielsen with the Regiment *Danmark* at Kohtla-Järve in February 1944. The kneeling man is Finn Jensen

(Right and below) Danish SS volunteers in Narva, 1944

Danmark soldiers in the city of Narva, 1944

(Left and below) Danes in Narva, 1944

European SS volunteers rescue some church bells from the ruins at Narva, 1944

Arne Kanstrup. He came the long way from 1/*Freikorps Danmark* to 1/SS-Pz.Gren.Rgt.24 *Danmark* and eventually to 7/SS-Pz.Gren.Rgt.24 *Danmark*. He was so badly wounded in the right arm in November 1944 that he could not return to the front

Holger Mogensen, another veteran of the *Freikorps*, with his girlfriend. He fell at Narva

The grave of *Obersturmführer* Johannes Frederiksen at Kreenholm, Narva, Estonia. The Danish *Ostuf* Frederiksen served with 16/SS-Pz.Gren.Rgt.24 *Danmark* and fell in action on 3rd February 1944. He was part of the colour guard at the last parade of the *Freikorps Danmark* in Grafenwöhr 20th May 1943

CHAPTER VII

The Battle for the Tannenberg Positions

The massive Soviet summer offensive, which tore a 400km chunk out of Army Group Centre in late 1944, indirectly threatened the stability of Army Group North and the Narva Front. The possibility now clearly existed that the German and European forces operating in the Baltic states could be permanently isolated from the rest of the Eastern Front. In addition, it was learned from prisoners that a new, massive Red Army assault on the Narva Front was in the offing. This was accentuated by increasingly heavier bombing attacks on Narva and the surrounding towns and by more small unit probing attacks.

Therefore, other plans had to be drawn up. The Narva bridgehead positions simply would not be tenable for long in the face of a full-scale enemy attack. Thus the HQ of Armee-Abteilung *Narwa* and III (Germanische) SS-Panzerkorps, which was now under the temporary command of *SS-Obergruppenführer* Matthias Kleinheisterkamp, devised secondary defensive lines 25kms due west of the River Narva, which were referred to as the Tannenberg Positions. In this area the terrain ranged from slightly hilly country near the northern coast to swampy ground in the south which hindered motor traffic. Other than that, defensive preparations in the area were rather minimal.

By early July it was decided to begin a systematic withdrawal of all the forces from Narva and the bridgehead back to the Tannenberg Positions as soon as the enemy's offensive intentions could be ascertained. This would be a rather tricky undertaking, since any miscalculation could lead to disaster. Now all that could be done was to await further developments - which were not long in coming. On 11th July 1944, the southern wing of the 18 Armee, to which III (Germanische) SS-Panzerkorps was subordinated, was attacked in force by the Soviet 2nd Baltic Front. This precipitated a withdrawal in that sector to the Marienburg Line that ran along the railway line from Pskov to Jēkabpils. This made it clear that the days of occupation of the Narva area were numbered.

17th July saw another strong enemy assault on the *Danmark* positions around Outpost *Sunshine*. Once again violent fighting raged and the foremost positions were lost. This time *SS-Untersturmführer* Spleth led the counterattack that threw back the communists but he was killed in the process. However, after a vicious hand-to-hand engagement, the lines were regained and many enemy soldiers were killed or captured. These new captives in particular revealed that a full-scale Red Army attack would soon follow. As a result III (Germanische) SS-Panzerkorps troops were put on a higher state of alert.

On 19th July the decision to fall back on the Tannenberg Positions was made, although the full evacuation would not get underway until the enemy approached closer to Narva. Still, support units began aligning themselves for a rapid withdrawal and work began in earnest on defences in the Tannenberg sector. Although the exact date of the Red Army attack was not known, everyone now knew that it was imminent. The withdrawal from the Narva bridgehead positions to the west bank of the river was initiated on 23rd July.

On the next day, 24th July 1944, a massive, two-pronged Soviet attack on the Narva Front began. The assault featured two pincer movements, one to the far north aimed at Riigi - Narva-Jõesuu and another to the south directed towards Vaivara. The aim was to break through at both points and then unite the two pincers behind the bulk of the Armee-Abteilung *Narwa*. Fortunately there were obstacles in the way of this. The southern wing of the attack had to move through marsh and swamp country that was being defended by the combat-hardened veterans of the East Prussian 11 Infanterie-Division. Although massive infantry and armoured forces were thrown into this onslaught, the Red Army were not able to make any initial headway whatsoever against the stubborn East Prussians. This sector held; the southern pincer would not be able to help with the planned envelopment of Armee-Abteilung *Narwa*!

Unfortunately the same could not be said of the northern pincer. In the Riigi - Narva-Jõesuu area on the northern Gulf of Finland seacoast the enemy achieved a major breakthrough against troops of the 20 Waffen-Grenadier-Division der SS (*estnische Nr 1*). As these soldiers began to retreat westward they left vulnerable the northern flank of Armee-Abteilung *Narwa*. In the meantime, engineers, naval and penal troops had begun working around the clock to construct defences in the Tannenberg Positions. The key points here would be a pair of low hills, namely *Grenadier Hill* (*Grenadierhöhe*) and *Orphanage Hill* (*Kinderheimhöhe*)[7], which dominated the landscape. A Flemish SS battalion from the 6 SS-Freiwilligen-Sturmbrigade *Langemarck*[8], which had been sent as reinforcement to the Narva Front, was placed in position on the critical Orphanage Hill.

At 2330 hours on 24th July 1944, the evacuation of the Narva bridgehead began with troops from the SS-Panzergrenadier-Regiment 24 *Danmark* (less its 7th Company) and I/SS-Pz.Gren.Rgt.49 *De Ruyter* crossing the River Narva bridges to the west. Soon after them came the entire SS-Panzergrenadier-Regiment 48 *General Seyffardt* and II/SS-Pz.Gren.Rgt.49 *De Ruyter* followed by 7/SS-Pz.Gren.Rgt.24 *Danmark*, which served as the rearguard. These troops were ordered to fall back only as far as Narva city on the west bank of the river and hold positions there for the next 24 hours.

The plan now was for the III (Germanische) SS-Panzerkorps troops to systematically fall back on a series of four designated 'delaying positions' in succession before going into the main Tannenberg defensive lines. At each position, the SS troops were supposed to hold the enemy as long as possible, if necessary, before going on to the next. Initially, this worked perfectly well, as the troops did not have to retreat under pressure, but during the latter phases of the operation this scheme would break down into a mad scramble which in turn would cause the tragic annihilation of the SS-Panzergrenadier-Regiment 48 *General Seyffardt*.

By midnight on 25th July 1944, the final withdrawal from Narva had been completed. The engineers from the *Nederland* Brigade stayed behind to blow up the river bridges, an operation which had to be carried out in the face of enemy fire after one of the bridges failed to blow! However the job was eventually accomplished and all

---

[7] The Estonian names for these are *Grenaderimägi* and *Lastekodumägi* respectively, the chain of hills being known as the *Sinimäed* (The Blue Hills).

[8] For further information on the 6th SS Brigade *Langemarck* at Narva, see: R Landwehr Lions of Flanders (1996) Shelf Books, UK (Stahlhelm Series 160).

troops were soon *en route* to the west. The first 'delaying position' designated 'Forward Point A' was at an old forest work camp at Vanaküla. Troops from SS-Panzergrenadier-Regiment 48 *General Seyffardt*, SS-Panzergrenadier-Regiment 24 *Danmark* and SS-Panzergrenadier-Regiment 49 *De Ruyter* reached this area at various times on 25th July.

To the north, the Soviets had established a large bridgehead across the River Narva at Riigi; on 25th July, Estonian SS troops were able to contain this intrusion but on 26th July, the Red Army broke out, driving the Estonian volunteers back, and the race was on to see who would reach the Tannenberg Positions first! All day long, the troops covering the withdrawal (from the various engineer companies and the SS-Panzer-Abteilung 11 *Hermann von Salza*) had continuously to fight off the enemy while trying to save themselves in the process. They were in turn supported by Stuka dive-bombers from the Luftwaffe who tried to zero in on the communist spearheads.

Still the situation was extremely dangerous. At the delaying position known as 'Forward Point D' on the Lipsu road, SS-Panzer-Abteilung 11 *Hermann von Salza* along with two Estonian volunteer companies fighting together as SS-Kampfgruppe *Kausch*, was bypassed and encircled by enemy advance elements. A call for help went out and troops from the SS-Pionier-Bataillon 11 responded; in heavy close-combat, Kampfgruppe *Kausch* was rescued - but it had almost ended in disaster. Some of the other retreating units would not be so lucky!

CHAPTER VIII

Defence of the Tannenberg Line

The *Nordland* divisional staff had begun its withdrawal from Narva to the Repniku forest camp (codenamed 'Wartburg') early in the morning of 25th July 1944. The divisional HQ was fully relocated to the settlement of Saksamaa, a little over a kilometre to the west of Vaivara by 1100 hours. By the afternoon most of SS-Panzergrenadier-Regiment 24 *Danmark* had reached the railway lines in the Tannenberg Positions. 11/SS-Pz.Gren.Rgt.24 *Danmark*, under *SS-Hauptsturmführer* Trautwein was, however, sent back into position in the Repniku forest by the divisional staff to hold open a route for the still retreating SS-Panzergrenadier-Regiment 23 *Norge*.

At 1700 hours on 25th July, the units of III (Germanische) SS-Panzerkorps were ordered to begin falling back to 'Grid Line 61', running from Narva-Jõesuu to Soldino, commencing at 1800 hours. 7/SS-Pz.Gren.Rgt.24 *Danmark* led by *SS-Untersturmführer* Madsen would again be the rearguard for the rest of the regiment, which would be following the railway lines to the west. To the north, the *Nederland* Brigade had also begun the second phase of its withdrawal but the enemy here had made serious inroads around and at 'Blocking Point A' at Vanaküla. Parts of the SS-Panzergrenadier-Regiment 49 *De Ruyter* along with *Nordland* Flak troops were cut off and had to be rescued by other elements of the *Nederland* Brigade. But even more ominous was the failure of the SS-Panzergrenadier-Regiment 48 *General Seyffardt* to reach its assigned defensive positions by midnight on 25th July. Earlier in the evening of the 25th, this regiment had taken an unauthorised rest to await the arrival of a detached rearguard company that had straggled far behind. This proved to be a fatal pause. A strong Red Army advance force swiftly moved in and cut the main east-west highway which was the withdrawal route for the regiment. It was then forced to abandon heavy weapons and supplies and take to the woods to the south. It was in this area, in the forests to the east of Repniku, that the SS-Panzergrenadier-Regiment 48 *General Seyffardt* met its doom. On 26th July it was enveloped by overwhelming enemy forces and tried desperately to fight its way out of the entrapment. No progress was made.

In the afternoon hours, between 1400 and 1700 hours, the regiment was split into small kampfgruppen which were ordered to try and break out on their own. Few of them made it. Only about 20% of personnel ever made it back to the German lines. The rest were either killed on the spot or later perished in Soviet captivity. Efforts by the rest of the brigade to locate and rescue the SS-Panzergrenadier-Regiment 48 *General Seyffardt* on 26th July had proved equally futile and had almost cost the loss of the *Nederland*'s reconnaissance and *sturmgeschütz* companies as well.

Elsewhere, by the morning of 26 July, all other troops assigned to Armee-Abteilung *Narwa* had successfully completed the first phase of their withdrawal from the River Narva front. However, enemy troops quickly penetrated some of the defensive lines held in the north by the 20 Waffen-Grenadier-Division der SS (*estnische Nr 1*) and to the south of the railway lines in the sector of SS-Panzergrenadier-Regiment 24 *Danmark*. This latter move cut off the still retreating III/SS-Pz.Gren.Rgt.23 *Norge*, which had to be rescued by a vigorous counterattack against the Soviet spearheads by 11/SS-Pz.Gren.Rgt.24 *Danmark* under *SS-Hauptsturmführer* Trautwein. *Danmark* grenadiers managed to restore the old defensive lines and reopen the escape route for III/SS-Pz.Gren.Rgt.23 *Norge*.

To the north a link-up was eventually secured with the Estonian SS troops and their positions were assumed by the *Nederland* Brigade: the Estonians were subsequently sent south into the - as yet - un-threatened swampland along the southern reaches of the River Narva. On 26th July the Red Army also began a heavy bombardment of the high ground within the Tannenberg Positions; targeting especially the old orphanage buildings which dominated the top of Orphanage Hill. This position in particular was critical, since it dominated all the nearby roads. In the course of the day the orphanage buildings were reduced to rubble and the Flemish SS defenders from 6 SS-Freiwilligen-Sturmbrigade *Langemarck* took some serious casualties, including the wounding of the battalion commander and his adjutant. Also lost in the intense artillery barrage was the observation post of the 13th (Heavy Weapons) Company of Regiment *Danmark* which had been set up on top of the hill. The company commander, *SS-Hauptsturmführer* Meggl, was killed in the shelling.

The Tannenberg defensive lines were anchored by a series of three hills, running west to east as follows: Hill 69.9, Grenadier Hill and Orphanage Hill. To the south of these hills was an open plain, through which the main Estonian east-west railway lines ran, while to the north was more easily defended high ground stretching to the Gulf of Finland. The most dominant feature to the north-west was a long stretch of hilly terrain known as the 'Swedish Wall'. The III (Germanische) SS-Panzerkorps positions in this sector took the shape of a reversed letter 'L', stretching south from the Gulf of Finland to a point south of the railway lines, where the defensive positions then veered west. The sector to the north of the three main hills was held by the *Nederland* Brigade, with the Regiment *De Ruyter* HQ located near Hill 69.9. Regiment *Danmark* was given the critical open area to the south and south-east of the hills.

Apart from II/SS-Pz.Gren.Rgt.23 *Norge*, which defended Grenadier Hill, the rest of the SS-Panzergrenadier-Regiment 23 *Norge* was situated near the railway lines towards the south-west where it eventually linked up to the East Prussian 11 Infanterie-Division. The most exposed part of the front was the juncture between II/SS-Pz.Gren.Rgt.49 *De Ruyter* (*SS-Hauptsturmführer* Frühauf) and III/SS-Pz.Gren.Rgt.24 *Danmark* (*SS-Sturmbannführer* Kappus), which straddled the main east-west Estonian highway, with II/SS-Pz.Gren.Rgt.49 *De Ruyter* to the north of the road and III/SS-Pz.Gren.Rgt.24 *Danmark* to the south. This would be the softest target for the enemy on the eastern sector of the Tannenberg front.

Just after darkness fell on the evening of 26th June 1944, the Soviets began their first assault on the Tannenberg Positions. The enemy offensive plan was simple: overwhelm the front-line defences, seize the main road and drive down it to the west. A task force of five tanks with accompanying Red Army infantry, followed closely by another armoured contingent, led the way, completely smashing through the positions of a Kriegsmarine infantry company that had been given the task of guarding the highway in the III/SS-Pz.Gren.Rgt.24 *Danmark* sector. These new 'infantrymen' had been poorly trained and had never seen action on land before. The enemy breakthrough force

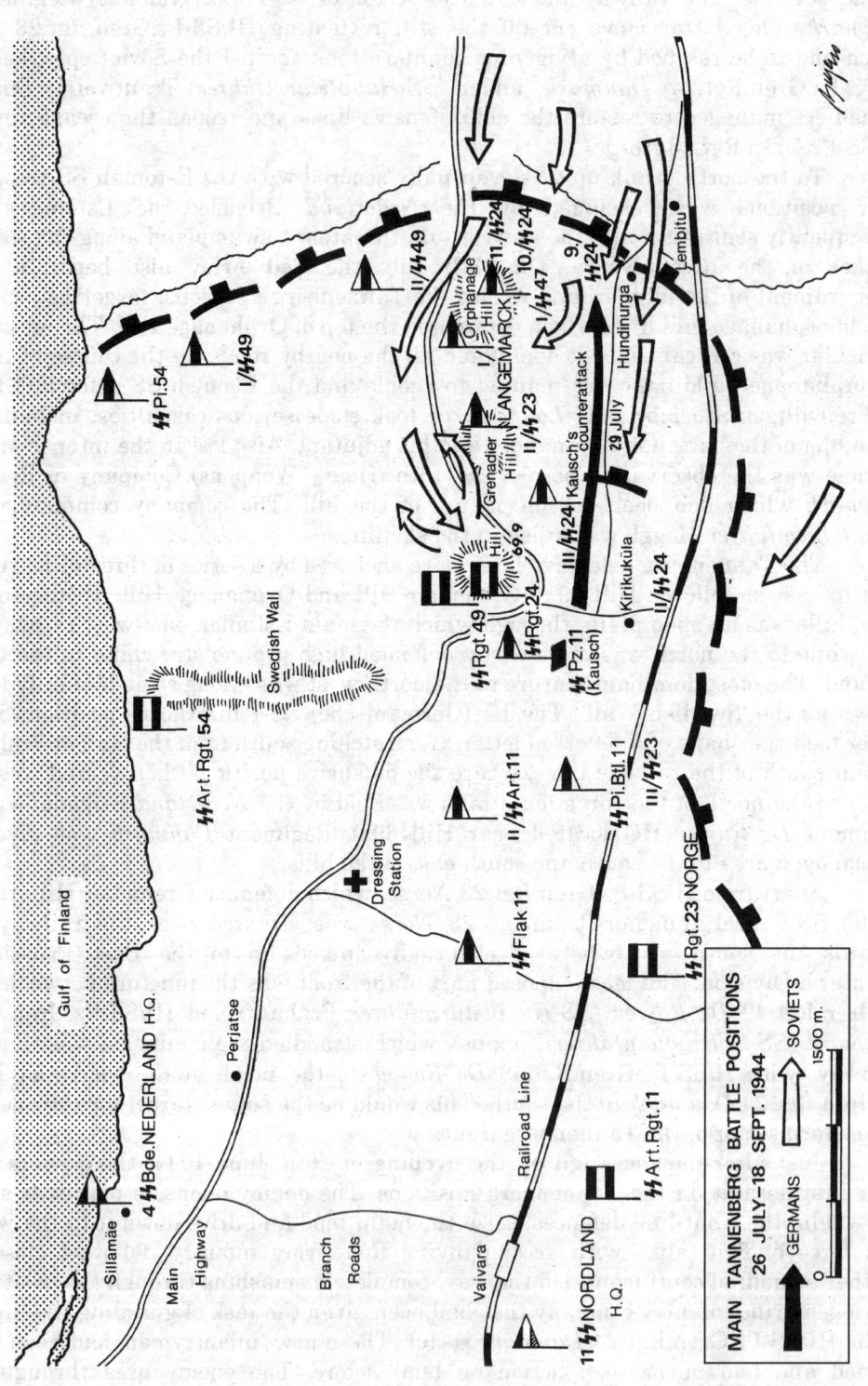

therefore had an easy task and was able to drive through to Orphanage Hill before coming to a halt.

The situation immediately became critical. The *Nordland* Divisional headquarters called upon the Regiment *Danmark* reserves, 11th Company and the tank destruction platoon, to deal with this dangerous inroad. After a short situation briefing the *Danmark* soldiers went on the attack. The tank destruction platoon, carrying personal anti-tank weapons (*Panzerfaust* and *Panzerschreck*) crept up close to the enemy tanks and within minutes had set them all ablaze. As violent explosions rocked the eastern slope of Orphanage Hill, the men of 11/SS-Pz.Gren.Rgt.24 *Danmark* wiped out the communist infantry escort and helped restore the old defensive lines some 300m to the east of the orphanage. The commander of the *Danmark* tank destruction platoon, 20 year old *SS-Unterscharführer* Mellenthin, personally destroyed seven enemy tanks in the action and disabled three others. Naturally, the successful operation brought about a heavy enemy mortar barrage in retaliation.

At 0600 hours on 27th July, a general Soviet artillery bombardment of the Tannenberg Positions began, suggesting that another attack was imminent. III (Germanische) SS-Panzerkorps countered this shelling with its own barrage from truck-mounted rocket-launchers of SS-Vielfach-Werfer-Batterie 521. These were of deadly effectiveness and played a key role in the successful defence of the sector.

At 0900 hours the Red Army came again, sending strong armoured and infantry forces slamming into the Regiment *Danmark* positions around the Tirtsu Road that were defended by the 10/ and 11/SS-Pz.Gren.Rgt.24 *Danmark*. Fully 30 'Stalin' and T-34 tanks moved to within 70m of 11th Company's positions and the CO, *SS-Hauptsturmführer* Trautwein was badly wounded. When the tanks opened fire, the men of 11th Company jumped up and began running away, but in a few minutes they came to their senses and went back on the attack with *Panzerfäuste*. With spectacular courage and élan, the *Danmark* volunteers literally shot up the Soviet tank force; after fourteen tanks had been destroyed, the others headed for the rear. Once again a crisis was successfully overcome.

Later on the 27th, both 10/ and 11/SS-Pz.Gren.Rgt.24 *Danmark* became isolated after the enemy advance forces filtered past them. Literally cut off from each other and the rest of the regiment, the two companies fought on steadfastly for the next few days until only a handful of survivors remained. Elsewhere, 9/SS-Pz.Gren.Rgt.24 *Danmark* was pulled out of the regiment's northern wing to help repel an advancing enemy force on Hundinurga. Violent fighting broke out here that soon spread throughout the sectors of II/SS-Pz.Gren.Rgt.24 *Danmark* and III/SS-Pz.Gren.Rgt.23 *Norge*. In a short time the entire front of III (Germanische) SS-Panzerkorps was engaged and the villages of Auvere, Lembitu and Sooküla had to be evacuated.

It became clear that this was now the battle that everyone had anticipated; a merciless life and death struggle that would determine the fate of Estonia and perhaps the whole Baltic region. Huge packs of onrushing Soviet tanks now ploughed into the *Danmark* lines; there were too many to stop at once and the positions of III/SS-Pz.Gren.Rgt.24 *Danmark* were overrun. The surviving grenadiers fought valiantly on in small groups or tried to defend the nearby high ground. The Red Army juggernaut now swept up and around Orphanage Hill, where the Flemish volunteers of 6 SS-Freiwilligen-Sturmbrigade *Langemarck* grimly held their ground. The fighting raged all the way to the *Nederland* positions in the far north; by the afternoon of 27th July, all of III (Germanische) SS-Panzerkorps' combat troops were trying desperately to hang on. The *Nordland* Division launched a prompt counterattack with 12 *sturmgeschütze* that successfully stopped the forward penetration of the enemy armour through the middle of the Tannenberg Positions.

Elsewhere the situation remained critical. The III/SS-Pz.Gren.Rgt.24 *Danmark* command post near Hundinurga to the south of Orphanage Hill was besieged. The battalion staff, consisting of *SS-Hauptsturmführer* Meier and 19 men were determined to resist until the end. They sent out a desperate call for assistance and fortunately one nearby unit, 7/SS-Pz.Gren.Rgt.23 *Norge* was able to respond. Attacking briskly from a wooded area to the north-west, the *Norge* grenadiers broke through the enemy encirclement and liberated the HQ. On the south-eastern section of the Tannenberg Positions, *SS-Hauptsturmführer* Heinz Hämel's II/SS-Pz.Gren.Rgt.24 *Danmark* also became totally engulfed in fighting by noon on 27th July. The battalion's companies were situated as follows: 5/ and 6/SS-Pz.Gren.Rgt.24 *Danmark* in the main defensive lines, 7/SS-Pz.Gren.Rgt.24 *Danmark*, which had covered the retreat from Narva, in reserve to the west of Hill 69.9, and 8/SS-Pz.Gren.Rgt.24 *Danmark* in firing positions around the Vaivara church, with its mortar section set up in a gravel pit to the south-west of Hundinurga. As the fighting raged, reinforcements were called for and these appeared in the form of I/Waf.Gren.Rgt.d.SS 47 from the 20 Waffen-Grenadier-Division der SS (*estnische Nr 1*), which had been battered during the Narva withdrawal but was still combat-worthy, and a part of 9/SS-Pz.Gren.Rgt.24 *Danmark*. Using these troops and with the support of 8th Company's mortars, Hämel was able to launch a counterattack and drive back the Red Army forces in his sector, but in the process he was badly wounded. While the Soviets managed to seize the south-eastern sector of Orphanage Hill, the ruins of the orphanage building on the summit remained firmly in the hands of the Flemish SS volunteers. The Flemings, along with Estonian SS reinforcements, *Nordland* combat engineers and grenadiers from III/SS-Pz.Gren.Rgt.24 *Danmark* were able somehow to hold on to a firm defensive line running from the hill to the village of Tirtsu.

Meanwhile, at around noon on 27th July, the *Nordland* commander, *SS-Brigadeführer* von Scholz held a situation conference at the *Danmark* regimental HQ on the south-west slope of Hill 69.9. A decision was made to send assault parties of combat engineers behind the lines to place 'booby traps' and gather intelligence. As always, "Alte Fritz" (von Scholz) sought out the opinions of his subordinates. Once the conference broke up, von Scholz left to inspect the heavy weapons positions of 13/SS-Pz.Gren.Rgt.24 *Danmark* under *SS-Hauptsturmführer* Lärum, which were located nearby. Just as von Scholz began conversing with Lärum near the 13th Company command post, a heavy enemy artillery barrage on the company positions suddenly began and von Scholz was seriously wounded in the head by a shell fragment. On the advice of *Nordland*'s senior medical officer, Swiss-born *SS-Obersturmbannführer* Dr Franz Riedweg, von Scholz was evacuated from the *Nordland* field hospital to a specialised surgery station at Rakvere, accompanied by the wounded *SS-Hauptsturmführer* Hämel. "Alte Fritz" would die *en route*. He was an irreplaceable man who would be posthumously decorated with the Swords to the Knight's Cross (Oakleaves 12th March 1944) by the Führer.

Later that night, *Nordland* engineers and Estonian SS volunteers from I/Waf.Gren.Rgt.d.SS 47 attempted to regain the lost sectors of Orphanage Hill. But confusion reigned supreme and the attack eventually failed with the engineers mis-identifying enemy troops as their own and suffering near-disastrous consequences as a result. The Estonians advanced too far and the battalion was cut off and largely destroyed. The survivors later regrouped with the Flemish SS troops in the ruins of the orphanage.

CHAPTER IX

Fighting for Destiny

By now nearly all of the combat units of III (Germanische) SS-Panzerkorps were down to half-strength or less. At Narva, the Soviets had rebuilt the river bridges and were pouring troops across. 11 Guards Divisions and 6 Soviet tank divisions were now massed against the Tannenberg Positions. All that *SS-Obergruppenführer* Steiner could do was to concentrate his artillery, heavy weapons and armoured vehicles and use them to focus on the most critical spots along the defensive perimeter. Hopefully that, along with the supreme morale and fighting ability of the European SS volunteers, would be enough to save the day. Otherwise the consequences were grim: the gateway to the major portion of Europe would be wide open.

On 28th July 1944 the battle for the Tannenberg Positions resumed with the greatest of ferocity. The *Danmark* heavy weapons companies, 8/, 12/ and 13/SS-Pz.Gren.Rgt.24 *Danmark* were now grouped together under the command of *SS-Hauptsturmführer* Lärum in an area stretching from the south-east of Hill 69.9 to Kirikuküla. The *Norge* heavy weapons were also assembled in a similar manner nearby. With the loss of *SS-Brigadeführer* Fritz von Scholz, the *Nordland* Division was now under the control of a former Army officer, *SS-Brigadeführer* Joachim Ziegler, who had been the III (Germanische) SS-Panzerkorps chief-of-staff. His previous position was in turn taken over by *SS-Obersturmbannführer* Bockelberg.

In the morning of 28th July the Red Army overran most of the remaining Flemish and Estonian SS positions on Orphanage Hill. These were retaken by a counterattack led by II/SS-Pz.Gren.Rgt.23 *Norge*, in which the battalion commander, *SS-Sturmbannführer* Scheibe, was wounded. But the European defenders were too weak to hold on and eventually were pushed completely off the hill.

The focal point of the defence next became the neighbouring Grenadier Hill. Thanks to the efforts of the Estonian SS troops a stable defensive line was finally formed along the crest of the hill and the enemy advance was at least temporarily halted. To the east of Orphanage Hill, some of the *Nordland* defensive positions were still holding out. 11/SS-Pz.Gren.Rgt.24 *Danmark* held out until the 29th; when reduced to 12 combat capable men it had to make a run for the lines of the *Nederland* Brigade. One of the Danish volunteers, *SS-Rottenführer* Jørgensen, was badly wounded in the escape effort and 'finished himself off' while being held by his younger brother. Afterwards, his brother broke down and ran off towards the enemy which created a diversion and probably saved the lives of his comrades who were then able to scramble into the *Nederland* positions.

Fierce fighting raged around III/SS-Pz.Gren.Rgt.24 *Danmark*'s positions at Hundinurga on the 28th but, using hand-held weapons, the *Danmark* grenadiers were able to drive back a Red Army tank force. Two *Nordland sturmgeschütze*, held in reserve near the III/SS-Pz.Gren.Rgt.24 *Danmark* command post, set up an ambush which accounted for many of the enemy armoured vehicles. The battle continued to the north and east of Hundinurga; at one point the battalion HQ was threatened but was rescued by a prompt counterattack by 7/SS-Pz.Gren.Rgt.23 *Norge*, which eliminated a Soviet tank force in close-combat. The only casualty at the III/SS-Pz.Gren.Rgt.24 *Danmark* command post was *SS-Untersturmführer* Elfsen who had been picked off by a sniper.

To the east of Hundinurga the village of Tirtsu had been lost, and in the afternoon of 28th July a *Danmark* platoon accompanied by a Panther from SS-Panzer-Abteilung 11 *Hermann von Salza* was ordered to retake the town. The enemy fire soon drove the Panther to cover but the *Danmark* grenadiers kept advancing and when they got close to Tirtsu they were surprised to see all of the enemy defenders suddenly taking to the hills. The *Danmark* platoon then reoccupied the positions around Tirtsu which was equivalent to an entire regimental sector! When expected supporting troops did not materialise on the next day, however, the *Danmark* troops were forced to withdraw under renewed enemy pressure.

At sunset on 28th July, 7/SS-Pz.Gren.Rgt.24 *Danmark*, with 50 of its own men and 20 Flemish SS volunteers, launched an attack aimed at regaining Orphanage Hill. But the Soviets were ready and drove back the SS attackers in a hail of defensive fire, wounding the company commander, *SS-Untersturmführer* Madsen, in the process. As night fell on the 28th, enemy incursions were still in place all along the south-eastern perimeter of the Tannenberg Positions. The next day, 29th July, was likely to be a day of decision. The choice was a simple one: either the European SS troops would hold their ground or perhaps all of Estonia and the Baltic region would be lost to the Red Army. It boiled down to that!

On the morning of the 29th a heavy enemy artillery barrage fell on the eastern Tannenberg Positions, to be quickly followed by aerial bombing runs on Grenadier Hill. Once the smoke had cleared from the bombing run the enemy ground attack commenced, spearheaded by no fewer than 100 tanks! For the Red Army this was clearly to be their 'day of decision!' The III (Germanische) SS-Panzerkorps artillery units responded in kind to the enemy onslaught and managed to inflict enormous casualties but without significantly slowing the Soviet advance.

To the east of Orphanage Hill the remaining isolated SS *hedgehog* defensive positions were slowly eliminated by the Red Army. This included one *hedgehog* manned by survivors from 11/SS-Pz.Gren.Rgt.24 *Danmark*. The company CO, *SS-Hauptsturmführer* Trautwein, was wounded early in the battle but continued to fight on before eventually being killed by the foe. All of his successors were also wounded one by one. On Grenadier Hill, Flemish, Estonian, German and Norwegian SS troops held out in isolated bunkers and trenches. Orders could no longer get though to them so they were strictly on their own.

Near the north-east corner of Grenadier Hill was an anti-tank battery from 6 SS-Freiwilligen-Sturmbrigade *Langemarck*, which had been reduced to one gun and one gunner: the brave Flemish volunteer, *SS-Sturmmann* (later *Unterscharführer*) Remi Schrijnen. As 30 enemy tanks lumbered towards him, he lined up his shells on the ground next to his weapon and went to work. Before long most of the enemy armour would either be destroyed, damaged or driven off. One last tank made it to within 50m of Schrijnen's gun before he was able to blow it up! Even though wounded, Schrijnen remained at his post throughout the fighting and would eventually receive a well-earned Knight's Cross.

To the north and north-east the troops of the *De Ruyter* Regiment of the *Nederland* Brigade fought desperately to stave off the foe. The regimental commander, *SS-Obersturmbannführer* Hans Collani, formerly of the *Leibstandarte SS Adolf Hitler*, fell badly wounded and shot himself when it appeared the Red Army would overrun his command post. As it turned out they were not able to; the resistance of the Dutch and German SS grenadiers was too fierce.

In the afternoon a counterattack by a combined *Nordland* armoured force led by *SS-Obersturmbannführer* Kausch, the commander of SS-Panzer-Abteilung 11 *Hermann von Salza*, finally turned the tide near Grenadier Hill in a very violent engagement. By evening, all of the hill was back in the hands of the Waffen-SS. 113 enemy tanks had been destroyed on the battlefield in the course of three days of fighting and a huge number of dead Red Army infantrymen were scattered all over.

Heavy, intense fighting continued for the next two days, but there were no more 'all out' enemy assaults. For the next few weeks there would, however, continue to be violent Soviet localised attacks. These were still very dangerous and had to be repulsed with great courage and sacrifice by the III (Germanische) SS-Panzerkorps grenadiers.

On 1st August 1944 the official communiqué of the German Army that was distributed to the news media, paid the following special tribute to the defenders of the Tannenberg Positions:

"In the land area out from Narva, the enemy has launched a great offensive and has absorbed high losses. During the past days, the III (Germanische) SS-Panzerkorps under the leadership of *General der Waffen-SS* Steiner with the Germanic Volunteer Divisions *Nordland* and *Nederland* and the 20 Waffen-Grenadier-Division der SS (*estnische Nr 1*) along with the East Prussian 11 Infanterie-Division and land-based naval and army artillery and mortar units, has played a prominent role in stopping the enemy in this sector".

In early August 1944, the focal point of the fighting for the Tannenberg Positions centred once again on Grenadier Hill and the village of Hundinurga. On 5th August another Soviet advance force had managed to isolate and threaten the small defensive force that held on to Grenadier Hill. After the wounding of the 'Hill' commander, *SS-Hauptsturmführer* Bachmeier, the situation became desperate. But this time a very unlikely band of heroes would emerge to save the day. These were the disciplinary cases from all of the III (Germanische) SS-Panzerkorps units who had been organised into SS-Bewährungskompanie 103[9].

In a violent counterattack, SS-Bewährungskompanie 103 managed to throw the Red Army back off Grenadier Hill and with the help of small surviving contingents from 10/ and 11/SS-Pz.Gren.Rgt.24 *Danmark* and some regimental staff members, were then able to restore contacts between the hill and the garrison at Hundinurga. Hundinurga was now very ably defended by soldiers from 9/ and 7/SS-Pz.Gren.Rgt.23 *Norge*, and the 20 Waffen-Grenadier-Division der SS (*estnische Nr 1*).

After the fighting the soldiers of SS-Bewährungskompanie 103 were declared 'rehabilitated' and were reinstated with their old ranks and decorations. The remnants of both 10/ and 11/SS-Pz.Gren.Rgt.24 *Danmark* were withdrawn from the front to be

---

[9] A unit made up from officers under suspended sentence of court martial. They were given the chance to 'redeem' themselves in combat. For more information on such units see Ingo Petersson A Special Kind of Crowd (Forthcoming) Shelf Books Ltd, UK (Stahlhelm Series 138).

reformed. They would each receive new Danish commanders: *SS-Untersturmführer* Jessen and *SS-Obersturmführer* Thorkildsen, respectively.

During lulls in the combat action in August, efforts were made to rebuild the strength of the units of III (Germanische) SS-Panzerkorps. Most of the individual companies, which had contained up to 200 men each only a month or so earlier, had now been reduced to 50 men or less - a striking testimony to losses suffered by the European SS volunteers during this successful defensive effort. Through their stalwart performance, comradeship and total sacrifice, the soldiers of the SS-Panzergrenadier-Regiment 24 *Danmark* and their comrades in the *Nordland* Division and III (Germanische) SS-Panzerkorps, had demonstrated the tangible existence of a true, idealistic multinational European community united to effectively fight one of the true scourges of the 20th Century: Soviet Communism.

On the left is Jorgen Henrik Johansen, a veteran of the *Freikorps Danmark* who became the *Kammerwart* (supply clerk) of II/SS-Pz.Gren.Rgt.24 *Danmark*. On the right is the Danish volunteer Hansen from Copenhagen

SS-Oberscharführer Albert Hektor, a platoon leader in 7/SS-Pz.Gren.Rgt.24 *Danmark* after receiving the Knight's Cross on 23rd August 1944. He was later acting commander of 15/SS-Pz.Gren.Rgt.24 *Danmark*

Workshop activity. The man facing the camera is *Oberscharführer* Albert Jensen

(Above) Left to right: *Unterscharführer* Kaj Olesen (known as Germaner-Ole), a mechanic with 8/SS-Pz.Gren.Rgt.24 *Danmark*, *Unterscharführer* Preben Sommer as acting transport officer with II/SS-Pz.Gren.Rgt.24 *Danmark*, and *Oberscharführer* Albert Jensen, master mechanic and foreman with the workshop of II/SS-Pz.Gren.Rgt.24 *Danmark*. All three proudly wear their old *Freikorps* cuff-titles with the new sonnenrad collar insignia and Danish arm shields. Olesen and Jensen both wear trade badges for mechanics below their arm shields

(Right) II/SS-Pz.Gren.Rgt.24 *Danmark* workshop. In the centre is *Oberscharführer* Albert Jensen while on the right is mechanic Nissen

(Left) Members of the II/SS-Pz.Gren.Rgt.24 *Danmark* workshop. Note the sign with the Dannebrog and numeral 'II' for II Battalion The encircled letter 'I' stood for I-Staffel (workshop)

The *Nordland* divisional sign on a *Danmark* truck

Attending to a Schwimmwagen in the workshop. Note the Dannebrog on the lower right side

Danmark transport column. The truck is hauling an infantry gun

A ***Danmark*** transport column moving out; the trucks are hauling field guns

CHAPTER X

Relocation to Latvia

When the great Soviet summer offensive that had begun on 22nd June 1944 overwhelmed the front lines of the German Army Group Centre, troops from III (Germanische) SS-Panzerkorps were needed to help rectify the situation in Latvia to prevent the isolation of Estonia. The primary unit called upon was the SS-Panzer-Aufklärungs-Abteilung 11 under *SS-Sturmbannführer* Rudolf Saalbach, which was rushed by express train from the Narva Front to the Daugavpils sector in Latvia in early July 1944. Here it was retitled Panzergruppe *Saalbach* and it was used along with regular Army elements to counterattack Soviet advance forces over a wide area in Latvia.

However, this was not enough to prevent communist breakthroughs and by mid-August the Red Army were racing into southern Estonia and threatening the city of Tartu. Again, III (Germanische) SS-Panzerkorps was asked to provide troops to help the situation and on the night of 15th/16th August, Kampfgruppe *Wagner*, formed from parts of the *Nordland* Division and *Nederland* Brigade, and using all the remaining *Nordland* armoured vehicles, was rushed from the Tannenberg Positions towards Tartu. Fortunately, by now the Tannenberg front had calmed down enough to allow for the siphoning off of some of III (Germanische) SS-Panzerkorps' valuable combat troops.

Whilst not able to prevent the loss of Tartu, Kampfgruppe *Wagner*, supplemented by I Bataillon from the 5 SS-Freiwilligen-Sturmbrigade *Wallonien* led by Léon Degrelle, was able to stabilise the front along the River Em by early September. In the process of some very heroically fought engagements, the soldiers of Kampfgruppe *Wagner* managed to eliminate a dangerous Soviet bridgehead across the Em and effectively halt the enemy advance in the area. This saved Estonia for the time being, but soon increasing pressure elsewhere would force the total evacuation of the small Baltic state.

On 14th September 1944, the commander of Army Group North, *Generaloberst* Schörner, made the decision - against orders - to begin the evacuation of Armee-Abteilung *Narwa* and III (Germanische) SS-Panzerkorps from Estonia. All the evidence indicated that the Soviets were preparing a massive assault on the Estonian positions that could no longer be repelled by the weakened defensive forces. Adolf Hitler, who had earlier rejected a withdrawal from Estonia on the grounds that holding Estonia protected vital eastern Baltic shipping lanes, agreed to *Generaloberst* Schörner's decision once he learned that Finland was going to unilaterally surrender to the Soviets. That move alone would have doomed Estonia.

So under the codename Operation Tree Bough (*Aster*), the evacuation procedure got underway immediately. III (Germanische) SS-Panzerkorps received its orders to pull out in the evening of 15th September, at which contingency plans for just such an occurrence were put into effect. Whilst some support units immediately got underway for the west, the combat troops remained in place until the night of 18th/19th September, when their disengagement began.

The destination for III (Germanische) SS-Panzerkorps was the western port city of Pärnu. The troops would fall back in small assembly groups to temporary positions to the east of Rakvere. Soldiers from the II Armeekorps would stay in defensive positions until sometime on 19th September, thus helping to protect the initial withdrawal of III (Germanische) SS-Panzerkorps. SS-Panzergrenadier-Regiment 24 *Danmark* led off the III (Germanische) SS-Panzerkorps retreat at 1800 hours on 18th September. Unit by unit followed on an agreed time schedule so that, by 2000 hours, most of the troops of the *Nordland* Division and *Nederland* Brigade were in transit towards the west.

As it happened, SS-Panzergrenadier-Regiment 24 *Danmark* reached its designated embarkation area only to find that the expected motorised transport had not materialised on time. This delay meant that 6/SS-Pz.Gren.Rgt.24 *Danmark*, serving as the regimental rearguard, might have to fight its way out. 6th Company had remained behind on Hill 69.9 while *Danmark*'s *Maschinenpistolezug* (MPi-Zug - Machine Pistol Assault Platoon) and Pionierzug (Pi-Zug - Engineer Platoon) had stayed in place on Grenadier Hill. Their job was to hinder and slow down any possible enemy pursuit. To further this objective, small groups of *Danmark* volunteers were also scattered throughout the old defensive lines to put on a show of resistance in case the Red Army turned up. To assist the rearguard and expend all their ammunition so it would not have to be transported on the march to Pärnu, the *Danmark* heavy weapons companies (13th and 14th) kept a heavy supporting fire until 2030 hours. These elements, having used up all their ammunition, then joined the rest of *Danmark* on its westward retreat.

6/SS-Pz.Gren.Rgt.24 *Danmark* finally withdrew from Hill 69.9 at 2200 hours on the 18th, still leaving behind the *Danmark* Pionierzug under *SS-Hauptscharführer* Christensen and its Maschinenpistolezug led by *SS-Hauptscharführer* Schwabenburg. They stayed in place for another hour, at the time constituting the easternmost element of the German Armed Forces on the whole Eastern Front! It was not long before the Red Army got wind of events and small scale enemy harassing operations soon developed. By the time Regiment *Danmark* crossed the bridge to the south of Sillamäe, Estonia, continuous explosions and burst of flame from the enemy side could be seen in the distance.

The rest of the withdrawal for III (Germanische) SS-Panzerkorps troops continued without serious incident. During the morning of 19th September the *Danmark* grenadiers reached Kohtla-Järve and by noon had arrived in Rakvere. When they reached the vicinity of Pärnu, special rations and extra supplies, that would have otherwise have had to have been destroyed, were liberally distributed to the SS troops.

The only unit of Armee-Abteilung *Narwa* which seemed to have had serious difficulty during the retreat was Division zbV 300, composed of Estonian Frontier Guards led by the staff of the destroyed Luftwaffe 13 Feld-Division, supplemented by German Jäger troops and scattered Waffen-SS members, including the competent Danish *SS-Obersturmbannführer* Rantzau-Engelhardt. This large but poorly-equipped and ill-trained division had some 17,000 troops split into two brigades that maintained a 50km front in the swamps along the Narva from just north of Lake Peipus to south of the Tannenberg Positions. The brigades were known as 'North' and 'South' respectively due to their positioning on the front lines and Brigade North came under the command of *SS-Obersturmbannführer* Rantzau-Engelhardt.

Division zbV 300 began its withdrawal along narrow log roads through the swamps on 18th September. The retreat soon became chaotic as the pony carts and marching troops of the formation soon became tangled in massive traffic jams. During the initial stages of the division's retreat, the SS-Panzer-Aufklärungs-Abteilung 11 of the *Nordland* Division tried to keep the Soviet follow-up forces at bay. But by 19th September the enemy inroads all around were too numerous to block and the SS-Panzer-Aufklärungs-Abteilung 11, in danger of being cut off, had to withdraw from the sector, leaving Division zbV 300 on its own.

To try and protect itself the division formed three kampfgruppen of about 600 men each, based around German troop cadres. But the formation could not move fast enough to avoid being encircled by Soviet pincers and the bulk of it soon disappeared into the swamplands. The survivors would go on to fight underground against the Soviet occupation forces until well into the 1950s. Small parts of Division zbV 300, including a kampfgruppe led by *SS-Obersturmbannführer* Rantzau-Engelhardt, did however make it through to safety in western Estonia.

In the meantime *SS-Sturmbannführer* Saalbach's SS-Panzer-Aufklärungs-Abteilung 11, continued to cover the withdrawal of the III (Germanische) SS-Panzerkorps forces. The SS troops were now either evacuated by ship from Pärnu to Riga or proceeded south down the coast into Latvia and by 20th/21st September the communists were in hot pursuit. A small defensive perimeter around Pärnu was maintained for about three days by troops from the *De Ruyter* Regiment of the *Nederland* Brigade and part of SS-Panzer-Aufklärungs-Abteilung 11, until the sea evacuation had been completed. These troops then proceeded down the coast, sending out tank destroyer teams to slow down the Red Army. They eventually crossed the Latvian border on 25th September, about three days after the bulk of the *Nordland* Division had already gone into Latvia.

Also safely reaching Latvia was the 20 Waffen-Grenadier-Division der SS (*estnische Nr 1*), which was then shipped from Riga to Germany for reformation; it would, of course, never return home. To the north, *SS-Obergruppenführer* Steiner had helped to oversee the successful sea evacuation of Tallinn. Needless to say the Estonians were very upset by developments but Steiner promised to take as many of them out of the country as possible, and more than 80,000 troops and civilian refugees were safely shipped out of Tallinn alone. In the wake of the German retreat all of the important oil refineries and industrial facilities in Estonia also had to be destroyed, a task carried out to a large degree by III (Germanische) SS-Panzerkorps engineers. The withdrawal from Estonia was a sad end to what had been a noble and heroic defensive effort but, in the final analysis, there was no other option. The skilled soldiers from Armee-Abteilung *Narwa* had been saved to fight another day, and that was what mattered most.

On the morning of 22nd September 1944, most of the *Nordland* Division was in combat readiness positions about 30kms to the north-east of Riga, the Latvian capital. Orders now came for the division to relocate to the south-east of Riga during the afternoon and take up new 'blocking positions' against the advancing Soviets. The relocation took place during a furious enemy aerial bombardment of Riga and its suburbs. By evening, the *Nordland* Division was in place in a forested area between the Rivers Daugava and Kekāva, with the divisional command post situated in the town of Gulbji. The headquarters for III (Germanische) SS-Panzerkorps was now in the Latvian town of Tigurgas.

On 23rd September 1944, the *Nordland* Division was ordered to launch a counterattack against nearby Soviet incursions. Spearheading the operation was the Regiment *Danmark* which was given the assignment of regaining the villages of Lidakas and Vaici and clearing the enemy out of the woods along the east bank of the River Kekāva. III/SS-Pz.Gren.Rgt.24 Danmark was ordered to advance from the regiment's left flank, which was situated to the north-east of Lidakas, and take that town while II/SS-Pz.Gren.Rgt.24 Danmark, moving out of the regiment's right flank from the north-east of Vaici, was to seize that village. Following that the two battalions were to link up.

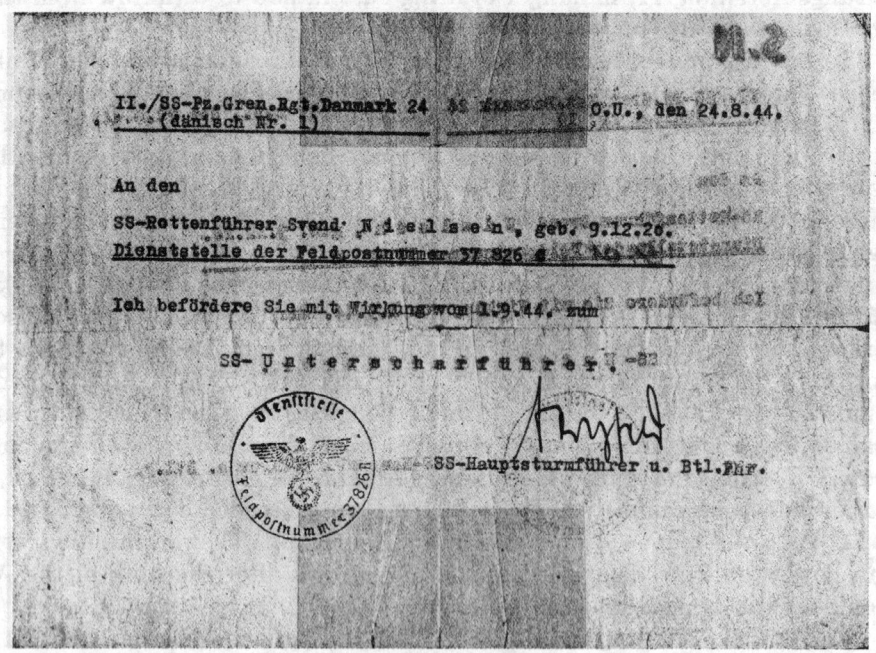

Document authorising the promotion of *SS-Rottenführer* Svend Nielsen from II/SS-Pz.Gren.Rgt.24 *Danmark* to *SS-Unterscharführer* signed by the battalion commander (probably *SS-Hauptsturmführer* Albert Bergfeldt)

The *Danmark* assault was to be supported by tanks and *sturmgeschütze* from the 14 Panzer-Division. In the meantime, the regimental heavy weapons companies, 13th and 14th, would be held back to protect the flanks of the attacking battalions. Other elements of the *Nordland* Division and the neighbouring 11 Infanterie-Division and 225 Infanterie-Division would be brought into action as the fighting developed. Their main objective would be to secure the Cempulli-Baldone road to prevent the enemy from using it for a flank attack on the advancing SS troops.

The *Danmark* grenadiers took up their attack positions during the night of 22nd/23rd September. The actual assault, with support from the *Nordland* artillery and the Luftwaffe, got underway at 0930 hours on the 23rd, even though the armour from the 14 Panzer-Division had been late in getting into position. III/SS-Pz.Gren.Rgt.24 *Danmark* immediately went forward into Lidakas and took the town in hand-to-hand combat. 6/ and 11/SS-Pz.Gren.Rgt.24 *Danmark* were then ordered to clear the last few hundred metres to the bank of the River Kekāva but they were initially kept pinned down by accurate enemy machine gun and artillery fire. This brought the III/SS-Pz.Gren.Rgt.24 *Danmark* attack to a temporary halt and the Red Army began to prepare for a counterattack of their own. Fortunately tanks and *sturmgeschütze* from the 14 Panzer-Division now arrived and they were able to drive back the first wave of Soviet attackers. A lengthy artillery duel between both sides now developed which effectively kept the III/SS-Pz.Gren.Rgt.24 *Danmark* grenadiers pinned down where they were for the next few hours. In the meantime several weak Red Army attacks were broken up.

At around 1300 hours a Stuka dive-bomber attack softened the enemy resistance and the III/SS-Pz.Gren.Rgt.24 *Danmark* attack, led by *SS-Hauptsturmführer* Ternedde, got underway again. This time 6th and 11th Companies were put into reserve and other companies spearheaded the drive. A considerable amount of additional ground was gained until the advance halted permanently at about 1700 hours. II/SS-Pz.Gren.Rgt.24 *Danmark,* although also engaged, had played a subordinate role in the fighting and had despatched troops (including 6th Company) to support the III/SS-Pz.Gren.Rgt.24 *Danmark* effort. By the time the fighting had wound down the SS-Panzergrenadier-Regiment 24 *Danmark* had taken some 300 casualties - a rather heavy price to pay. As a result all the regimental reserves, including staff, signals and supply troops had to be rushed up to the front to help defend the newly-won ground. Even then, the regimental commander, *SS-Obersturmbannführer* Albrecht Krügel, was not at all certain that *Danmark* could hold its gains if the Soviets counterattacked in force.

While *Danmark* had attacked the enemy from the north and east, SS-Panzergrenadier-Regiment 23 *Norge* with the support of the remaining armour from SS-Panzer-Abteilung 11 *Hermann von Salza*, was to attack from the Dekmeri-Katlapaji line in the west. The idea was to trap the massive Red Army forces between SS-Panzergrenadier-Regiment 23 *Norge* and SS-Panzergrenadier-Regiment 24 *Danmark*, and the 11 Infanterie-Division and 225 Infanterie-Division who were holding blocking positions farther to the east. The *Norge* attack, beginning at 1400 hours on the 23rd, proceeded through the woods against an enemy tank brigade equipped with American-supplied Sherman tanks along with some Stalin models. The fighting in the *Norge* sector raged until 25th September by which time all objectives had been secured and the Red Army tank brigade had been annihilated. The *Norge* grenadiers now effected a position running from Dekmeri-Asenbergi and by 26th September were able to link up with the *Danmark* soldiers in a newly solidified battle line.

On the 26th, III/SS-Pz.Gren.Rgt.23 *Norge* had its positions penetrated by a Soviet attack force, but the battalion regrouped and threw out the Red Army in a violent counterattack led personally by the battalion commander, *SS-Hauptsturmführer* Martin Gürz. Gürz was killed in the action but, for his heroic actions in saving the front, he was posthumously decorated with the Knight's Cross.

Having brought stability to the front to the south-east of Riga, the units of III (Germanische) SS-Panzerkorps were now relieved and were withdrawn through Riga to an assembly area around Dobele, near the city of Tukums. Part of the SS-Panzergrenadier-Regiment 24 *Danmark* was now quartered in barracks buildings in Jelgava, which two years before had been occupied by troops from the *Freikorps Danmark*, so it was familiar ground for some of the 'old sweats'.

On 28th September the III (Germanische) SS-Panzerkorps troops took up defensive positions to the south-west of Riga. Then, on 30th September, the Red Army onslaught on the new lines began. For more than two weeks the European SS volunteers put up a valiant resistance, but it became increasingly clear that there was too much territory to defend against all too powerful enemy forces. Therefore, on 6th October 1944, Army Group North began Operation Thunder (*Donner*), the phased withdrawal into the defensible western Latvian province of Kurzeme or Kurland. It was a good strategic move, the German-European forces in Kurland would be able to hold until the very end of the war without being defeated on the battlefield. The downside of the situation was that Kurland would become totally isolated; there would be no land bridge to friendly territories to the south, north or east, and the pocket would have to be supplied by sea and air. However the troops in Kurland would tie down vast Soviet forces which otherwise would have been free to wage the onslaught on East Prussia and Germany proper.

By 12th October 1944, the units of the *Nordland* Division and *Nederland* Brigade had fallen back into the southern sector of the Kurland sector. On the 13th the last bridges over the River Daugava to Riga were blown up and the Latvian capital was abandoned to the Red Army. *Generaloberst* Schörner, commanding Army Group North, submitted plans to the Führer's HQ for an immediate breakout towards East Prussia to be spearheaded by III (Germanische) SS-Panzerkorps and I Armeekorps under *General* Busse.

It was a desperate scheme that would have meant blocking some 60 Red Army Guards and infantry divisions plus 13 tank brigades that had been arrayed along the Baltic coast to the south and around the land perimeter of Kurland. Success would have been far from certain. The plan was subsequently rejected by the Führer; Kurland was not to be abandoned! Given the situation that then existed on the Eastern Front, it proved to be the proper decision.

CHAPTER XI

Kurland

On the Kurland Front

By 12th October 1944, the units of III (Germanische) SS-Panzerkorps had all entered the southern sector of the Kurland Pocket. Behind them, the Red Army were busily putting one Latvian village after another to the flame; it was to be the beginning of a savage reign of terror for any Latvian civilians that remained.

The ultimate enemy objective now was to attempt to seize the last major Latvian port, Liepāja, upon which the defence of the Kurland Pocket depended. However this target would remain out of communist hands until the end of the war, thanks to the stalwart efforts of the European defensive forces. By 15th October 1944, the battalions of the *Nordland* Division and *Nederland* Brigade were able to form a cohesive, linked front for the first time in weeks. From north to south the unit positions ran as follows:

- **II/SS-Pz.Gren.Rgt.23** *Norge*: in place to the south of the 30 Infanterie-Division, along the railway line running to the east of Priekule-Vaiņode, including Hill 39.1.
- **III/SS-Pz.Gren.Rgt.23** *Norge*: in place to the south of the main railway line, with its key defensive strongpoint being Horse Head Hill (*Pferdekopfhöhe*).
- **II/SS-Pz.Gren.Rgt.24** *Danmark*: holding positions on a line running from the villages of Klein-Trekni to Trusi-Trekni.
- **III/SS-Pz.Gren.Rgt.24** *Danmark*: located to the south-west of II/SS-Pz.Gren.Rgt.24 *Danmark*, in Grudulis, Kirkstal and the swamps south of Purmsāti.
- **SS-Pionier-Bataillon 54**: situated in the hills to the north-east of Kalēti.
- **II/SS-Pz.Gren.Rgt.49** *De Ruyter*: in place along the railway lines to the east of Annenhof.
- **III/SS-Pz.Gren.Rgt.49** *De Ruyter*: positioned along the Priekule-Skuodas railway line near Ozoli, with Hill 17.1 being the strongpoint in the sector.
- **SS-Kampfgruppe** *Aigner* (consisting of all the remaining combat capable troops of the *Nederland* Brigade): on a line running from near Ozoli too the River Apše on the Lithuanian frontier where it was connected to the 11 Infanterie-Division.

Corps, division and brigade headquarters elements were clustered in close proximity with the III (Germanische) SS-Panzerkorps HQ at Goldnieki, the *Nordland* HQ in Maki, between Liepāja and Priekule, and the *Nederland* HQ in a group of houses to the south-east of Susta. The front lines between II/SS-Pz.Gren.Rgt.23 *Norge* and the 30 Infanterie-Division were reinforced by elements from the 4 Panzer-Division during the later part of 15th October.

On 16th October 1944, the newly established positions of SS-Panzergrenadier-Regiment 23 *Norge* and *Danmark* came under a furious enemy onslaught. In violent fighting, the Red Army managed to make a substantial penetration between II and III Battalions of SS-Panzergrenadier-Regiment 23 *Norge*. The *Norge* grenadiers put up a desperate resistance and all of the officers in 10/SS-Pz.Gren.Rgt.23 *Norge* were killed. The communist incursion would be sealed off and eliminated by SS assault troops on 17th October, but heavy combat in the sector would rage for the next five days.

Regiment *Danmark*'s sector was also hit by aggressive enemy attacks on 16th October. The Red Army objective was to take the village of Trekni and seize the road to Purmsāti. The Danish and German SS volunteers quickly came under heavy pressure and were soon fighting for survival. 11/SS-Pz.Gren.Rgt.24 *Danmark* was initially able to hold on by sending continuous rounds of heavy weapons fire at near point-blank range into the oncoming foe. After taking horrendous casualties, the communists decided to temporarily move their attack elsewhere!

The Soviets next hit the juncture between 10th and 11th Company and succeeded in making a breakthrough. *Danmark*'s Maschinenpistolezug, led by *SS-Untersturmführer* Schwabenberg, counterattacked against the penetration force but it was driven back into the positions of 11/SS-Pz.Gren.Rgt.24 *Danmark* after quickly losing 4 men killed and 14 more wounded. Later in the day, the Maschinenpistolezug again tried to restore a links with 10th Company, not knowing that 10th Company had been forced to shift its positions another 2000m further away. This gap had already been occupied by the foe and it proved to be too much for the 29 surviving members of the Maschinenpistolezug to deal with. After a brisk fire-fight they again withdrew into 11/SS-Pz.Gren.Rgt.24 *Danmark*'s lines.

At 1600 hours on 16th October, another massive direct enemy assault began on 11/SS-Pz.Gren.Rgt.24 *Danmark*'s positions. To compound the problems of the defenders, the company's heavy machine guns had begun to run low on ammunition. As a result, the company commander, *SS-Hauptscharführer* Albrecht (no officers were left!) went around to each machine gun emplacement to personally help direct their fire, which had to be as accurate as possible. By bringing the lightly wounded into the lines, 11th Company was once again able to hold on, but towards dusk the enemy again began trying to infiltrate the lines. This time individual Red Army soldiers had begun swimming through the small streams in the area to get close in and around the 11/SS-Pz.Gren.Rgt.24 *Danmark* positions. Getting exasperated, Albrecht fired a flare in order to obtain close artillery support from II/SS-Art.Rgt.11, which soon responded. The subsequent accurate shelling soon brought the Soviet efforts in the area to a close for the day.

During the night of 16th/17th October 1944, the commander of III/SS-Pz.Gren.Rgt.24 *Danmark*, *SS-Hauptsturmführer* Rudolf Ternedde, reorganised the positions of his companies. Fresh ammunition and supplies were sent up to the front and the wounded were finally evacuated. 13/SS-Pz.Gren.Rgt.24 *Danmark*, led by a Danish NCO, *SS-Oberscharführer* Noach, was brought out of reserve and placed directly in the battalion lines. Thus, when the Red Army resumed their attack after daybreak, they were met with massed heavy weapons fire from 13th Company. This brought their onslaught to a halt. But it also meant that the II/SS-Pz.Gren.Rgt.24 *Danmark* positions would now have to be softened up. As a result, at 0900 hours on the 17th, the Soviets sent a heavy barrage of artillery and mortar fire towards the II/SS-Pz.Gren.Rgt.24 *Danmark* sector. Following about twenty minutes of this, the Soviet infantry was back charging the *Danmark* lines, shouting "Urrah, Urrah". Again, they did not get very far. This time, III/SS-Pz.Gren.Rgt.24 *Danmark* also added its firepower to the defensive effort and the assault soon collapsed. After a few more enemy probing attacks on 18th and 19th October, the Regiment *Danmark* sector became fairly quiet.

Following a few calm days, a fairly weak Red Army force was able to slip through the gap between II/ and III/SS-Pz.Gren.Rgt.24 *Danmark* and seize part of the vital Gramzda-Purmsāti road. In the process, the village of Trekni was also infiltrated by the enemy. This set off alarm bells and precipitated an immediate response from the *Nordland* Division. A quick counterattack by the Swedish Company (3/SS-Pz.Aufkl.Abt.11), led by the Swedish *SS-Obersturmführer* Pehrsson, was not able to dislodge the enemy incursion. As a result a much stronger Red Army force was then able to move into the salient.

The Danish *SS-Hauptsturmführer* Per Sørensen (from II/SS-Pz.Gren.Rgt.24 *Danmark*) was instructed to put together a kampfgruppe to restore the links between II/ and III/SS-Pz.Gren.Rgt.24 *Danmark*. He assembled a force from 5/SS-Pz.Gren.Rgt.24 *Danmark*, the Maschinenpistolezug (*SS-Untersturmführer* Schwabenberg) and the *Alarmkompanie* (Emergency Company, led by *SS-Hauptsturmführer* Roßmann) along with assorted transport and support troops. A scouting party from *Danmark*'s Alarmkompanie endeavoured to restore physical contact between the two battalions on 23rd October, but it was not able to achieve its objective and had to withdraw from its advance positions under the cover of darkness, having lost 1 killed and 4 wounded.

The situation remained the same until 26th October 1944, when strong enemy artillery fire hit the positions of 6/SS-Pz.Gren.Rgt.24 *Danmark*. This was followed by another ground attack and a temporary breakthrough was made. During the afternoon, a counterattack by the II/SS-Pz.Gren.Rgt.24 *Danmark* reserves under the battalion commander, *SS-Hauptsturmführer* Albert Bergfeldt, was able to expel the Red Army and restore the lines. However, it was becoming obvious from the activity of the other side that the enemy had something big in mind soon!

The Second Battle of Kurland

On 27th October 1944, the Second Battle of Kurland got underway with the massed salvo of more than 2,000 Soviet artillery pieces directed at the centre of the Kurland front. This was followed by the onslaught of 45 Red Army Guards Divisions and 1 Tank Corps, with 2 other Tank Corps in support. The attack hit with overwhelming force all along the front. The battalions of SS-Panzergrenadier-Regiment 23 *Norge* were unable to hold their positions and were forced to give ground, losing all contact with the 30 Infanterie-Division to the north. At the HQ of Regiment *Danmark*, the CO, *SS-Obersturmbannführer* Albrecht Krügel, monitored the radio messages from his battalions and companies and soon became alarmed by the gravity of the situation. At 0930 hours, 5th Company reported being under attack but still holding; at 1030 hours, II Battalion radioed that the enemy penetration had been made in 6th Company's lines near the village of Kelputi, while 7th Company was still holding. Half-an-hour later, the reports became more desperate: 5th Company reported that it was still holding, but that the enemy had broken through 6th Company and was now in their rear.

SS-Obersturmbannführer Krügel who had moved the regimental command post up to Hill 28.3 to be closer to the action, had only one reply to all of the radio messages:

"Hold your positions!" The *Danmark* Alarmkompanie reported coming under attack at 1110 hours in Kelputi. At the same time, with 10/SS-Pz.Gren.Rgt.24 *Danmark* and that part of 11/SS-Pz.Gren.Rgt.24 *Danmark* located south of the Gramzda-Purmsāti Road, had begun to give ground and fell back into the forest to the south-west of Grudulis. At 11th Company's main positions along both sides of the road at Trekni, which it held with the Maschinenpistolezug, motorised enemy forces were observed flooding past on both sides. *SS-Obersturmbannführer* Krügel radioed 11th Company to "Hold under all circumstances!" But this was no longer becoming an effective option if any troops were to be saved!

What happened next was observed by the rangefinder for II/SS-Art.Rgt.11. He reported the following to the *Danmark* HQ at 1140 hours: "The enemy has broken through in the sector of 5th Company and the Alarmkompanie". Five minutes later he reported that these troops had been overwhelmed and the position of the Maschinenpistolezug was unclear. Faced by overwhelming enemy infantry and tank forces, running low on ammunition and absorbing high casualties, the *Danmark* grenadiers in this sector could do no more. By following a concrete drainage pipe that ran beneath the Trekni road they were able to reach the observation post of II/SS-Art.Rgt.11. By now, 11/SS-Pz.Gren.Rgt.24 *Danmark* and the Maschinenpistolezug had been reduced to mere remnants, with only 2 NCOs and 7 men left in the former and 1 Norwegian officer, 2 NCOs and 6 men left in the latter. Joined by survivors from 12/SS-Pz.Gren.Rgt.24 *Danmark*, a withdrawal was now carried to the forest south of Grudulis; wounded soldiers being carried along in tarpaulins.

At 1300 hours the battle shifted to the main point in the *Danmark* lines: Hill 28.3, which was defended by Kampfgruppe Sørensen. 5/SS-Pz.Gren.Rgt.24 *Danmark* held the north-western part of the hill and it had the support of 6/, 7/ and 8/SS-Pz.Gren.Rgt.24 *Danmark*, which were all in the nearby vicinity. The orders from *SS-Obersturmbannführer* Krügel were to "Hold Hill 28.3 under all circumstances!" He saw to it that two *sturmgeschütze* were brought up to support the defensive effort. This, along with the appearance of the *Danmark* Alarmkompanie, allowed the SS volunteers to hold the position for the rest of the day.

Early in the morning of 28th October, a large Soviet assault force bore down on Hill 28.3 and drove the *Danmark* defenders from their main positions. With the help of the *sturmgeschütze* however, the *Danmark* grenadiers were able to regain the lines in a swift counterattack a short time later. The enemy objective then became to try and outflank the hill. A Red Army spearhead managed to penetrate the juncture between 5/ and 6/SS-Pz.Gren.Rgt.24 *Danmark*, and began threatening the heavy weapons positions to the rear.

SS-Obersturmbannführer Krügel then came to the conclusion that the regimental positions were untenable. He ordered the withdrawal of the heavy weapons sections under the cover of fire from the *sturmgeschütze* and two Flak guns from 14th Company which had been re-deployed from the anti-aircraft to the ground role. By late afternoon on 28th October, the entire regiment was in retreat towards Purmsāti. The Soviets followed close behind and managed to seize the Purmsāti railway station before the *Danmark* grenadiers could get into position to defend it. At dusk, *SS-Obersturmbannführer* Krügel tried to form a new defensive line along the railway tracks that ran north-south from Priekule to Skuodas. But everything remained in flux and the lines were far from stable. On his way to find the SS-Panzergrenadier-Regiment 24 *Danmark*, the *Nordland* divisional adjutant, *SS-Sturmbannführer* Witten, drove into the Red Army lines at Purmsāti in his Schwimmwagen. His driver later made it back to the *Danmark* lines where he reported that both Witten and his aide had been killed by the Soviets.

Purmsāti

During the night of 28th/29th October 1944, the commanders of the *Nordland* Division and the SS-Panzergrenadier-Regiment 24 *Danmark* visited the front-line positions near Purmsāti and devised a plan to link up with SS-Pionier-Bataillon 54 to the south. In order to do this, reinforcements were brought in from the *Nordland* Division's SS-Feldersatz-Bataillon 11 which had been stationed near Auce, and 40 of these troops were assigned to Kampfgruppe *Sørensen*. This command now consisted of a selection of troops from 5/SS-Pz.Gren.Rgt.24 *Danmark*, SS-Artillerie-Regiment 11, the Alarmkompanie and SS-Wirtschaft-Bataillon 11.

However, serious problems developed early in the day of 29th October when the 40 man reserve platoon that had been assigned to Kampfgruppe *Sørensen* was decoyed into an enemy ambush leading to the loss or capture of most of these soldiers. To offset this small disaster the entire 3rd Company from SS-Feldersatz-Bataillon 11 was then assigned to the kampfgruppe, deployed in and around the Purmsāti schoolhouse. In the course of the morning of 29th October a major battle developed between the Purmsāti schoolhouse and railway station with the fighting flaring up and down the main street in Purmsāti. With the help of two roaming *sturmgeschütze* from the *Nordland* Division, the *Danmark* defenders were able to drive off the initial Soviet assault on the town but the railway station went up in flames during the counterattack by the SS grenadiers. At around midday on the 29th, the Red Army were back with tanks and infantry and this time moved directly towards the Purmsāti schoolhouse. The soldiers of Kampfgruppe *Sørensen* went after the tanks with *Panzerfäuste* and destroyed or crippled 4 of them in short order causing the infantry escort to fall back. The battle for Purmsāti continued through 31st October and although the fighting was often intense, the Soviets were unable to make any headway with their attacks.

The last effort by the communists to take the town came in the form of a suicidal infantry assault launched after an artillery barrage at 1600 hours on the 31st. This was a half-hearted effort in which Red Army infantrymen were clearly being forced forward into the zone of fire of the SS defenders by the political commissars behind them. The slaughter was dreadful. Following this fiasco and the sealing off of another enemy penetration to the north of Purmsāti in which every enemy tank that had pushed forward was destroyed, the battle for the town finally drew to a close. With élan, courage and skilful, hands-on leadership by the officers and NCOs, SS-Panzergrenadier-Regiment 24 *Danmark* had decisively won the day!

For their heroic deeds during the battle, *SS-Hauptsturmführer* Per Sørensen, *SS-Hauptsturmführer* Rudolf Ternedde (CO of III/SS-Pz.Gren.Rgt.24 *Danmark*) and *SS-Unterscharführer* Alfred Jonstrup were all awarded the Honour Roll Clasp of the German Army. Sørensen and Jonstrup would be the only two Danes to receive this prestigious decoration. Alfred Jonstrup was a veteran of the old *Freikorps Danmark* and had helped rescue the body of the fallen *Freikorps Danmark* commander, *SS-Obersturmbannführer* C F von Schalburg in 1942. On 27th October 1944 he was assigned to carry a message across the Purmsāti battlefield concerning the repositioning of the *Danmark* Alarmkompanie (Kompanie Roßmann). In the course of carrying out his mission, a shell splinter hit Jonstrup in the face causing a severe wound to his chin and lower jaw. Despite his condition, Jonstrup successfully brought his message to the regimental command post and filled out a report before seeking medical care. He would

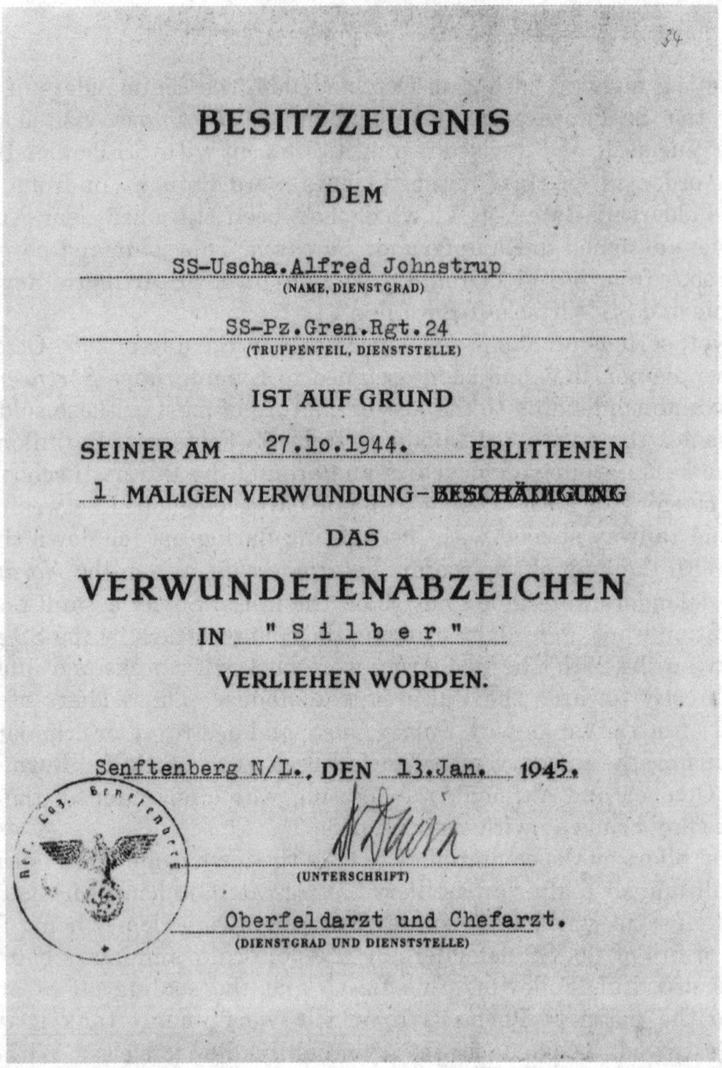

BESITZZEUGNIS

DEM

SS-Uscha.Alfred Johnstrup
(NAME, DIENSTGRAD)

SS-Pz.Gren.Rgt.24
(TRUPPENTEIL, DIENSTSTELLE)

IST AUF GRUND

SEINER AM 27.10.1944. ERLITTENEN

1 MALIGEN VERWUNDUNG – ~~BESCHÄDIGUNG~~

DAS

VERWUNDETENABZEICHEN

IN "Silber"

VERLIEHEN WORDEN.

Senftenberg N/L., DEN 13.Jan. 1945.

(UNTERSCHRIFT)

Oberfeldarzt und Chefarzt.
(DIENSTGRAD UND DIENSTSTELLE)

Authorisation for the award of the Silver Wound Badge to *Unterscharführer* Alfred Jonstrup signed by the Chief Medical Officer at the military hospital in Senftenberg. This was the wound he received during the act which won him the Honour Roll Clasp.

be maimed for life by his terrible wound but his actions on that day may well have saved the front.

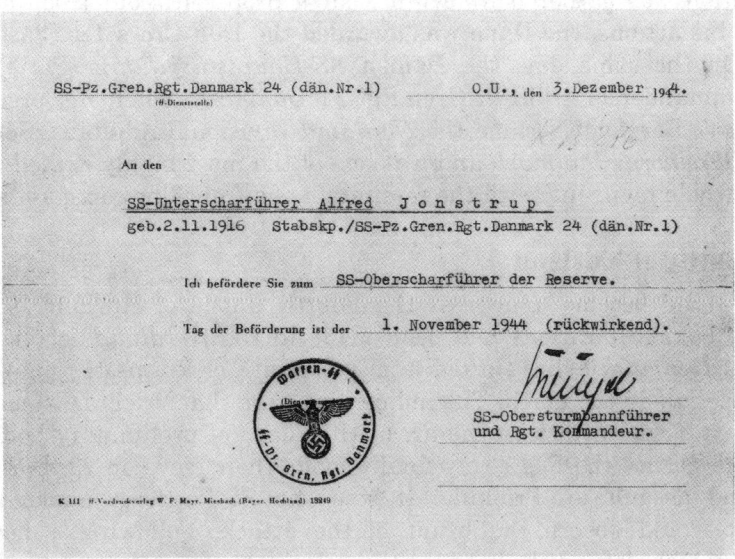

Document authorising the retroactive promotion of *SS-Unterscharführer* Alfred Jonstrup from the Staff Company of Regiment *Danmark* to the rank of *SS-Oberscharführer der Reserve*. It is signed by the regimental CO, *Ostubaf* Albrecht Krügel

The Third Battle of Kurland

SS-Obersturmbannführer Albrecht Krügel, the *Danmark* CO, was decorated with the Oakleaves to the Knight's Cross in November 1944 and was given a home leave. His role as regimental commander was temporarily assumed by *SS-Obersturmbannführer* von Bock und Pollach, the *Nordland* Division's Chief-of-Staff (Ia). Fortunately the next two months brought a period of relative calm to the III (Germanische) SS-Panzerkorps sector, enabling units to be reinforced and occasionally rotated out of the line. Even the Third Battle of Kurland, which began on 21st December, bypassed the sector held by III (Germanische) SS-Panzerkorps. Instead, the brunt of this fighting fell on the VI Waffen-Armeekorps der SS (*Lettisches*)[10] and the Latvian SS volunteers did a splendid job in helping repel this latest Soviet onslaught.

Three months of fighting in Kurland had inflicted a little over 70,000 casualties on the German-European side and perhaps as much at ten times as many on the enemy, but the Red Army still remained the stronger force! As December passed on, the principle combat activity in the III (Germanische) SS-Panzerkorps sector revolved around the sending out of scouting parties to investigate the enemy positions and movements.

By early January 1945 it was becoming evident that Soviet activity was increasing in the sectors opposite the *Nordland* Division. On 9th January, strong enemy heavy weapons fire was directed on the house held by a squad from 8/SS-Pz.Gren.Rgt.24

---

[10] 6th (Latvian) SS Corps

Danmark in Purmsāti in which the Danish squad leader, *SS-Unterscharführer* Laursen was mortally wounded. On 12th January, another Danish volunteer, on his own initiative, went out behind the enemy lines and brought back a Russian prisoner. So much information was gathered from him that a proposed scout troop operation was cancelled. For his actions, the Dane was awarded the Iron Cross 1st Class and given a home leave. On the same day, the Danish *SS-Hauptsturmführer* Per Sørensen was named the commander of II/SS-Pz.Gren.Rgt.24 *Danmark*, when his predecessor, *SS-Sturmbannführer* Bergfeldt became the *Nordland* Divisional Adjutant. Sørensen was a veteran of the *Freikorps Danmark* and was one of the most highly skilled and qualified officers in the whole regiment, with the reputation of a front-line commander.

The Fourth Battle of Kurland

What would become known as the Fourth Battle of Kurland began on 20th January 1945. Some alterations had been made in the *Nordland* sector, with III/SS-Pz.Gren.Rgt.24 *Danmark* being shifted from just south of Purmsāti to new positions to the south of Priekule in the north. The indications were that Priekule would be the focal point of the next Soviet attack in the area. After days of preliminary bombardment of the *Nordland* positions, the Red Army finally made their move on 23rd January with a massive ground assault on Priekule. It was the SS-Panzergrenadier-Regiment 24 *Danmark* that would absorb the brunt of the attack. Following a heavy artillery bombardment which left such heavy accumulations of smoke as to destroy local visibility, 40 enemy tanks and accompanying Red Army infantry zeroed in on Priekule.

The grenadiers from 6/SS-Pz.Gren.Rgt.24 *Danmark* were able to blunt the first enemy wave by destroying all of the 10 tanks advancing on the company positions, in close combat and mowing down the infantry escort. But somewhat later in the day a force of 30 Soviet tanks that had been repulsed by the soldiers of 7/ and 11/SS-Pz.Gren.Rgt.24 *Danmark*, again hit the 6th Company lines. These were just too many for the 6/SS-Pz.Gren.Rgt.24 *Danmark* grenadiers to handle and the company positions were quickly overrun. Breaking though the lines, the Soviet armour was now able to hit 7/ and 11/SS-Pz.Gren.Rgt.24 *Danmark* in the flank and roll up both company lines in succession. Contingents of motorised Red Army infantry quickly followed and the whole *Nordland* sector to the north of Purmsāti was soon in jeopardy.

Heavy weapons fire from 8/SS-Pz.Gren.Rgt.24 *Danmark* (*SS-Untersturmführer* Birkedahl-Hansen) and 13/SS-Pz.Gren.Rgt.24 *Danmark* slowed the enemy just enough to permit the regrouping of II/ and III/SS-Pz.Gren.Rgt.24 *Danmark* in new defensive positions in and around Purmsāti. It was hoped to be able to prepare a counterattack with the help of the adjoining II/SS-Pz.Gren.Rgt.23 *Norge*, but there were simply not enough troops left to do more than hang on. For instance, 6/SS-Pz.Gren.Rgt.24 *Danmark* had been reduced to 1 officer and 3 men (!), whilst 7/SS-Pz.Gren.Rgt.24 *Danmark* only had 1 officer and 14 men. Most of the other *Danmark* companies, including 8th Company, had been reduced roughly 50% in size with substantial losses to vehicles and equipment. III/SS-Pz.Gren.Rgt.24 *Danmark* reported the loss of most of its officers and had to abandon its positions to the south of Purmsāti.

Fortunately the depleted SS-Panzergrenadier-Regiment 24 *Danmark* was given some respite during the night of 23rd/24th January 1945, when much of the 14 Panzer-Division moved into the regimental sector to prepare for a counterattack. This would literally save the day for III (Germanische) SS-Panzerkorps. The tanks from 14 Panzer-Division were able to stabilise the front and bring relief to the hard-pressed 23 SS-Freiwilligen-Panzergrenadier-Division *Nederland* to the south.

At the conclusion of the Fourth Battle of Kurland, the decision was made to withdraw the badly battered III (Germanische) SS-Panzerkorps to Germany, commencing on 28th January 1945, for what was hoped would be a protracted period of refitting and reinforcement. But the situation even in eastern Germany was becoming more critical every day and it would not be long before the combat-hardened European SS volunteers would be back in action in even more desperate fighting!

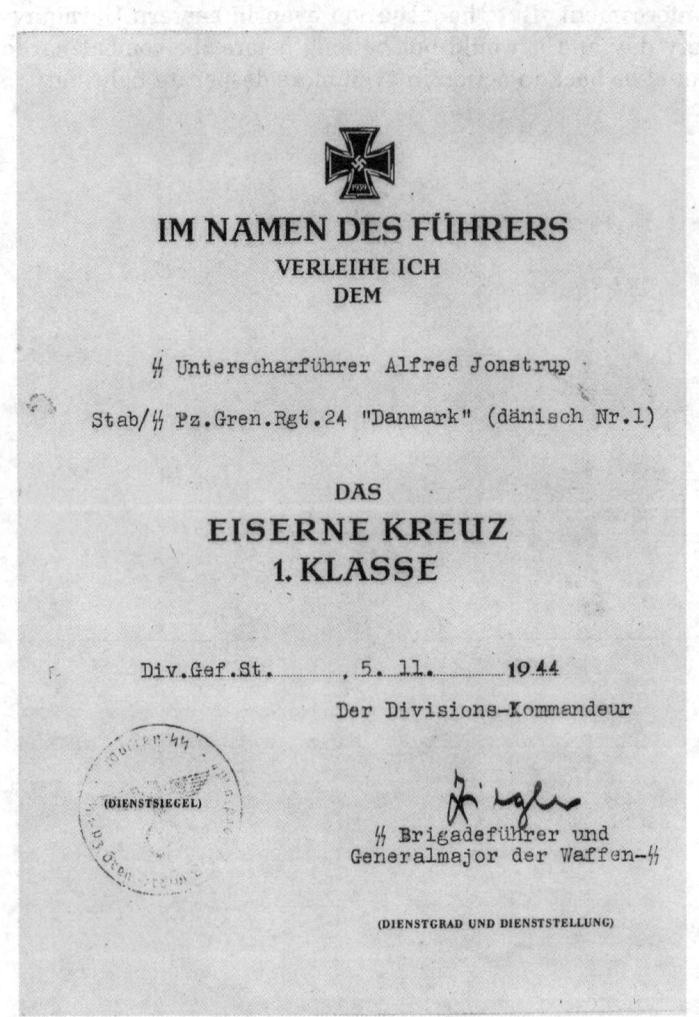

Citation for the Iron Cross 1st Class given to *Unterscharführer* Alfred Jonstrup of the Staff of SS-Pz.Gren.Rgt.24 *Danmark*. The signature is that of the commander of the *Nordland* Division, *SS-Brigadeführer* Joachim Ziegler

SS-*Sturmmann* Alfred Jonstrup. He was a veteran of the Russo-Finnish War and the *Freikorps Danmark*. Jonstrup served with the Staff Company of Regiment *Danmark* and was awarded the coveted Honour Roll Clasp of the German Army on 25th December 1944. On 2nd June 1942, whilst serving with the *Freikorps*, Jonstrup had dragged the body of the legendary Danish *Sturmbannfuhrer* von Schalburg out of an exposed area and back to the lines

Alfred Jonstrup after being very badly wounded in the face on 27th October 1944. Despite the fact that his jaw was shot to pieces and he was unable to speak, he insisted upon writing down the information he was carrying to the *Danmark* headquarters. For this he received the Honour Roll Clasp and a promotion to *Oberscharführer der Reserve*, even though he never again returned to active duty. (The documents for his wound badge and his promotion are reproduced on pages 128-9)

(Above and above left) *SS-Untersturmführer* Erik Erikson, born 11th February 1917 in Århus, Denmark. Erikson had volunteered for the Waffen-SS on 26th June 1940 and had then served with the *Wiking* Division. From 1st February 1943 until 31st July 1943 he attended the 9th SS Wartime Officer's Training Class at the SS-Junkerschule Bad Tölz. Then from September 1943 until April 1944, *Untersturmführer* Erikson served as a platoon leader with 10/SS-Pz.Gren.Rgt.24 *Danmark*. His decorations included the Iron Cross 2nd Class, the Infantry Assault Badge in Bronze, the Wound Badge in Black and the Winter War Medal 1941/42

(Left) *SS-Obersturmführer* Johannes Hellmers, a Danish volunteer and company commander in the *Nederland* Division who was awarded the Knight's Cross

SS-Obersturmführer Christian Dall. A Nordschleswiger, Dall volunteered for the SS in the summer of 1940. He first went to 1/Rgt. *Nordland* at Klagenfurt, Austria and then served with 13/Rgt. *Nordland*. After graduating from SS-Junkerschule Bad Tölz in 1943, he went to Croatia with the III (Germanische) SS-Panzerkorps. In the spring of 1944 he became the CO of 13/SS-Pz.Gren.Rgt.23 *Norge*. He ended the war as a kampfgruppe commander in the 38 SS-Pz.Gren.Div. *Nibelungen*. His wartime decorations included: Iron Cross 1st and 2nd Class, Close Combat Clasp in Silver, Infantry Assault Badge in Silver, Tank Destruction Badge, Wound Badge in Silver, Winter War Medal 1941/42, and the Croatian Order of the Iron Trefoil 4th Class

SS-Untersturmführer Kaj Gustav Feilberg. A Danish volunteer, Feilberg joined Regiment *Nordland* in Vienna An the autumn of 1940. In 1943 he went to SS-Junkerschule Bad Tölz in the same class as Christen Dall. After graduating he was sent to the SS-Panzer-Aufklärungs-Abteilung 11 where he served as a platoon leader with the 4th Company. Following the war, Feilberg was convicted for having committed a murder during the German occupation. All the evidence would suggest that he was innocent but, as a result, Feilberg was forced into hiding in Germany where he remains to this day

SS-Unterscharführer Fritz Ihle, a Nordschleswiger who joined 4/Rgt. *Nordland* in Klagenfurt, Austria in 1940. He later went to 7/ Rgt. Nordland in Vienna but was with 15/ Rgt. *Nordland* in 1941 during the advance into Russia. In 1943 when the III (Germanische) SS-Panzerkorps was raised, Ihle as an *Unterscharführer* was transferred to the 2/SS-Pz.Gren.Rgt.24 *Danmark*. However due to his experience with the recce company of the old Nordland Regiment he was soon sent to 2/SS-Pz.Aufkl.Abt.11 where he remained for the rest of the war. His wartime decorations were: Iron Cross 2nd Class, Infantry Assault Badge in Bronze, Tank Battle Badge in Bronze, Wound Badge in Black and Winter War Medal 1941/42. After the war, Fritz Ihle was told by his old Spieß from 2/SS-Pz.Aufkl.Abt.11 that he had been promoted to *Oberscharführer* and decorated with the Iron Cross 1st Class on the Führer's birthday (20th April 1945). However, Ihle was in hospital and this was never brought to his attention. As he was not informed during wartime he does not wish to recognise the promotion or decoration now

Leave request for health reasons, (i.e. recovery from a wound), forwarded to the commander of 2/SS-Pz.Gren.Rgt.24 *Danmark* by *Unterscharführer* Fritz Ihle. It is countersigned by the company medical officer

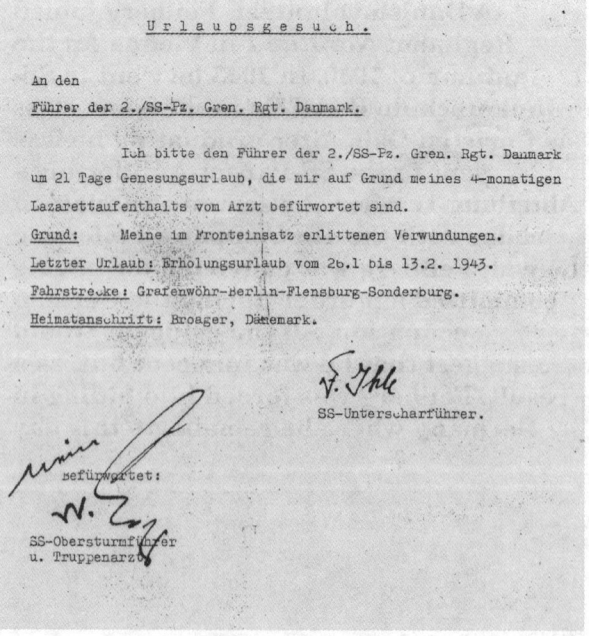

SS-Standartenoberjunker Fritz Weber. Weber was another Nordschleswiger who volunteered for the SS-VT in 1939 and became one of the very few Danes to participate in the Western Campaign of 1940 with 1/SS-Rgt. *Germania*. He later went into Russia with the same company. In 1943 he was transferred to the III (Germ) SS-Pz.Kps where he served with the Staff Company of the 11 SS-Freiw.Pz.Gren.Div. *Nordland* as an Unterscharführer and leader of the heavy mortar platoon. After Narva and some fighting in Latvia, Weber left for the SS-Junkerschule Bad Tölz in the autumn of 1944. In 1945, as a Standartenoberjunker (officer designate) he was transferred to the 38 SS-Pz.Gren.Div. *Nibelungen* where he was placed in charge of a platoon of Dutch SS recruits. Weber's wartime decorations were the following: the Iron Cross 2nd Class, Infantry Assault Badge in Bronze, Wound Badge in Silver, and the Winter War Medal 1941/42

SS-Rottenführer Egon Larsen. Larsen volunteered for the SS in the autumn of 1940 and he went to 7/Rgt. Nordland in Vienna. In the autumn of 1943 he was back in Vienna as a pupil at the *Kraftfahrtechnische Lehranstalt der SS* (KTL der SS) which was a motorised vehicle technical school. Here he was educated as a Panzerwart or tank mechanic. He then joined the schwere SS-Panzer-Abteilung 503 (Heavy Tank Detachment 503) with the III (Germanische) SS-Panzerkorps. Late in the war this unit became II/SS-Pz.Rgt.11 *Hermann von Salza*, at least on paper, when *Hermann von Salza* was authorised to expand into a regiment

CHAPTER XII

Battles in Pomerania

On 28th January 1945, the surviving remnants of the III (Germanische) SS-Panzerkorps were withdrawn from their front-line positions near Priekule, Latvia under the cover of darkness. The European SS force was then shipped back to Stettin, Germany from the Latvian port of Liepāja. During the rushed embarkation process, two trucks belonging to SS-Panzergrenadier-Regiment 24 *Danmark* slipped off the docks into the water and were lost to further use!

While most elements of the Corps made it safely to Stettin, one troopship, the *Moira*, carrying many soldiers from the 23 SS-Freiwilligen-Panzergrenadier-Division *Nederland* was torpedoed and lost with all hands. Many Corps elements that had earlier been sent to Germany for reformation were new grouped at the Hammerstein Training Ground to join the main body of the III (Germanische) SS-Panzerkorps to the east of Lake Madü along the River Ihna. Due to the crisis in this sector, any reformation of the Corps units from Latvia would have to be done on the move. There would be no time for any prolonged rest or refitting. The Corps, which now incorporated regimental kampfgruppen from both the Flemish 27 SS-Freiwilligen-Grenadier-Division *Langemarck*, 28 SS-Freiwilligen-Grenadier-Division *Wallonien* and the 10 SS-Panzer-Division *Frundsberg*, came under the aegis of the newly created 11 Panzer-Armee, under the command of *SS-Obergruppenführer* Steiner. His temporary replacement as CO of III (Germanische) SS-Panzerkorps was an Army officer, *General* Martin Unrein.

On a front running west-east from Lake Madü to the town of Hassendorf, the Corps deployed the following formations in early February 1945:

- part of 10 SS-Panzer-Division *Frundsberg*
- SS-Kampfgruppe *Wallonien*
- parts of 4 SS-Polizei-Panzergrenadier-Division and 10 SS-Panzer-Division *Frundsberg*
- SS-Kampfgruppe *Langemarck*
- 11 SS-Panzergrenadier-Division *Nordland*
- 23 SS-Freiwilligen-Panzergrenadier-Division *Nederland*
- SS-Panzerjäger-Abteilung 11
- Führer-Begleit-Division and Führer-Grenadier Division
- 281 Infanterie-Division

The Corps objective was to eventually go on the offensive and push back the advancing Red Army to the south. The first order of business was to stabilise the front

Battles in Pomerania

and maintain the Arnswalde salient which bulged out of the main River Ihna lines towards the south-east.

This was not an easy task. The roughly 15,000 European SS troops in the sector were faced by more than 90,000 Red Army soldiers, massed in 9 full divisions! After several days of furious fighting, the Soviets were able to complete an entrapment of the town of Arnswalde. A surrender ultimatum was then issued to the Arnswalde garrison commander on 13th February 1945, but was refused. Instead, III (Germanische) SS-Panzerkorps was ordered to go over to the offensive, relieve Arnswalde and clear out the enemy forces on the south bank of the Ihna. To this end the bulk of the 10 SS-Panzer-Division *Frundsberg* was brought in.

Attack on the Arnswalde Salient

The SS relief attack towards Arnswalde got underway on 16th February 1945, after combat engineers had managed to span the River Ihna with heavy makeshift bridges. Spearheading the assault was II/SS-Pz.Gren.Rgt.24 *Danmark* led by the redoubtable Danish *SS-Sturmbannführer* Per Sørensen, and II/SS-Pz.Gren.Rgt.23 *Norge*. Armoured vehicles from *Nordland* Division and the Führer-Begleit-Division under *Generalmajor* Remer[11] closely supported the attack of the European SS battalions. The first objective was to regain the town of Reichenbach.

After II/SS-Pz.Gren.Rgt.23 *Norge* was slowed down by fierce communist resistance at Schlagenthin, it was left to II/SS-Pz.Gren.Rgt.24 *Danmark* to secure Reichenbach. Led by its 6th and 7th Companies with 5th Company in close support and 8th Company in reserve, the battalion smashed into the town throwing back the enemy before them. *SS-Sturmbannführer* Sørensen personally led the advance assault platoon that seized the south part of the town. While under fire, the *Danmark* grenadiers had to rescue desperate women and children who had been trapped in a truly hellish inferno - the whole town was soon ablaze!

After the town had been taken, the *Danmark* CO, *SS-Obersturmbannführer* Albrecht Krügel came forward to confer with *SS-Sturmbannführer* Sørensen. The decision was made to continue and seize the woods and high ground around the town to which the enemy had retreated. At 1300 hours on the 16th, the *Danmark* soldiers continued their attack and within 45 minutes had secured all of their objectives. The Regimental and II Battalion command posts now moved into what was left of Reichenbach. It was soon discovered that most of the town's inhabitants had been murdered by the Red Army in a series of horrible atrocities, which no one would ever have to answer for! The farms and yards of the dead residents were however filled with livestock that had to be immediately evacuated by the *Nordland* commissary troops.

By the afternoon of the 16th, the Waffen-SS spearheads were advancing to the south of Lake Ihna in all sectors, but the enemy defensives grew stronger by the minute. SS-Panzergrenadier-Regiment 23 *Norge* was unable to take Schlagenthin quickly, which in turn caused SS-Panzergrenadier-Regiment 24 *Danmark* to slow its advance. As a result, *Danmark* remained on the high ground to the south of Reichenbach for most of the day. Schlagenthin finally fell to the *Norge* grenadiers in the evening. Despite this, many of the day's objectives of III (Germanische) SS-Panzerkorps had not been achieved.

On 17th February, the offensive continued, although it soon bogged down in the west along the shores of Lake Madü. In the *Nordland* sector, SS-Panzergrenadier-Regiment 23 *Norge* rushed out from Schlagenthin and established a 'security line' from

---

[11] Remer was the officer who had averted the take-over in Berlin by the conspirators of the 20th July Bomb Plot. His loyalty to Hitler had gained him an immediate promotion and this exalted appointment.

Stolzenfelde to Marienwerder. Regiment *Danmark* was given the mission of regaining the towns of Bonin and Schönwerder, an effort that hinged on the ability of I/SS-Rgt.66 of the 27 SS-Freiwilligen-Grenadier-Division *Langemarck* to take Gut Marienfelde on *Danmark*'s right flank. III/SS-Pz.Gren.Rgt.24 *Danmark*, ably led by *SS-Hauptsturmführer* Rudolf Ternedde, was able to take Bonin in difficult fighting, but the advance on Schönwerder was placed on hold until the Flemish SS volunteers of the *Langemarck* Division secured Gut Marienfelde. The estate finally fell to the Flemings late in the afternoon, just before *SS-Sturmbannführer* Sørensen's II/SS-Pz.Gren.Rgt.24 *Danmark* was about to assist.

Once Gut Marienfelde was secured, Regiment *Danmark* was able to turn its attention to Schönwerder. Again, Sørensen's II Battalion led the way, quickly overrunning the initial enemy defences on the flat ground outside the town. The secondary defences - a well prepared line of bunkers - were somewhat more difficult to 'crack'. But the grenadiers from 6/ and 7/SS-Pz.Gren.Rgt.24 *Danmark*, along with the close support of three *Nordland sturmgeschütze*, were able to systematically drive the Red Army from their dug-outs. Inside the bunkers large quantities of weapons and supplies were found, including a vast amount of tinned foodstuffs marked "Made in USA". Needless to say most of this lend-lease bounty was appropriated by the SS soldiers before the commissary officers got their hands on it!

As the *Danmark* attack group advanced down the road to Schönwerder, the escorting *Nordland sturmgeschütze* fell one by one to well-placed land mines. This, combined with a furious heavy weapons barrage from the Red Army, bogged down the attack. Some *Nordland* armoured cars tried to break into the town from the east, but they too were driven back. Another conference between *SS-Obersturmbannführer* Krügel and *SS-Sturmbannführer* Sørensen was held towards the end of the day and the further course of the assault was plotted, although it had to be postponed until the next day due to the onset of darkness.

During the night, *SS-Sturmbannführer* Sørensen threw out a piquet line along the Stargard-Arnswalde railway line and sent out a squad to link up with III/SS-Pz.Gren.Rgt.24 *Danmark* to the east. 16 (Pi)/SS-Pz.Gren.Rgt.24 *Danmark* was also brought out of reserve and placed in the front lines between II/SS-Pz.Gren.Rgt.24 *Danmark* and I/SS-Rgt.66. In the course of 18th February, II/SS-Pz.Gren.Rgt.24 *Danmark*, led by *SS-Untersturmführer* Madsen's 7th Company, which first penetrated the final enemy defensive line, was able to seize most of Schönwerder.

At 1600 hours on 17th February, seven tanks from the *Nordland* Division smashed their way into Arnswalde in a daring attack; the siege was lifted and the primary Corps objective was obtained. 18th February saw heavy fighting for the town as a narrow 'escape corridor' was built from the main III (Germanische) SS-Panzerkorps lines into the town to evacuate civilians and the wounded. The rest of the day saw only small gains made all along the front and by 19th February, static warfare had again begun to set in.

Despite some spectacular achievements, including the destruction of 17 enemy tanks and the capture of 3 more by the *sturmgeschütze* of SS-Panzerjäger-Abteilung 11, the Waffen-SS offensive had clearly come to a halt. While few reinforcements could be brought up on the German side, the Soviets quickly began a massive increase in manpower and material in their lines. In the course of 19th and 20th February, heavy fighting raged for both Arnswalde and Schönwerder. On the 21st, the Regiment *Danmark* was subjected to an enormous enemy artillery bombardment, but the SS troopers grimly hung on to their positions. Only the livestock in the vicinity were evacuated!

However, sad conclusions had to be drawn. The SS formations could no longer make any forward progress and they could hardly stay in extended, exposed positions to the south of the Ihna forever while the enemy grew progressively stronger. Therefore, on the afternoon of 21st February, *SS-Obergruppenführer* Steiner decided to begin the withdrawal of the 11 Panzer-Armee back to the north bank of the Ihna. There was no longer any doubt that the Soviets were too powerful to confront by head-on attack. But such was the despicable, barbaric nature of the foe, the battle had to continue to the bitter end - no matter what. There could be no compromise with these Bolshevik enemies of civilisation!

Following a methodical step-by-step plan, the troops south of the Ihna were withdrawn in three groups at hourly intervals, during the night of 21st February. Protection for the withdrawal was provided by an armoured kampfgruppe led by *SS-Obersturmbannführer* Groß. At midnight, *General* Unrein and what remained of the Arnswalde garrison reported to the III (Germanische) SS-Panzerkorps HQ in Tornow.

SS-Panzergrenadier-Regiment 24 *Danmark* covered the southern flank of the retreat and was the last unit to withdraw across the Ihna. II and III/SS-Pz.Gren.Rgt.24 *Danmark* did not leave their positions around Schönwerder until 2300 hours on the 21st. A small task force led by *SS-Untersturmführer* Gordon stayed behind to give the impression that the lines were still occupied. At 03:00 on 22nd February, the regimental commander shot up a flare to finally recall Gordon's rearguard troops.

In the dawn hours of the 22nd, *SS-Sturmbannführer* Sørensen gave the order to blow the last bridge over the River Ihna. However, just before the charges were detonated, 10/SS-Pz.Gren.Rgt.23 *Norge* suddenly appeared on the south bank of the river and was allowed to cross. The bridge was then sent flying into the air with an enormous roar!

Between 23rd-28th February 1945, the units of III (Germanische) SS-Panzerkorps began pulling back so as to defend the approaches to the important cities of Stargard and Stettin. On the 24th, SS-Panzergrenadier-Regiment 24 *Danmark* was moved into new defensive positions to the south of Stargard. III Battalion moved into the western sector running from Lange-Berge to Streesen, while II Battalion was deployed to the east in an area running from Streesen to the Faule Ihna, adjoining the right flank of SS-Kampfgruppe *Wallonien* from the 28 SS-Freiwilligen-Grenadier-Division *Wallonien*.

The preparations for the Soviet offensive against Stargard and the River Ihna sector began in earnest on 28th February 1945. III/SS-Pz.Gren.Rgt.24 *Danmark* reported heavy incoming artillery fire on its positions, a sure sign that a large attack was in the offing. A Soviet ground attack was launched against a portion of the front held by the 23 SS-Freiwilligen-Panzergrenadier-Division *Nederland* but this was repulsed. Several smaller probing attacks were also noted.

The Red Storm Breaks

On 1st March 1945, the storm broke. The greatest massed enemy artillery bombardment that anyone had witnessed during the war, was unleashed upon the III (Germanische) SS-Panzerkorps positions. It was followed up by an enormous ground attack. Even this could not break the spirit of the European SS defenders, who continued to put up a strong resistance wherever they could. However, the odds were just too great. By noon Corps units were in retreat all along the front and Red Army forces closed in on the town of Schöneberg.

Once again, the tenacious soldiers of the *Nordland, Nederland, Langemarck* and *Wallonien* Divisions were able to regroup and slow the onslaught. The fighting was of the most desperate nature imaginable and disasters were often averted only by a hairsbreadth. In the afternoon of 1st March, the transport column of SS-Panzergrenadier-Regiment 24 *Danmark* was situated in Barskewitz when sentries spotted a breakthrough Soviet tank force heading directly towards them. The alarm was raised and the chase was on! Under enemy fire the *Danmark* convoy just managed to reach the safety of the town of Dahlow. It was a situation that was common all over the front, as support troops tried to get out of the way of the advancing foe. For a while, confusion and chaos reigned supreme and only the firm and tenacious resistance of the veteran SS troops prevented a complete disaster.

In the night of 1st/2nd March, the Regiment *Danmark* was withdrawn from its positions to the south of Stargard with orders to relocate near Dahlow to the north-east, where the regimental support troops were. During the process of moving through Stargard, the CO of II/SS-Pz.Gren.Rgt.24 *Danmark*, *SS-Sturmbannführer* Sørensen, received an emergency directive from a military policeman sending his battalion to Freienwalde to assist the hard-pressed 23 SS-Freiwilligen-Panzergrenadier-Division *Nederland*.

Elsewhere on 2nd March 1945, troops from the *Wallonien* Division steadfastly blocked the Soviet advance to the south-east of Stargard, while to the north-east, armoured units from the *Nordland* Division prepared a counterattack to help stave off enemy pressure on Highway 158, the main route to Stargard. The immediate objective was to retake the town of Büche to the south-east. This job was given to III/SS-Pz.Gren.Rgt.24 *Danmark*, which moved into position on two sides of the town. With the help of 3 *Nordland* tanks, the *Danmark* grenadiers recaptured the town and the surrounding area.

9/SS-Pz.Gren.Rgt.24 *Danmark,* under *SS-Untersturmführer* Birkedahl-Hansen, had the job of occupying Büche itself. What they found in the town was almost too much, even for these hardened soldiers: the women and children of the town had all been brutally murdered and their mutilated bodies were strewn about everywhere. It was a sickening spectacle and yet *another* atrocity that the USSR would never have to answer for! As 9/SS-Pz.Gren.Rgt.24 *Danmark* moved into Büche, 5 destroyed Soviet tanks in the town were still burning. With the help of two anti-tank guns, 9th Company managed to repel enemy armoured and infantry counterattacks throughout the night.

But at 0600 hours on the 3rd of March, a Soviet tank force again approached the Büche Bridge. One of the tanks was blown up by an anti-tank gun and another was destroyed by a platoon leader's Panzerfaust, but 9/SS-Pz.Gren.Rgt.24 *Danmark* was no longer strong enough to hold the whole town. *SS-Untersturmführer* Birkedahl-Hansen pulled his depleted command back into the northern part of Büche. Orders soon arrived for the company to begin a withdrawal to Marienfließ. But this town was also under enemy attack and could not be held much longer either! Therefore, 9/SS-Pz.Gren.Rgt.24 *Danmark*, with a strength of only 20 fit men, fell back on the town of Trampke and continued retreating from there.

To the west of Trampke, 9th Company ran into the remnants of the 10th, which had also taken heavy losses. The commander of 10/SS-Pz.Gren.Rgt.24 *Danmark*, *SS-Untersturmführer* Thorkildsen, combined both of the companies and assumed overall command. He immediately set up a blocking position to slow the enemy advance. When some of the Red Army tanks appeared, grenadiers from 9/SS-Pz.Gren.Rgt.24 *Danmark* went after them with *Panzerfäuste* and succeeded in driving them back. Some respite had been gained. Later in the day, the survivors of III/SS-Pz.Gren.Rgt.24 *Danmark* regrouped at an interception point near Dahlow.

Elsewhere, in the north-eastern part of the town of Freienwalde, II/SS-Pz.Gren.Rgt.24 *Danmark* was taken out of Corps reserve and placed in the front line, next to 23 SS-Freiwilligen-Panzergrenadier-Division *Nederland*. 6/ and 7/SS-Pz.Gren.Rgt.24 *Danmark* were deployed on the south and north sides of the Steinhöfel-Nöblin road respectively. But before the SS grenadiers could dig in, an enemy armoured spearhead appeared. The battalion CO, *SS-Sturmbannführer* Sørensen, immediately ordered his troops to fall back to the outskirts of Freienwalde.

For some of the *Danmark* grenadiers the order came too late. 1st Platoon of 6/SS-Pz.Gren.Rgt.24 *Danmark,* led by *SS-Oberscharführer* Pösch, found itself cut off, with the enemy attacking from three sides and the Groß Starlitz Lake to its back! The Waffen-SS volunteers put up a fierce resistance and actually drove back the enemy infantry. However, the Red Army moved up some armour and placed them in a semicircle around 200m away from the trapped platoon. Without anti-tank weapons there was no way to resist these monsters. The 6/SS-Pz.Gren.Rgt.24 *Danmark* grenadiers then attempted an immediate breakout using machine-pistols, hand grenades and pistols. With great skill, determination and courage, the platoon fought their way along the south side of the lake. *SS-Oberscharführer* Pösch and four of his men successfully made their way to Freienwalde, but five soldiers from the platoon were captured by the Soviets and another was killed.

The fight for the outskirts of Freienwalde raged throughout the day. Massive heavy weapons fire from both sides dominated the battle, but the European SS defenders held their positions like a wall of steel. The communists were not able to gain any ground. Troops from II/SS-Pz.Gren.Rgt.24 *Danmark* and SS-Pionier-Bataillon 54 firmly held the main front to the east of Freienwalde, while 5/SS-Pz.Gren.Rgt.24 *Danmark* held down the left flank to the north of the town.

SS-Sturmbannführer Sørensen now became the Freienwalde garrison commander. While the town held out throughout the day, the flimsy defensive line between Freienwalde and Stargard had been pierced at many points by the foe. At 1700 hours, *SS-Obersturmführer* Schoofs, the adjutant of SS-Pionier-Bataillon 54, reported to *SS-Sturmbannführer* Sørensen that the Soviets had broken through on a wide front to the north taking Voßberg and overrunning the Freienwalde-Stargard road. Scouts from the 23 SS-Freiwilligen-Panzergrenadier-Division *Nederland* noticed a strong Red Army force assembling before Freienwalde under the partial cover of darkness. The situation began to look critical! After assessing the options, *SS-Sturmbannführer* Sørensen decided on an early morning withdrawal, commencing at 0230 on 4th March, towards Kannenberg, which was still being defended by elements of the *Nordland* Division, including SS-Panzer-Regiment 11 *Hermann von Salza*[12]. The battalion fell back in stages to Kannenberg and helped to defend the town during the day. However the unexpected evacuation of the city of Stargard left Kannenberg suddenly vulnerable and at 2100 hours on the 4th, the town had to be abandoned.

II/SS-Pz.Gren.Rgt.24 *Danmark* reached the village of Wittenfelde on the morning of 5th March and immediately began digging in around Hill 84. To the battalion's north were elements of the 23 SS-Freiwilligen-Panzergrenadier-Division *Nederland*, while the Fallschirmjäger-Regiment *Schacht* defended the nearby road to Falkenberg. Fighting for the area went on all day. At one point Hill 84 fell to the Red Army but it was regained by the II/SS-Pz.Gren.Rgt.24 *Danmark* grenadiers in a fierce counterattack.

---

[12] SS-Panzer-Abteilung 11 *Hermann von Salza* had been merged with SS-Schwere-Panzer-Abteilung 503 in Pomerania to form SS-Panzer-Regiment 11 *Hermann von Salza*

5/SS-Pz.Gren.Rgt.24 *Danmark* eventually had to be detached to help block a soviet inroad near the Massow Forestry House. Meanwhile, III/SS-Pz.Gren.Rgt.24 *Danmark*, situated to the east of Mulkenthin, was able to stop Soviet armoured attacks all day. Despite the fact that its companies had been reduced to around 30 men, each holding 900m sectors, the Danes and volksdeutsche in the battalion were able to drive back or destroy wave after wave of enemy tanks. The sheer courage and heroism of these men, armed with *Panzerfäuste* and often in solitary positions, cannot be underestimated. They did their duty to the utmost of their ability! Elsewhere on the Ihna Front on 5th March 1945, around Lübow, Saarow and Seefeld, the soldiers of the 28 SS-Freiwilligen-Grenadier-Division *Wallonien*, personally led by *SS-Standartenführer* Léon Degrelle, stopped massive, continuous onslaughts of Soviet infantry and tanks in another epic display of valour. Everywhere they were deployed, the European volunteers of the Waffen-SS held on under tremendous enemy pressure.

6th March 1945 saw the fighting continue and even intensify. Late in the day the town of Massow came under Red Army attack from three sides. *SS-Brigadeführer* Wagner, commanding 23 SS-Freiwilligen-Panzergrenadier-Division *Nederland*, conferred with his officers and *SS-Sturmbannführer* Sørensen from II/SS-Pz.Gren.Rgt.24 *Danmark*. Orders from higher authorities were specific: "Hold your positions!". Wagner decided the only way that this could be achieved was to split all of the regular units up into 'partisan groups' - independent detachments that were to keep on fighting even if the town and main lines were lost. To this end, all of the reserve and support troops would have to be thrown into battle. There would be no holding back any longer; this would be a total and absolute resistance.

Thankfully, the Massow defenders received a reprieve from III (Germanische) SS-Panzerkorps HQ at 0300 on 7th March, when orders were received permitting the troops to withdraw to Resehl to set up a more secure defensive line. II/SS-Pz.Gren.Rgt.24 *Danmark* was the first unit to reach Resehl and at 0900 hours, 5th and 7th Companies were sent into the southern part of the town. Here they found that a contingent of 60 Soviet troops had already moved in behind the designated front! 7th Company grenadiers immediately launched an assault that succeeded in totally eliminating this enemy incursion.

Later on 7th March, the *Nederland* positions around Daarz and Rosenow collapsed in the face of severe enemy pressure. With the fall of Daarz, Soviet forces were able to advance unimpeded on Resehl and, by 1630, II/SS-Pz.Gren.Rgt.24 *Danmark* and the neighbouring Army Aufklärungs-Abteilung 115 were forced to fight off assaults from three sides. On other sectors on 7th March, SS-Panzergrenadier-Regiment 23 *Norge* found itself fighting for its very existence along the Stettin Autobahn, while III/SS-Pz.Gren.Rgt.24 *Danmark* was pushed back into a forested area by Red Army tanks and infantry. However the battalion was able to rally with the help of two stray Army tanks and it carried out a counterattack that halted the enemy advance. Meanwhile, the *Nordland* divisional HQ had relocated to Hinzendorf, but was forced to move to nearby Karlsbach when enemy artillery set the whole town on fire. Hinzendorf subsequently burned to the ground.

To the east of Karolinenhorst, one of the more bizarre incidents of the entire war took place. The right flank of III/SS-Pz.Gren.Rgt.24 *Danmark*, comprised of the Pionierzug and Maschinenpistolezug, was suddenly attacked by charging Soviet horsed cavalry! The mounted troopers were allowed to get within 150m of the III/SS-Pz.Gren.Rgt.24 *Danmark* positions before the SS grenadiers, with the support of *infanteriegeschütze*, opened fire. Within seconds one of the last cavalry charges of modern times collapsed in absolute carnage. Not one of the valiant (but stupid)

Battles in Pomerania 145

cavalrymen survived. Afterwards, III/SS-Pz.Gren.Rgt.24 *Danmark* joined up with the SS-Fla-Abteilung 11 in Augustwalde before retreating to Hohenkrug.

The Altdamm Bridgehead

At 0200 hours on 8th March, *SS-Sturmbannführer* Sørensen reported with II/SS-Pz.Gren.Rgt.24 *Danmark* to the *Nederland* divisional command post at Lüttgenhagen. At this point, the battalion was technically subordinated to the 23 SS-Freiwilligen-Panzergrenadier-Division *Nederland*. The Danish battalion was directed to take up positions in Christinenberg on the shores of Lake Damm by 0700 hours. This was part of the defensive perimeter being formed around Altdamm, which would become the last sizeable pocket of resistance across the northern Oder River. Once Altdamm was lost, the Oder, running from south to north, would be the last defensive line of consequence in eastern Germany. As they arrived, the *Nordland, Nederland, Wallonien* and *Langemarck* units were all placed in positions around what would become known as the Altdamm Bridgehead. III/SS-Pz.Gren.Rgt.24 *Danmark*, along with parts of SS-Pionier-Bataillon 11 and SS-Fla-Abteilung 11, took its place in the southern part of the bridgehead.

At noon on 8th March, a strong enemy assault force slammed into II/SS-Pz.Gren.Rgt.24 *Danmark* and once again, *SS-Sturmbannführer* Sørensen was forced to order a withdrawal. However, the sector commander, *Major* Schacht (CO of Fallschirmjäger-Regiment *Schacht*) ordered the battalion to turn around and counterattack. To this end a company from the 10 SS-Panzer-Division *Frundsberg* was assigned to assist II/SS-Pz.Gren.Rgt.24 *Danmark*. But due to heavy, concentrated Soviet artillery fire, the attack never got off the ground. To add insult to injury, 6/SS-Pz.Gren.Rgt.24 *Danmark* lost its 'cook wagon' to a direct hit from a Red Army anti-tank gun later that evening! On 9th March 1945, the withdrawal from the outlying areas of the Altdamm front continued. At 1400 hours the town of Friederichsdorf was abandoned in a fighting withdrawal covered by troops on the Christinenberg Road from 6/ and 7/SS-Pz.Gren.Rgt.24 *Danmark* and the Maschinenpistolezug, with the help of two tanks. By that evening the total strength of both companies and the independent platoon had been reduced to 2 officers, 5 NCOs and 30 men. At full strength, these elements would have contained probably around 350 men!

10th March saw more enemy probing attacks, while the Waffen-SS grenadiers attempted to strengthen the Altdamm perimeter. At 0700 hours on 11th March a strong Soviet force assaulted *SS-Sturmbannführer* Sørensen's ad hoc *Danmark* command near Oberhof. The *Danmark* soldiers fought with the usual skill and steadfastness and blunted the initial onslaught. But they really had no defence against the massed heavy weapons fire that followed. In this intense barrage the company commanders of 6/, 7/ and 8/SS-Pz.Gren.Rgt.24 *Danmark* were all wounded and the 8th Company had no officers or senior NCOs left to lead it, even though it was the only element in the battalion now even vaguely intact. The battalion adjutant, *SS-Untersturmführer* Rasmussen had to be dispatched to take charge of it. A quick survey of II/SS-Pz.Gren.Rgt.24 *Danmark*'s combat strength, less 8th Company, was not encouraging. *SS-Sturmbannführer* Sørensen realised that he really only now had 20 fit men left! The battalion had sacrificed itself almost to the point of elimination. It was certainly a tribute, however much unwanted, to the supreme efforts of the II/SS-Pz.Gren.Rgt.24 *Danmark* volunteers!

By 12th March, enemy pressure again forced III/SS-Pz.Gren.Rgt.24 *Danmark* back along Highway 104 from Augustwalde towards Altdamm, where a final compressed bridgehead across the River Oder was beginning to take shape. III/SS-Pz.Gren.Rgt.24

Danmark along with parts of SS-Fla-Abteilung 11, took up temporary blocking positions near Hohenkrug, but these elements were soon pushed back to the north-west towards Rosengarten. The Regiment *Danmark* command post now relocated to Stutthof, somewhat farther to the north. But the enemy followed quickly and managed to again push back parts of III/SS-Pz.Gren.Rgt.24 *Danmark*. However the 10th and 11th Companies launched yet another swift counterattack and regained the lost positions, which were held successfully until the night of 14th/15th March, when the final withdrawal to Altdamm began. In the meantime, the northern Altdamm front held up fairly well from 12th to 15th March 1945, thanks in large part to effective support from the mortar section of 8/SS-Pz.Gren.Rgt.24 *Danmark*, led by *SS-Oberscharführer* Vandborg. On 15th March, the bulk of III/SS-Pz.Gren.Rgt.24 *Danmark* arrived to take up defensive position on both sides of the main Altdamm railway station. Farther to the east, some anti-tank trenches were manned by 11/SS-Pz.Gren.Rgt.24 *Danmark* and the Maschinenpistolezug. They were both soon pushed back. 11th Company, temporarily led by *SS-Untersturmführer* Kruse, just managed to avoid being overrun, while the Maschinenpistolezug barely managed to escape an airborne 'Molotov Cocktail' attack on its trenches.

At noon on 15th March, the Altdamm railway station was lost to a superior communist attack force; III/SS-Pz.Gren.Rgt.24 *Danmark* was just too weak to hold on to its positions. A *Danmark* counterattack launched at 1500 hours also proved unsuccessful. On 16th March, the regimental commander, *SS-Obersturmbannführer* Albrecht Krügel, assembled the remnants of II/SS-Pz.Gren.Rgt.24 *Danmark* (10 men) and the Maschinenpistolezug (9 men) and personally led them in a desperate surprise attack aimed at regaining the railway station. In a frantic struggle, *SS-Obersturmbannführer* Krügel was killed and his men were forced to retreat to positions just west of the station. Albrecht Krügel would be posthumously decorated with the Oakleaves to the Knight's Cross on 28th March 1945.

The fighting for Altdamm reached its pinnacle during the next two days; the defenders from III (Germanische) SS-Panzerkorps were almost completely depleted but, as always, they fought with unbelievable courage and stamina. III/SS-Pz.Gren.Rgt.24 *Danmark* lost its positions near the railway station to a massive Soviet onslaught on 17th March and the commander of 11th Company, *SS-Obersturmführer* Thorkildsen, was killed. What was left of the regiment now regrouped in the Altdamm cemetery under the temporary command of *SS-Hauptsturmführer* Rudolf Ternedde. The net *Danmark* regimental combat strength, with several survivors from the decimated II Battalion having already retreated to Stettin, and including drivers and signallers, stood at only 50 men! Still this contingent would manage to hold its positions in Altdamm until 19th March 1945.

The final withdrawal from the Altdamm bridgehead took place during the night of 19th March. The remnants of Regiment *Danmark* pulled back from the cemetery but were caught by another artillery barrage, which killed six more men and wounded many others. It was as if the carnage would never end! In Pomerania the SS-Panzergrenadier-Regiment 24 *Danmark* had truly served its time in hell. As usual, the men of the *Danmark* Maschinenpistolezug brought up the rear, covering the retreat. Once they got over the Autobahn bridge across the Oder, the combat engineers blew it sky high. Somewhat further to the south a rearguard from the 28 SS-Freiwilligen-Grenadier-Division *Wallonien* with two tanks in support crossed the Altdamm railway bridge and it too was destroyed. The heroic epic struggle for Pomerania had come to an end; the surviving European volunteers of III (Germanische) SS-Panzerkorps now had to gird themselves for the last sacrificial battles for Europe and the Reich.

CHAPTER XIII

Berlin

To the East of Berlin

Prior to falling back across the Oder, defences had been prepared along the west banks by the staffs of 11 Panzer-Armee (*SS-Obergruppenführer* Steiner) and 3 Panzer-Armee (*General der Panzertruppen* von Manteuffel) and preparations had been made to quickly 'refresh' the depleted forces that had retreated from Pomerania. The remnants of III (Germanische) SS-Panzerkorps were sent to the towns of Wussow, Sommersdorf and Wattin, in order to refit under relatively peaceful circumstances. Fortunately the River Oder defences held throughout the latter part of March 1945 early April 1945.

11 SS-Freiwilligen-Panzergrenadier-Division *Nordland* began its reformation process in the area to the west of Schwedt-Bad Freienwalde. The divisional units were spread amongst the various villages in the vicinity, with the divisional HQ being established at Alt-Künkendorf. SS-Panzergrenadier-Regiment 24 *Danmark* began reassembling in the town of Hohenlandin. With the addition of some 200 excess personnel from SS-Panzer-Regiment 11 *Hermann von Salza*, which had to be downgraded to detachment size due to a shortage of armoured vehicles, Regiment *Danmark* was able to quickly bring its exhausted companies up to a strength of around 80 men each.

By mid-April the regiment had also received a considerable number of recovered wounded and also absorbed most of the members of a land-based Naval infantry battalion. As a result the regimental strength grew to about 1,500 personnel of all ranks. The new CO was *SS-Obersturmbannführer* Klotz, with *SS-Sturmbannführer* Sørensen in charge of II Battalion (partially motorised) and *SS-Sturmbannführer* Ternedde leading III Battalion (fully motorised). The I Battalion remained with 5 SS-Panzer-Division *Wiking*, which was now deployed in Austria.

On 16th April 1945, the *Nordland* Division was ordered back to the front line to the east of Berlin. On this day the great Soviet 'Berlin Offensive' was launched by Marshal Zhukov with a massive onslaught across the Oder by enormous Red Army formations. Despite furious German resistance, the communists were soon able to throw some 23 bridges across the river and move troops across at will. In the Küstrin bridgehead alone, the Soviets had more materiel (22,000 artillery pieces. 4,000 tanks and 5,000 aircraft) than the Wehrmacht could muster along the entire Eastern Front! In addition there were some 50 Guards Divisions in the area; the German-European forces were puny in comparison, but the effort had to be made to stop the enemy - there was simply no alternative.

By the night of 16th/17th April, III (Germanische) SS-Panzerkorps elements were all on the move to attempt to intercept and stop the communist onslaught. SS-Panzergrenadier-Regiment 24 *Danmark* was sent into the woods east of Strausberg in a defensive line facing to the east and north-east. The transport column had to ferry in III/SS-Pz.Gren.Rgt.24 *Danmark* first and then go back for II/SS-Pz.Gren.Rgt.24 *Danmark*; there were no longer enough vehicles for both battalions. 15/SS-Pz.Gren.Rgt.24 *Danmark* and the Ersatzkompanie had to walk to the new positions.

In the afternoon of 17th April, III/SS-Pz.Gren.Rgt.24 *Danmark* was able to repel a strong enemy attack near Hermersdorf with the assistance of an 88mm Flak battery and a contingent of Fallschirmjäger troops. But the 88mm Flak battery had to pull back when it ran out of ammunition; it would no longer be able to support the *Danmark* grenadiers. By the morning of 18th April, II/SS-Pz.Gren.Rgt.24 *Danmark* was concentrated near the town of Gielsdorf, while III/SS-Pz.Gren.Rgt.24 *Danmark* remained in the woods to the west of Hermersdorf. SS-Panzergrenadier-Regiment 23 *Norge* was located to the south of the *Danmark* positions, while a 500-man Hitler Youth kampfgruppe was in place to the north. Assorted elements from 9 Fallschirmjäger-Division helped to reinforce the *Nordland* lines.

As the day progressed, the German positions, under massive assault from both ground and air, began to crumble, starting with those of the Hitler Youth kampfgruppe. In addition, the wooded area in the *Danmark* sector had been set ablaze by the heavy shelling. III/SS-Pz.Gren.Rgt.24 *Danmark*, led by *SS-Sturmbannführer* Ternedde, was very hard hit and it was all he could do to keep his command together. Farther to the south, the SS-Panzergrenadier-Regiment 23 *Norge*, coming under attack from three sides, had to fall back on Strausberg.

During the night of 18th/19th April, III/SS-Pz.Gren.Rgt.24 *Danmark* and the regimental support units had to retreat through the burning forest to the south of Buckow and then back through Garzau to Hohenstein. While this was going on, II/SS-Pz.Gren.Rgt.24 *Danmark* had to stay in place to await the return of III Battalion's trucks to haul its troops to safety! 16 (Pi)/SS-Pz.Gren.Rgt.24 *Danmark* and the Maschinenpistolezug (as usual!) covered the withdrawal.

The morning of 20th April saw a massive Soviet artillery bombardment of the front lines between Gielsdorf and Strausberg, followed by the expected enormous ground attack. *SS-Sturmbannführer* Sørensen was in Gielsdorf, awaiting the arrival of most of II/SS-Pz.Gren.Rgt.24 *Danmark* (actually the trucks from III Battalion never arrived, so the retreat was carried out on foot). Sørensen had his battalion staff and 8/SS-Pz.Gren.Rgt.24 *Danmark* with him; also in and around the town were the soldiers from SS-Pionier-Bataillon 11. Believing that the rest of his battalion would never get through to the division on its own, Sørensen commandeered the *Nordland* engineers and together with 8/SS-Pz.Gren.Rgt.24 *Danmark* they made a reconnaissance to the north, hoping to contact the rest of the battalion.

Instead, *SS-Sturmbannführer* Sørensen and his troops ran into the vanguard of a huge Red Army tank force and received word that the *Nordland* Division was now in full retreat. Therefore he reluctantly fell back on Gielsdorf to await developments. Elsewhere, near Hohenstein, III/SS-Pz.Gren.Rgt.24 *Danmark* and the regimental staff bore the brunt of the communist onslaught. Everyone, including the regimental and battalion commanders, went into the front lines, grabbing whatever weapon was available. *SS-Obersturmbannführer* Klotz and *SS-Sturmbannführer* Ternedde were both wounded by fragments of a bursting artillery shell. Ternedde suffered with concussion, but Klotz was mortally wounded. In addition, three transport drivers were killed and the regimental adjutant was wounded in the same blast.

The wounded officers were sent back to a dressing station near the divisional HQ, but *SS-Obersturmbannführer* Klotz died *en route*. *SS-Sturmbannführer* Ternedde would be able to rejoin his command the next day after a brief rest. In the meantime, *SS-Sturmbannführer* Sørensen, along with 8/SS-Pz.Gren.Rgt.24 *Danmark* and the *Nordland* engineers had to fight their way back into Gielsdorf with the help of two *sturmgeschütze*. Sørensen then received a radio message placing him in command of the entire Regiment *Danmark* (the first Dane to hold that position) but he was first ordered to proceed to the *Nordland* command post. Escorted by part of the *Nordland* engineer battalion and the II/SS-Pz.Gren.Rgt.24 *Danmark* staff and signals troops, Sørensen reached the *Nordland* HQ at Strausberg airport at about 1000 hours on 20th April. Here Sørensen paused to pay his last respects to *SS-Obersturmbannführer* Klotz, whose body was lying in a Volkswagen command car.

Sørensen met with his replacement as II/SS-Pz.Gren.Rgt.24 *Danmark* commander, *SS-Sturmbannführer* Bergfeldt, but there was still one problem: the battalion was still largely missing! The battalion adjutant, *SS-Untersturmführer* Ellef Rasmussen was therefore sent out to the north to try and locate it. Rasmussen eventually found the 5th, 6th and 7th Companies of Regiment *Danmark*, but they would never again rejoin the rest of the regiment. Instead, Rasmussen led them in a kampfgruppe under the control of III (Germanische) SS-Panzerkorps. He was promoted in the field to *SS-Hauptsturmführer* by *SS-Obergruppenführer* Steiner, and he led his reduced battalion in the Eberswalde and Nieder-Finow bridgeheads and along the Stör Canal line. The three *Danmark* companies involved gradually retreated to Schwerin where they surrendered to the Americans in May 1945.

SS-Sturmbannführer Sørensen next met with the *Nordland* commander, *SS-Brigadeführer* Ziegler, and then set up his regimental command post next to that of III/SS-Pz.Gren.Rgt.24 *Danmark*, which was temporarily being led by *SS-Untersturmführer* Dirksen. At midday, the whole area came under enemy bombardment and by early afternoon a Red Army advance force had penetrated to the airfield. 16 (Pi)/SS-Pz.Gren.Rgt.24 *Danmark* and the Maschinenpistolezug, supported by 88mm flak guns, went into action and swiftly knocked out three Soviet tanks and eliminated the enemy inroad. It was another brilliant, textbook tactical operation, that had been carried out over and over again by the *Danmark* grenadiers in the previous months but, as was often the case, it could do nothing more than buy a few more hours of precious time. Elsewhere the Russian advance continued unabated.

In the evening of 20th April, the *Nordland* Division began yet another withdrawal, this time to Altlandsberg. Regiment *Danmark* followed, taking up positions in the village of Buchholz. Nobody stayed in place for long; to the north the Red Army had routed a Luftwaffe infantry force and secured the road to Strausberg. *SS-Brigadeführer* Ziegler again ordered a withdrawal to avoid entrapment. Regiment *Danmark* regrouped to the west of Altlandsberg and to the south of Lake Strausberg. For a time it was cut off from the division, but eventually orders came through calling for the regiment to reoccupy Buchholz. Erring on the side of cautioun, *SS-Sturmbannführer* Sørensen sent only a scouting party back towards the town accompanied by a tank and a *sturmgeschütz*. It would be a futile mission; the Red Army were there in strength and it would be impossible to throw them out.

The Soviets were now throwing out large armoured spearheads in an effort to quickly reach Berlin and envelope the weak German-European forces still active to the east of the city. Regiment *Danmark*'s transport column. which evacuated the town of Mahlsdorf during the night of 20th/21st April, found itself relentlessly pursued by an enemy force led by 4 tanks. The truck drivers had to take evasive action through the nearby woods.

The still recuperating *SS-Sturmbannführer* Ternedde, who was with the column, soon got fed up with the dangerous game that was going on, stopped the trucks and sent the drivers out with *Panzerfäuste* to take care of the pursuing tanks. In a short time two of the enemy armoured vehicles were knocked out and the other two withdrew. The pressure was off - temporarily. Ternedde now instructed the *Danmark* drivers to proceed along the shore of Lake Müggel to Grunewald near Berlin.

That same evening, after giving up on Buchholz, *SS-Sturmbannführer* Sørensen, along with 8/SS-Pz.Gren.Rgt.24 *Danmark*, the Maschinenpistolezug, the *Danmark* engineers (16th Coy), signals and staff troops, travelled along the autobahn to Herzfelde. In the course of the morning of 21st April, much of the *Nordland* Division regrouped in a 'cloverleaf' area along Reich Autobahn 1 just outside Berlin. The formation again had been incredibly depleted and many elements were missing.

During the afternoon, another Soviet penetration near Neuenhagen was reported and the tired *Danmark* grenadiers were once again called upon to meet the emergency. The men of the Maschinenpistolezug and 16 (Pi)/SS-Pz.Gren.Rgt.24 *Danmark*, loaded into armoured personnel carriers and escorted by two *Nordland sturmgeschütze*, were driven along the Dahlwitz-Hoppegarten branch road until they came across the new Red Army inroad. Once again they went into action with the incredible combat skills honed from being in almost continual action for the past two years.

Two out of four enemy tanks were quickly liquidated in close combat and the others pulled away. The breakthrough was again temporarily blocked. But by evening, the Soviets were back, in force, and there would be no stopping them again. One more time the courageous *Danmark* grenadiers had to fall back. It was a repeat of the same scenario that had happened again and again over the previous several months.

But a new drama was developing. The final struggle for Berlin itself now loomed on the horizon, and the battered remnants of the 11 SS-Panzergrenadier-Division *Nordland* and the SS-Panzergrenadier-Regiment 24 *Danmark* were both called upon to fall back into the city's suburbs for the ultimate battle for Germany and Europe. The heroic, sacrificial last stand of the European Waffen-SS was about to begin! Four years of savage warfare against a barbaric foe on the Eastern Front had come down to this; the course of Western civilisation lay square in the balance and no matter what happened, there would be no turning back!

The Final Cataclysm

In the course of 22nd April 1945, the *Nordland* Division conducted a series of retreats back into the Tiergarten in Berlin itself. For the most part, the division would now be deployed in small, emergency kampfgruppen that would be gradually destroyed in the course of the battle for the German capital. During the afternoon of 22nd April and the morning of the 23rd, *Nordland* was heavily engaged in trying to defend the area around the Karlshorst race track, but ammunition dwindled and the divisional commander became more and more disillusioned with his task. *SS-Brigadeführer* Ziegler had no desire to have the remnants of his Division *Nordland* destroyed in Berlin. In the face of what appeared to be a hopeless situation he became increasingly despondent and as a result his command suffered.

Nordland slowly pulled back, on *SS-Brigadeführer* Ziegler's orders, to the Neukölln district of Berlin, where the divisional HQ was set up. The Regiment *Danmark* was employed holding a bridgehead across the River Spree in Oberschöneweide. After driving off two enemy assaults, the *Danmark* grenadiers were hit with a massive artillery barrage and the order was given to retreat across the Spree bridges, after which they were blown up.

SS-Sturmbannführer Sørensen next led Regiment *Danmark* into the crumbling ruins of Niederschöneweide, but in the process contact was lost with divisional HQ. A little further to the north, SS-Panzergrenadier-Regiment 23 *Norge* also found itself cut off from the *Nordland* staff. In between the two Scandinavian SS-Regiments were members of the SS-Pionier-Bataillon 11, which was soon assaulted by the Red Army crossing the Spree in rubber boats. However, the engineers were able, at least, to hold on to the river bank.

During the night of 23rd/24th April, *SS-Sturmbannführer* Sørensen travelled to the *Nordland* HQ in Neukölln to give a situation report to *SS-Brigadeführer* Ziegler. The main problem was that no-one really had any idea of the overall picture in Berlin, resulting in universal confusion. Ziegler was now very depressed and he painted a gloomy picture of the prospects for Sørensen. The Danish *Sturmbannführer* then returned to the *Danmark* command post, located in a partially-collapsed brewery.

Meanwhile, the *Nordland* engineers found themselves unable to cope with the Russian assault teams that were endeavouring to cross the Spree, and it was not long before the enemy had secured a number of crossing points. Once again, everyone started to pull back. *SS-Brigadeführer* Ziegler decided to relocate his HQ in a large inner city store building.

In the Niederschöneweide area 'all hell broke loose', and Regiment *Danmark* was forced to withdraw across the Landwehr Canal. It then built up a new defensive line in a semicircle around the Köllnische Heide railway station. But the main fighting in the *Nordland* sector was now in the Treptow Park area, which was defended by SS-Pionier-Bataillon 11, assisted by the few remaining armoured vehicles from SS-Panzer-Regiment 11 *Hermann von Salza*. Led by *SS-Obersturmbannführer* Kausch, the *Hermann von Salza* tanks launched the last *Nordland* armoured attack of the war and were finally able to halt the enemy advance in the area.

In the meantime, Regiment *Danmark*, now re-designated as a kampfgruppe, endeavoured to hold on to its positions around the railway station and a nearby subway station. Another tragedy now assailed the regiment. *SS-Sturmbannführer* Sørensen climbed up a lamp-post in an effort to observe enemy troop movements and a few seconds later a single shot rang. He toppled to the ground with a bullet to the heart, the victim of a sniper.

Per Sørensen was the last official regimental commander and, like all his predecessors, was killed in the line of duty. Sørensen may well have been the most capable and respected Danish officer in the Waffen-SS. In the eyes of many, he qualified for a Knight's Cross on more than one occasion. In four years of near continuous combat on the Eastern Front, Sørensen and his soldiers always accomplished whatever task was set before them. He was clearly a 'giant' among many 'giants' in the European Waffen-SS.

SS-Sturmbannführer Sørensen's body was placed in a Schwimmwagen from 13/SS-Pz.Gren.Rgt.24 *Danmark*, and driven to the *Nordland* command post near Neukölln, accompanied by his personal aide for many years, *SS-Unterscharführer* Scholles. Needless to say, Sørensen was an irreplaceable individual. However, someone had to command what was left of Regiment *Danmark*, and the task now fell temporarily to *SS-Obersturmführer* Petersen, the commander of 14 (Flak)/SS-Pz.Gren.Rgt.24 *Danmark*.

The body of Sørensen was taken to Pichelsdorf, where the *Nordland* mortuary detachment was in operation. On the next day he would be buried in an 'ammunition crate' coffin in the Plötzensee cemetery. An eight-man honour guard of old veterans of the *Freikorps Danmark* was rounded up to participate in the funeral ceremony. The eulogy which follows was spoken by the German *SS-Sturmscharführer* Hermann:

> "We are standing here by the grave to take our last departure from a courageous Danish comrade, the foremost officer and leader of the Regiment *Danmark*, Per Sørensen! I must, even in this hour, give the thanks of my people for you and your many Danish comrades who have stood so loyally beside us. I would like to wish from my heart that you find peace in our bleeding city!"

As Hermann spoke the coffin was lowered into the grave. He then saluted and the honour guard fired three salvoes over the open grave. Then a woman tossed flowers into the grave and each SS man in attendance passed by and threw in a handful of earth. The ceremony concluded with the singing of Ich hatt' einen Kameraden accompanied by the loud crash of enemy artillery fire in the background.

In the meantime the battle continued. 16 (Pi)/SS-Pz.Gren.Rgt.24 *Danmark* and the still largely intact Maschinenpistolezug, now reinforced by some Naval infantry, were sent to defend the Jungfernheide. The rest of the SS Regiments *Norge* and *Danmark* had atrophied to absolute minimal strength. When the last *Norge* commander, *SS-Obersturmbannführer* Körbel, was severely wounded, the command of what was left of both of the heroic Scandinavian SS Regiments passed to *SS-Sturmbannführer* Ternedde. The *Danmark* regimental adjutant, *SS-Hauptsturmführer* Lührs was so now badly wounded that he could not be evacuated. He took his own life.

The final battles for the Spree and Teltow Canal sectors began in earnest on 25th April. On this same day the despondent *SS-Brigadeführer* Ziegler was removed from the command of the *Nordland* Division and sent to the Führer Bunker where he was placed under house arrest for 'insubordination'. He was replaced by the dynamic 'inspector' of the French Waffen-SS, *SS-Brigadeführer und Generalmajor der Waffen-SS* Dr Gustav Krukenberg, who had just arrived in Berlin with a contingent of French SS volunteers from 33 SS-Freiwilligen-Grenadier-Division *Charlemagne*. Krukenberg was appalled by the poor deployment of what was left of the Division *Nordland* and he wasted no time in reorganisation. He immediately placed his French SS troops in the front lines, where they would begin there own personal epic over the next few days, including the elimination of more than 60 Red Army tanks!

Last Battles

The Neukölln sector of Berlin was now being defended by III/SS-Pz.Gren.Rgt.24 *Danmark*, regimental kampfgruppen under *SS-Untersturmführer* Christensen and *SS-Oberscharführer* Illum, SS-Kampfbataillon *Charlemagne* and assorted Volkssturm units. To the north-west of Neukölln, at the Jungfernheide, 16 (Pi)/SS-Pz.Gren.Rgt.24 *Danmark* and the Maschinenpistolezug dug in to await the enemy advance. 25th April 1945 marked the closing of the ring on Berlin; the city was now totally encircled. For the European defenders there was only one option: to fight it out to the bitter end!

By 26th April, most the *Nordland* survivors had been pulled back to the inner city, with elements of the division taking up the defence of the Reichs Chancellery itself. Regiment *Danmark* formed a new 100-man kampfgruppe from the transport and support troops and lightly wounded, under the signals officer from II Battalion, *SS-*

Untersturmführer Bachmann. This troop was deployed in a defensive line around the Hallescher Platz, linking with another part of the Division *Nordland* at the Cottbuses Tor.

As the Soviet assault wave swept into central Berlin on 27th April, great gaps were quickly torn in the weak German defensive positions. Kampfgruppe *Bachmann*, joined by the men of the 13/SS-Pz.Gren.Rgt.24 *Danmark*, who were now fighting as infantry, and all of the remaining *Danmark* soldiers, were forced back to the Belle-Alliance-Platz, where they would make their stand. Elsewhere, two *infanteriegeschütz* from 8/SS-Pz.Gren.Rgt.24 *Danmark* defended the Anhalt railway station with the remnants of *SS-Sturmbannführer* Saalbach's SS-Panzer-Aufklärungs-Abteilung 11.

In the afternoon of 27th April, the *Danmark* defenders began receiving enemy tank fire on Belle-Alliance-Platz and by 1430 hours, the Soviets were crossing the River Spree at will, sending more tanks and infantry across. It was time once again for another counterattack by the *Danmark* grenadiers. With the usual valour and consummate courage, the *Danmark* troops, led by *SS-Untersturmführer* Dirksen, shot up the Red Army armoured spearhead and yet again drove back the foe; but they could not clear the communist infantry that had infiltrated the ruins all around. The SS men were finally forced to retreat to a point some 200m south of the Kochstraße where they carried on a close range machine-pistol and hand grenade duel with the foe until well into the evening.

On 28th April, the *Danmark* soldiers fought it out along the Friedrichstraße and the Kochstraße subway station. As the 28th progressed, they were forced back south to the corner of Friedrichstraße and Puttkamerstraße. Here *SS-Untersturmführer* Bachmann was wounded and put out of action. Nearby, around the Reichsbank, the last elements of both Regiments 23 *Norge* and 24 *Danmark* were now combined under the command of *SS-Sturmbannführer* Ternedde. They took part in the defence of the last few square kilometres of the city that still remained in German hands.

Bitter fighting raged throughout the *Nordland* sector on 29th April, but still the beleaguered European volunteers held out and for one last time, stopped the enemy advance. On the 30th the situation became increasingly chaotic. The numerous wounded could no longer be evacuated because there was nowhere left to send them! Near the Tiergarten, *SS-Obersturmführer* Birkedahl-Hansen, commander of 8/SS-Pz.Gren.Rgt.24 *Danmark*, who was ill from an attack of jaundice, led yet another *ad hoc* kampfgruppe of support troops in an attempt to block a Soviet breakthrough near the Berlin Zoo. A limited counterattack was made but had to be called off as darkness set in.

SS-Obersturmführer Birkedahl-Hansen now found himself isolated from the rest of the regiment. However he would eventually lead one of the few successful *Nordland* breakouts from Berlin and reach Warnemünde. Along with *SS-Rottenführer* Egon Larsen from SS-Schwere-Panzer-Abteilung 503, he would then take a rowing boat across the Baltic to Denmark only to be tossed into a Danish prison. However, that was preferable to Soviet captivity!

At 2000 hours on 30th April, *SS-Sturmbannführer* Ternedde was called into the *Nordland* command post for a final briefing by *SS-Brigadeführer* Krukenberg. Here he received news of Hitler's death and 'breakout' orders for what was left of the twin Scandinavian Panzergrenadier regiments. In concert with the rest of Schwere SS-Panzer-Abteilung 503 and the few remaining armoured scout cars from SS-Panzer-Aufklärungs-Abteilung 11, the European SS troops were to advance north along the Finow Canal with the objective of eventually reaching Armee-Abteilung *Steiner*. The main problem was to get the word out to the isolated groups of fighting men who were still scattered throughout the inner city ruins.

Eventually, every *Nordland* trooper that could be located began to move towards the Weidendamm Bridge. To complicate the task were the numerous civilian refugees who followed along after the soldiers. Shortly after midnight on 1st May 1945, the desperate escape effort got underway. The last *Nordland* armoured vehicles tried to cross the Weidendamm Bridge but immediately drew intense fire from all sides. The foot soldiers were not able to proceed into that inferno and, although they attempted to return fire, it was too dark to pinpoint the enemy positions with any accuracy.

As a result the 'breakout' force broke up into small clusters of men who went out to find other ways to safety. A group of 50 men and a *sturmgeschütz*, led by the former *Nordland* commander, *SS-Brigadeführer* Ziegler, tried to advance cautiously down the Prinz-Albrecht-Straße. All the while groups of a few men each peeled off from the main body to find their own way out. Some did, but most were not so fortunate. *SS-Brigadeführer* Ziegler and *SS-Sturmbannführer* Saalbach, were both killed at this point.

By first light on 1st May, the 'breakout' effort had ended and most of the survivors now had to find cover to protect themselves for at least another day. With few exceptions, organised defence no longer existed in Berlin. The city had now been officially 'surrendered' by the garrison commander, *General* Krebs, and by evening on 1st May, Soviet loudspeakers, set up throughout the ruins, called on the remaining defenders to surrender. They were promised 'honourable captivity' and a 'speedy return home', both of which promises were broken. As the Berlin PoWs would find out, there would be a slight 10-year stopover in Siberia, for some slave labour, before the promised homecoming came to pass!

As dusk descended on 2nd May 1945, the bulk of the German military forces in Berlin formed ranks and marched into captivity. Perhaps as many as 10,000 soldiers and civilians continued to resist until they ran out of ammunition. The final breakout attempt was made during the night of 2nd May when an assortment of approximately 1,000 European soldiers, including Spaniards and Latvians, tried to follow the subway tunnels out of the city. Few made it. The last handfuls of French and Latvian SS men in the city then finally surrendered to the Red Army; the Latvians removing their insignia in an attempt to pass themselves off as Germans.

While this was going on, a few elements of the *Nordland* Division that never made it into the city also met their fate. The division's emergency reserve company was destroyed in the fighting from the Ketzin bridgehead whilst part of the divisional staff and most of the supply units entered American captivity at Ludwigslust. On 2nd and 3rd May 1945, the troops from II/SS-Pz.Gren.Rgt.24 *Danmark* under *SS-Hauptsturmführer* Ellef Rasmussen, who had become separated from the rest of the regiment, surrendered to the Allies in the Dömitz-Ludwigslust sector. They had undergone many hair-raising battles before being able to join the rest of III (Germanische) SS-Panzerkorps to the west of Berlin.

With that surrender and the eventual capitulation of I/SS-Pz.Gren.Rgt.24 *Danmark* with the *Wiking* SS-Division in Austria, the saga of SS-Panzergrenadier-Regiment 24 *Danmark* came to a close. The Danes and their European comrades marched off into history, leaving behind an incredible record of bravery and achievement under the most intense adversity imaginable. All of the regimental commanders, save *SS-Sturmbannführer* Ternedde, whose position was somewhat limited, had been killed in succession. At all times from beginning to end, Regiment *Danmark* did its duty, often at enormous cost, but always with a great impact on the enemy. As long as courage, military skill and idealism are recognised, the Regiment *Danmark* grenadiers will be remembered.

For the survivors it would be a difficult road ahead. Most of the Germanic volunteers would be imprisoned by their own governments. Some would even be executed. In all cases, everyone would be smeared with the tar-brush of 'criminality' by the victors. As the European Waffen-SS volunteers languished and died in concentration camps and prisons, the fruits of the Soviet liberation became apparent as a third of Germany was physically eliminated and half of Europe vanished into cruel communist slavery, not to emerge again for nearly half a century. Millions of innocent souls and the finest soldiers in Europe would die after the war, either directly or indirectly, at the hands of the 'liberators'.

It remains to be seen if Western civilisation itself will survive the great Allied victory of World War II. However one thing is certain: the heroic, idealistic saga of the European Waffen-SS volunteers will live as long as history itself is still preserved and recorded!

SS-Obersturmführer Albert Bergfeldt. As *Hauptsturmführer* he briefly served as commander of II/SS-Pz.Gren.Rgt.24 *Danmark* in 1945

SS-Hauptsturmführer Rudolf Ternedde. He was first the commander of 6/SS-Pz.Gren.Rgt.24 *Danmark* and later took charge of III/SS-Pz.Gren.Rgt.24 *Danmark*. He ended the war in Berlin as the commander of a kampfgruppe composed of the survivors of both Regiments *Danmark* and *Norge*

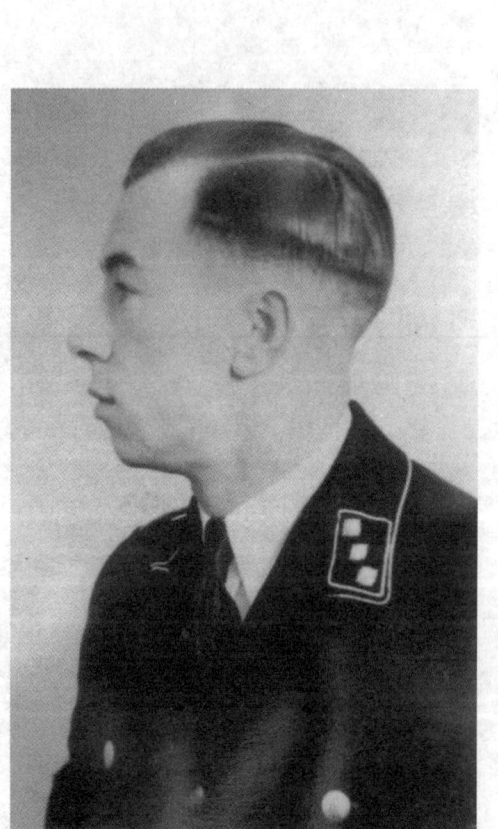

SS-Obersturmbannführer Rudolf Klotz (shown here as an *Untersturmführer* in the pre-war Allgemeine-SS) who commanded Regiment *Danmark* from 16th March 1945 to 21st April 1945 when he fell in action. *Ostubaf* Klotz won the German Cross in Gold for his actions in Slovakia with the SS-Panzergrenadier Regiment *Schill* on 14th November 1944

(Left) *SS-Obersturmführer* Fritz Sidon, a veteran of the SS-Regiment *Deutschland* who joined Regiment *Danmark* in January 1944, serving as an adjutant to *Hauptsturmführer* Per Sørensen, the CO of I/SS-Pz.Gren.Rgt.24 *Danmark*. When I/SS-Pz.Gren.Rgt.24 *Danmark* was temporarily disbanded, Sidon became the commander of 9/SS-Pz.Gren.Rgt.24 *Danmark*. While holding this position he won the prestigious Honour Roll Clasp on 5th November 1944

(Above and left) *SS-Untersturmführer* Ellef Rasmussen, a Danish veteran of 5 SS-Pz.Div. *Wiking* who transferred into the Regiment *Danmark*. For a short time he served as CO of 8/SS-Pz.Gren.Rgt.24 *Danmark* before serving as an adjutant to II/SS-Pz.Gren.Rgt.24 *Danmark* commanders *Hauptsturmführer* Heinz Hämel and *Sturmbannführer* Per Sørensen. Rasmussen was decorated with both classes of Iron Cross, Close Combat Badge in Bronze, Infantry Assault Badge in Silver, Wound Badge in Gold and the Winter War Medal

(Left) *SS-Untersturmführer* Ove Lund. This Danish volunteer fell in action with the Regiment *Danmark* as an *Obersturmführer* on 25th December 1944

Late in the war, the *Nordland* Division received a new sonnenrad collar patch. This is shown at right, worn by *SS-Sturmmann* Svend Larsen, a former member of 2/*Freikorps Danmark*

On the motorcycle is Oberscharführer Albert Jensen. He also came from the *Freikorps* and as a Werkmeister (Workshop Foreman) led the I-Staffel of II/SS-Pz.Gren.Rgt.24 *Danmark*. He received both classes of the War Service Cross with swords. Jensen served with the regiment to its last battles in Berlin where he was wounded on 2nd May 1945

A Danish SS volunteer with a flare gun near Liepāja, Latvia on 6th November 1944.

(Erik Rundkvist Archives)

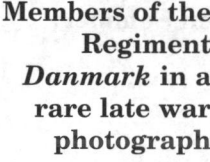

Members of the Regiment *Danmark* in a rare late war photograph

A late war photograph of *Danmark* troops wearing the sonnenrad collar patch. This was very rarely worn as the Danes considered themselves full SS men and preferred to wear the 'SS' runic patch

Another late war *Danmark* photo. On the far left is Kaj Olesen, known as "Germaner-Ole" (Germanic-Ole) because of his large size. He wears the sonnenrad collar patch.

On the right is *Unterscharführer* Preben Sommer

APPENDIX A

Awards and Decorations

Knight's Cross with Oakleaves (*Ritterkreuz mit Eichenlaub*)

SS-Obersturmbannführer	Albrecht Krügel	Kdr SS-Pz.Gren.Rgt.24 *Danmark*	18.11.1944

Knight's Cross[13] (*Ritterkreuz*)

SS-Obersturmführer	Walter Seebach	Fhr 5/SS-Pz.Gren.Rgt.24 *Danmark*	12.3.1944
SS-Hauptsturmführer	Heinz Hämel	Fhr II/SS-Pz.Gren.Rgt.24 *Danmark*	16.6.1944
SS-Unterscharführer	Egon Christophersen	Gruppenfhr 7/SS-Pz.Gren.Rgt.24 *Danmark*	11.7.1944
SS-Oberscharführer	Albert Hektor	Zugfhr 7/SS-Pz.Gren.Rgt.24 *Danmark*	13.8.1944

German Cross in Gold (*Deutsches Kreuz in Gold*)

SS-Obersturmbannführer	Hermenegild Graf von Westphalen	Kdr SS-Pz.Gren.Rgt.24 *Danmark* (Posthumous)	23.4.1944
SS-Hauptsturmführer	Per Sørensen	Fhr II/SS-Pz.Gren.Rgt.24 *Danmark*	14.10.1944
SS-Hauptsturmführer	Rudolf Ternedde	Fhr III/SS-Pz.Gren.Rgt.24 *Danmark*	14.11.1944

Honour Roll Clasp (*Ehrenblattspange*)

SS-Obersturmführer	Fritz Sidon	Fhr 9/SS-Pz.Gren.Rgt.24 *Danmark*	5.11.1944
SS-Hauptsturmführer	Per Sørensen	Fhr II/SS-Pz.Gren.Rgt.24 *Danmark*	17.12.1944
SS-Hauptsturmführer	Rudolf Ternedde	Fhr III/SS-Pz.Gren.Rgt.24 *Danmark*	17.12.1944
SS-Unterscharführer	Alfred Jonstrup	Gruppenfhr St.Kp/SS-Pz.Gren.Rgt.24 *Danmark*	25.12.1944

---

[13] In addition, two Danes won the Knight's Cross while serving with other formations:
SS-Obersturmführer Søren Kam (7.2.45) Fhr 1/SS-Pz.Gren.Rgt 9 *Germania*, 5 SS-Pz.Div *Wiking*
SS-Obersturmführer Johannes Hellmers (5.3.45) Chef 6/SS-Pz.Gren.Rgt.49 *De Ruyter*, 23 SS-Freiw.Pz.Gren.Div *Nederland*

APPENDIX B

Command Roster

SS-Panzergrenadier-Regiment 24 *Danmark*

Compiled by H T Nielsen
(Names and Dates of service are listed where known)

Commanders

SS-Obersturmbannführer	Hermenegild Graf von Westphalen	5.5.1943-9.4.1944
SS-Obersturmbannführer	Albrecht Krügel	9.4.1944-16.3.1945
SS-Obersturmbannführer	Rudolf Klotz	16.3.1945-21.4.1945
SS-Obersturmbannführer	Per Sørensen	21.4.1945-24.4.1945
SS-Obersturmführer	Petersen	24.4.1945-25.4.1945
SS-Sturmbannführer	Rudolf Ternedde	25.4.1945-2.5.1945

Regimental Adjutants

SS-Obersturmführer	Knud Thorgils	5.1943-6.1943
SS-Obersturmführer	Walter Seebach	6.1943-?
SS-Hauptsturmführer	Hermann Lührs	4.1945-24.4.1945

Staff Company Officers

SS-Untersturmführer	Erik Brørup	8.1943-?
SS-Untersturmführer	Jørgen Salskov	
SS-Untersturmführer	Poul Victor Broberg	
SS-Obersturmführer	Erik Vagn Fenger	

Medical Officers

SS-Hauptsturmführer	Dr Nagle	
SS-Sturmbannführer	Dr Heinz Schlegel	1.1944

Dentist

SS-Untersturmführer	Dr Wilhelm Schmidt

Orderly Officer

SS-Untersturmführer	Christian Ulrich Ditlev von Eggers	9.1943

Ib (Staff Quarters/Supply Officer):

SS-Obersturmführer	Hein

Transport Officer

SS-Hauptsturmführer	Willi Roßmann	6.1944

Maintenance Officers

SS-Hauptsturmführer	Heinrich Kogelgruber
SS-Untersturmführer	Hecht

I/SS-Pz.Gren.Rgt.24 *Danmark*

Commanders
SS-Obersturmbannführer	Knud Borge Martinsen	7.1943-?
SS-Sturmbannführer	Alfred Fischer	8.1943-?
SS-Hauptsturmführer	Kurt Wichmann	?-25.1.1944
SS-Hauptsturmführer	Per Sørensen	25.1.1944-?
SS-Obersturmführer	Geve Hans Ditlev Ahlefeldt-Laurvig	
SS-Sturmbannführer	Hermann im Masche	11.1944-18.3.1945

Battalion Adjutants
SS-Obersturmführer	Rudolf Rott	7.1943-?
SS-Untersturmführer	Peter Köppen	2.1944-10.1944

Orderly Officer
SS-Untersturmführer	Emil Freiherr Gyldenkrone	7.1943-?

Medical Officers
SS-Obersturmführer	Sedlacek	
SS-Obersturmführer	Dr Konrad Lotze	7.1943-?

Motorised Transport Officer
SS-Obersturmführer	Günther Wolff	7.1943-?

Maintenance Officer
SS-Untersturmführer	J Petersen

1/SS-Pz.Gren.Rgt.24 *Danmark*
SS-Hauptsturmführer	Per Sørensen	5.1943-25.1.1944
SS-Obersturmführer	Octavious Righardt Holger Norreen	10.1943-11.1943
SS-Untersturmführer	Hazal	

2/SS-Pz.Gren.Rgt.24 *Danmark*
SS-Untersturmführer	Hartvig Larsen	5.1943-?
SS-Untersturmführer	Hans Peter Jensen	

3/SS-Pz.Gren.Rgt.24 *Danmark*
SS-Obersturmführer	Heinz Hennecke	5.1943-25.1.1944
SS-Untersturmführer	John William Schröder	
SS-Obersturmführer	Fritz Sidon	

4/SS-Pz.Gren.Rgt.24 *Danmark*
SS-Obersturmführer	Helmut Stenger	5.1943-?

II/SS-Pz.Gren.Rgt.24 *Danmark*

Commanders

SS-Hauptsturmführer	Kurt Walther	5.1943-4.1944
SS-Hauptsturmführer	Heinz Hämel	4.1944-27.7.1944
SS-Hauptsturmführer	Albert Bergfeldt	27.7.1944-11.1944
SS-Sturmbannführer	Per Sørensen	1.1945-21.4.1945

Battalion Adjutants

SS-Obersturmführer	Knud Thorgils	5.1943-?
SS-Untersturmführer	Gerhard Szwerinski	?-6.1944
SS-Untersturmführer	Ellef Henry Rasmussen	?-11.3.1945,

Orderly Officer

SS-Untersturmführer	Gerhard Szwerinski	5.1943-?

Medical Officer

(A Luftwaffe Physician)

Motorised Transport Officer

SS-Obersturmführer	Werner Gerls	5.1943-?

Maintenance Officers

SS-Untersturmführer	Jørgen Salskov
SS-Obersturmführer	Walter Schäfer

5/SS-Pz.Gren.Rgt.24 *Danmark*

SS-Obersturmführer	Egil Poulsen	5.1943-.11.1943
SS-Obersturmführer	Walter Seebach	1.1944-?
SS-Hauptsturmführer	Gerd Fendler	1.1945-?
SS-Hauptsturmführer	Erich Seybt	2.1945-4.1945

6/SS-Pz.Gren.Rgt.24 *Danmark*

SS-Obersturmführer	Rudolf Ternedde	5.1943-?
SS-Untersturmführer	Kaj A H Bertramsen	
SS-Untersturmführer	Robert Spahn	?-23.1.1945
SS-Obersturmführer	Engelbrecht	2.1945-?
SS-Oberscharführer	Pösch	4.1945-?

7/SS-Pz.Gren.Rgt.24 *Danmark*

SS-Obersturmführer	Heinz Hämel	5.1943-?
SS-Untersturmführer	Erik Brørup	
SS-Untersturmführer	Robert L Hansen	
SS-Oberscharführer	Albert Hektor	13.2.1944-?
SS-Untersturmführer	Carsten Jørgensen	
SS-Untersturmführer	Mogens Karl Berthelsen	?-7.6.1944
SS-Untersturmführer	Leo Anton Nikolau Madsen	7.6.1944-28.7.1944
SS-Untersturmführer	Josef Stippernitz	4.1945-?

8/SS-Pz.Gren.Rgt.24 *Danmark*

SS-Obersturmführer	Ole Peter Kure	10.1943-1.1944
SS-Hauptsturmführer	Svend Sofus Lars Birkedal Hansen	?-4.1.1945

III/SS-Pz.Gren.Rgt.24 *Danmark*

Commanders
SS-Sturmbannführer	Per Neergaard-Jacobsen	5.1943-1.2.1944
SS-Sturmbannführer	Hans Kappus	6.1944-?
SS-Hauptsturmführer	Rudolf Ternedde	2.1945-25.4.1945
SS-Untersturmführer	Dirksen	

Battalion Adjutants
SS-Untersturmführer	Walter Landmesser	5.1943-?
SS-Untersturmführer	Wilhelm Efsen	6.1944-28.7.1944
SS-Untersturmführer	Lothar Krieger	4.1945-?
SS-Untersturmführer	Dirksen	24.4.1945-?

Orderly Officers
SS-Untersturmführer	V E Larsen	5.1943-.11.1943
SS-Obersturmführer	Octavious Righardt Holger Norreen	11.1943-?
SS-Untersturmführer	Erik Herlov Nielsen	?-29.1.1944

Maintenance Officer
SS-Obersturmführer	Hans Schramm	5.1943-?

9/SS-Pz.Gren.Rgt.24 *Danmark*
SS-Obersturmführer	H Meyer	5.1943-?
SS-Untersturmführer	Darm	2.1944-?
SS-Hauptsturmführer	Herbert Meier	
SS-Obersturmführer	Fritz Sidon	3.1944-?
SS-Obersturmführer	Knud Maagaard-Hansen	1.1945-23.1.1945
SS-Hauptscharführer	Pärschka	4.1945-?

10/SS-Pz.Gren.Rgt.24 *Danmark*
SS-Untersturmführer	Erik Vagn Fenger	5.1943-?
SS-Obersturmführer	Hugo C Jessen	8.1944-23.9.1944
SS-Obersturmführer	Knud Maagaard-Hansen	23.9.1944-.1.1945
SS-Untersturmführer	Hans Scheel	4.1945-?

11/SS-Pz.Gren.Rgt.24 *Danmark*
SS-Obersturmführer	Bent Worsoe Larsen	5.1943-1.2.1944
SS-Untersturmführer	Fritz Bünte	2.1944-?
SS-Hauptsturmführer	Paul Trautwein	7.1944-27.7.1944
SS-Untersturmführer	Kaj A H Bertramsen	27.7.1944-29.7.1944
SS-Obersturmführer	Poul Thorkildsen	8.1944-17.3.1945
SS-Untersturmführer	Jes Dirksen	4.1945-?

12/SS-Pz.Gren.Rgt.24 *Danmark*
SS-Obersturmführer	Johann Thorius	5.1943-?
SS-Hauptsturmführer	Herbert Meier	4.1945-?

Independent Companies

13/SS-Pz.Gren.Rgt.24 *Danmark* (Infantry Guns-Heavy Weapons):

SS-Hauptsturmführer	Erik Lärum	7.1944-.8.1944
SS-Hauptsturmführer	Günther Willenberg	8.1944-?
SS-Untersturmführer	Rolf Bachmann	12.1944-?

14 (Flak)/SS-Pz.Gren.Rgt.24 *Danmark* (Flak-Heavy Weapons):

SS-Untersturmführer	Heinrich Ernstmeier	?-1.2.1944
SS-Obersturmführer	H W Petersen	3.1945-4.1945

15/SS-Pz.Gren.Rgt.24 *Danmark*:
   Never Fully Formed

16/SS-Pz.Gren.Rgt.24 *Danmark* (Combat Engineers):

SS-Untersturmführer	Fahrenbacher	
SS-Untersturmführer	J I Frederiksen	
SS-Untersturmführer	Aronius	?-3.2.1944
SS-Untersturmführer	Henry Valdemar Christensen (Nicknamed Pi-Walde)	4.1945-?
SS-Untersturmführer	H W Petersen	

APPENDIX C

Orders of Battle

11 SS-Freiwillige-Panzergrenadier-Division *Nordland*

Divisional Commander
SS-Brigf u Gen.Maj d Waffen-SS Fritz von Scholz
SS-Brigf u Gen.Maj d Waffen-SS Joachim Ziegler
SS-Brigf u Gen.Maj d Waffen-SS Dr Gustav Krukenberg

SS-Panzer-Abteilung 11 *Hermann von Salza* (11th SS Tank Detachment)
Stabskompanie (HQ Company)
1/SS-Pz.Abt.11 (1st Tank Company)
2/SS-Pz.Abt.11 (2nd Tank Company)
3/SS-Pz.Abt.11 (3rd Tank Company)
4/SS-Pz.Abt.11 (4th Tank Company)

SS-Panzer-Aufklärungs-Abteilung 11 (11th SS Reconnaissance Detachment)
Stab (HQ)
zwei Spähwagen Kompanien (two Scout Car Companies)
zwei Kompanien geländegängige KFZ (two Cross-Country Lorry Company)
ein schwere kompanie (one Heavy Company)

SS-Pionier-Bataillon 11 (11th SS Engineer Battalion)
3 Pionier-Kompanien (three engineer companies)
1 Kolonne (column)

SS-Nachrichten-Abteilung 11 (11th SS Signals Detachment)
Funkkompanie (Radio Company)
Fernsprechkompanie (Telephone Company)

SS-Fla-Abteilung 11 (11th SS Anti-Aircraft Detachment)
drei schwere Batterien (three heavy batteries)
ein leichte Batterie (one light battery)

SS-Panzerjäger-Abteilung 11 (11th SS Anti-Tank Detachment)
Stab und versorgung (HQ)
3 Batterien (3 Batteries)

SS-Wirtschaft-Bataillon 11 (11th Service Battalion)
Stab (HQ)
4 Kompanien (4 Companies)

Feldlazarett (Field Hospital)

Feldgendarmerietrupp (Military Police Troop)

Instandsetzunghaltung-Abteilung (Maintenance Detachment)
    Stab (HQ)
    2 Werkstatt-Kompanien (2 Workshop Companies)
    Waffenmeisterzug (Armourer)

SS-Feldersatz-Bataillon 11 (11th SS Field Replacement Battalion)
    Stab (HQ)
    4 Kompanien (4 Companies)

SS-Artillerie-Regiment 11 (11th SS Artillery Regiment)
    I/SS-Art.Rgt.11 (I Detachment)
        1 (leFH)/SS-Art.Rgt.11 (1st light field howitzer battery)
        2 (leFH)/SS-Art.Rgt.11 (2nd light field howitzer battery)
        3 (leFH)/SS-Art.Rgt.11 (3rd light field howitzer battery)
    II/SS-Art.Rgt.11 (II Detachment)
        4 (leFH)/SS-Art.Rgt.11 (4th light field howitzer battery)
        5 (leFH)/SS-Art.Rgt.11 (5th light field howitzer battery)
        6 (leFH)/SS-Art.Rgt.11 (6th light field howitzer battery)
    III/SS-Art.Rgt.11 (III Detachment)
        7 (sFH)/SS-Art.Rgt.11 (7th heavy field howitzer battery)
        8 (sFH)/SS-Art.Rgt.11 (8th heavy field howitzer battery)
        9 (sFH)/SS-Art.Rgt.11 (9th heavy field howitzer battery)

SS-Panzergrenadier-Regiment 23 *Norge* (23rd SS Motorised Infantry Regiment)
    I/SS-Pz.Gren.Rgt.23 *Norge* (I Battalion)
    II/SS-Pz.Gren.Rgt.23 *Norge* (II Battalion)
    III/SS-Pz.Gren.Rgt.23 *Norge* (III Battalion)

SS-Panzergrenadier-Regiment 24 *Danmark* (24th SS Motorised Infantry Regiment)
    I/SS-Pz.Gren.Rgt.24 *Danmark* (I Battalion)
    II/SS-Pz.Gren.Rgt. 24 *Danmark* (II Battalion)
    III/SS-Pz.Gren.Rgt. 24 *Danmark* (III Battalion)

SS-Panzergrenadier-Regiment 24 *Danmark*

Commanders

SS-Ostubaf Hermenegild Graf von Westphalen	(5.5.1943-9.4.1944)
SS-Ostubaf Albrecht Krügel	(9.4.1944-16.3.1945)
SS-Ostubaf Rudolf Klotz	(16.3.1945-21.4.1945)
SS-Ostubaf Per Sørensen	(21.4.1945-24.4.1945)
SS-Ostuf Petersen	(acting 24.4.1945-25.4.1945)
SS-Stubaf Rudolf Ternedde	(25.4.1945-2.5.1945)

Staff

    Maschinenpistolezug (Machine-Pistol Assault Platoon)
    Pionierzug (Engineer Platoon)

I/SS-Pz.Gren.Rgt.24 *Danmark* (I Battalion)

    1/SS-Pz.Gren.Rgt.24 *Danmark* (1st Company)
    2/SS-Pz.Gren.Rgt.24 *Danmark* (2nd Company)
    3/SS-Pz.Gren.Rgt.24 *Danmark* (3rd Company)
    4/SS-Pz.Gren.Rgt.24 *Danmark* (4th Company)

II/SS-Pz.Gren.Rgt.24 *Danmark* (II Battalion)

    5/SS-Pz.Gren.Rgt.24 *Danmark* (5th Company)
    6/SS-Pz.Gren.Rgt.24 *Danmark* (6th Company)
    7/SS-Pz.Gren.Rgt.24 *Danmark* (7th Company)
    8/SS-Pz.Gren.Rgt.24 *Danmark* (8th Company)

III/SS-Pz.Gren.Rgt.24 *Danmark* (III Battalion)

    9/SS-Pz.Gren.Rgt.24 *Danmark* (9th Company)
    10/SS-Pz.Gren.Rgt.24 *Danmark* (10th Company)
    11/SS-Pz.Gren.Rgt.24 *Danmark* (11th Company)
    12/SS-Pz.Gren.Rgt.24 *Danmark* (12th Company)

13/SS-Pz.Gren.Rgt.24 *Danmark* (13th (Heavy Weapons) Company)

14 (Flak)/SS-Pz.Gren.Rgt.24 *Danmark* (14th (Anti-Aircraft) Company)

15/SS-Pz.Gren.Rgt.24 *Danmark* (15th (Motorcycle) Company)

16 (Pi)/SS-Pz.Gren.Rgt.24 *Danmark* (16th (Engineer) Company)

APPENDIX D

Waffen-SS Ranks

Waffen-SS ranks were based on both those of the pre-war Allgemeine-SS and the German Army and ranks such as *SS-Obermann* were introduced into the Waffen-SS so as to mirror exactly the Army system. In addition to this, officers from the rank of *SS-Brigadeführer* and above were deemed Generals of the Waffen-SS and held a dual title. For example, a Waffen-SS *Gruppenführer* was correctly referred to as *SS-Gruppenführer und Generalleutnant der Waffen-SS*.

In general there were six classes of rank in the Waffen-SS:

Höhere Führer	Senior Class Officers	SS-Oberstgruppenführer - SS-Standartenführer
Mittlere Führer	Middle Class Officers	SS-Obersturmbannführer - SS-Sturmbannführer
Untere Führer	Junior Class Officers	SS-Hauptsturmführer - SS-Untersturmführer
Unterführer	NCOs	SS-Hauptscharführer - SS-Unterscharführer
Mannschaften	Privates	SS-Rottenführer - SS-Mann

A basic comparison of ranks between the Waffen-SS, German and British Armies is given below:

Waffen-SS		German Infantry	British Infantry
		Generalfeldmarschall	Field Marshal
SS-Oberstgruppenführer	(SS-Obstgruf)	Generaloberst	General
SS-Obergruppenführer	(SS-Ogruf)	General	Lieutenant-General
SS-Gruppenführer	(SS-Gruf)	Generalleutnant	Major-General
SS-Brigadeführer	(SS-Brigf)	Generalmajor	Brigadier
SS-Oberführer	(SS-Obf)		
SS-Standartenführer	(SS-Staf)	Oberst	Colonel
SS-Obersturmbannführer	(SS-Ostubaf)	Oberstleutnant	Lieutenant-Colonel
SS-Sturmbannführer	(SS-Stubaf)	Major	Major
SS-Hauptsturmführer	(SS-Hstuf)	Hauptmann	Captain
SS-Obersturmführer	(SS-Ostuf)	Oberleutnant	Lieutenant
SS-Untersturmführer	(SS-Ustuf)	Leutnant	2nd Lieutenant
SS-Sturmscharführer	(SS-Stuscha)	Stabsfeldwebel	
SS-Hauptscharführer	(SS-Hscha)	Oberfeldwebel	Warrant Officer Class I
SS-Oberscharführer	(SS-Oscha)	Feldwebel	Warrant Officer Class II
			Colour-Serjeant
SS-Scharführer	(SS-Scha)	Unterfeldwebel	Serjeant
SS-Unterscharführer	(SS-Uscha)	Unteroffizier	Lance-Serjeant[14]
		Stabsgefreiter	
SS-Rottenführer	(SS-Rttf)	Obergefreiter	Corporal
SS-Sturmmann	(SS-Strm)	Gefreiter	Lance-Corporal
SS-Obermann		Obergrenadier	
SS-Mann		Grenadier	Private

---

[14] Technically, British 'Lance' titles were not ranks but appointments. A Lance-Serjeant was actually a 'Serjeant-candidate' with the rank of Corporal, similar to the German Army appointment *Fahnenjunker-Unteroffizier*. Furthermore, in reality, the British Army had 12 non-commissioned rank grades as opposed to the German 10. However, differences in organisation between the two armies make a more detailed comparison impossible.

APPENDIX E

Badges and Insignia

In common with other European volunteers, members of the SS-Panzergrenadier Regiment 24 *Danmark* wore SS uniform with special national insignia. The main items were the National Emblem, the Cuff-title, the Arm-shield and the Collar Patches. In addition to these, unit emblems were painted on vehicles and signposts etc. These latter are usually referred to as Formation Signs.

The National Emblem (Hoheitsabzeichen)

This was the national symbol of National-Socialist Germany - the eagle and swastika - and was worn in various forms by all branches of the armed forces. The version worn by the SS was worked in silver or light grey thread on a black backing and had stylised pointed wings. It was worn on the upper left arm.

The Hoheitsabzeichen as used by the SS

Cuff-Titles

The Cuff-title had originally been used by the Allgemeine-SS to denote the Standarte (Regiment). During the War the Waffen-SS expanded this system, allowing the cuff-title to represent many different types of unit. The Regiment *Danmark* used a title with *Danmark* in block letters, either in light grey thread or silver embroidery for officers and walking-out uniforms.

Variations of the cuff-title issued to SS-Pz.Gren.Rgt.24 *Danmark*.

Arm-shield

The arm-shield was used specifically by non-German volunteers to show their country of origin. The Danes wore a red shield with a white cross worked onto a black backing. It was worn directly below the National Emblem on the left arm.

Two different types of Danish arm shields. The elongated one was possibly privately made and was not common. The other format was the official one.

Collar Patches

In the SS, the left hand collar patch was used to denote rank, and the left was either a standard patch showing the SS runes or a specific unit related design. A sonnenrad (sun-wheel) collar patch was issued to all units of the 11 SS-Freiwilligen-Panzergrenadier-Division *Nordland*. Although intended to be worn throughout *Danmark* and *Nordland*, the SS runic collar patch was widely preferred by the soldiers and was worn whenever possible.

The Sonnenrad Collar Patch

Appendices

Formation Signs

There were two formation signs to be seen on vehicles of the *Nordland* Division, shown right, although the sonnenrad symbol was the 'official' one. However, from photographic evidence, it would appear that the Regiment *Danmark* vehicles usually displayed a sonnenrad, often without the shield, on the nearside mudguard and a Danish shield, similar to the arm-shield, on the offside. Examples are shown below.

APPENDIX F

Shelf Books General Translation Policy

The Treatment of Eastern European Placenames

Insofar as German-language primary sources bearing on the activities of the armed forces of the Third Reich have begun to appear in translation in recent years (mainly published in Canada and the USA) they have been flawed in their treatment of Eastern European placenames: these have been left exactly as found in the German text, with the result that the English eye encounters the unpronounceable "Wassiljewschtschina", or the unfamiliar "Charkow", hindering attempts to trace the course of the war on contemporary English-language atlases. SHELF policy is to attempt to get the English rendition as close to the original native-language version as possible, with exceptions given below.

Prior to 1945, extensive German settlement in the Eastern European lands and trade with their peoples resulted in the adoption of German names for local places which are distinctively different from those of the native languages. In some cases, these are simply Germanicisations of the local placenames which can readily be recognised therein. In others, particularly where the German is a translation of a Slavic, Baltic, Romanian or Magyar (Hungarian) locality, no similarity at all will be evident to the English reader. In still other cases, German settlers imported radically new names. These terms, therefore, occur in the primary sources: SHELF policy is to replace them with the native term, except in documents where such a transformation would be inauthentic, in which case, the native term is given in brackets following. Examples of such problems are:

Slovak:	Bratislava	**German**:	Preßburg
Polish:	Rzeszów	**German**:	Reichshof
Magyar:	Pécs	**German**:	Fünfkirchen
Magyar:	Székesfehérvár	**German**:	Stuhlweißenburg
Latvian:	Jelgava	**German**:	Mitau
Estonian:	Tallinn	**German**:	Reval
Russian:	Pskov	**German**:	Pleskau

In some particularly awkward cases the German text term is taken over from a third language, given the vicissitudes of history and the complexity of inter-ethnic penetration, thus:

- Lithuanian 'Kaunas' may be taken over into the German as 'Kowno' from the Russian-Polish in preference to the strictly-German 'Kauen'.
- The West Ukrainian (Galician) city of 'Lviv' is 'Lwów' to a Pole, 'Lvov' to a Russian, and 'Lemberg' to a German.
- The Latvian city of 'Daugavpils' (on the 'Daugava' river) is 'Dvinsk' (on the 'Western Dvina') to a Russian, 'Dünaburg' (on the 'Düna') to a German.
- 'Oradea Mare' (Romania) is 'Nagyvarad' to a Hungarian, 'Großwardein' to a German.

In such cases, Shelf policy is to choose the term used by the local ethnic group insofar as this enjoys the status of a 'Nation State' within the frontiers established around 1945, reinforced by the more recent break-up of the Soviet Empire (USSR), that is, the consolidation of the non-Russian identities of the Baltic, Ukrainian, Georgian, etc. nations.

As a result of the treaties of Versailles and St. Germain, many German-populated localities were lost to the German Reich or to the Habsburg successor state of Austria, soon after World War I. Since 1945, the whole of the historic German provinces of East Prussia, Pomerania and Silesia have been simply amputated from the main body of Germany and given by the victorious Allies to the Poles in compensation for the loss of correspondingly large swathes of their eastern marchlands (Kresy) to Stalin. The 1945 settlement confirmed the loss of the Sudetenland to Czechoslovakia (as it then was) and of West Prussia and *Danzig* to Poland. These displacements of frontiers were accompanied by the mass expulsion, and on occasion extermination of the German inhabitants of these regions. A similar fate befell the Volksdeutsche (ethnic Germans) of Romania (Banat and Transylvania (German 'Siebenbürgen')) of Yugoslavia, of Hungary (principally the Bácska) and *a fortiori* of the lands further east.

Naturally, German language texts utilise the placenames familiar to Germans for centuries, even though these will not now be found in contemporary atlases. However, to imply that German troops were fighting for their homes and families in Wroclaw, Kostrzyn, Kolobrzeg or Gdansk hardly seems appropriate: at the time these were Breslau, Küstrin, Kolberg and Danzig respectively.

The SHELF rule is therefore: places which were part of Germany before 1939, together with Danzig and West Prussia will be given in the German form; places never part of Germany in the local form consolidated since 1945 (1990) but placed in the gazetteer where helpful. A few hard cases - places incorporated into the Reich during the war years - for example Poznan (Posen), Lódz (Litzmannstadt) or Maribor (Marburg) will be dealt with in context.

Subsequent to this elimination of the German element in the Eastern European landscape, the collapse of Communism in the 1990s resulted in the redesignation of some historic cities purely for political reasons: thus, Leningrad reverted to being St. Petersburg, Gorkii to Nizhnyi Novgorod, Ordzhonikidze to Vladikavkaz, whereas Stalingrad had already become Volgograd (not the historic Tsaritsyn) somewhat earlier. However, for most people the siege of Leningrad and the Battle of Stalingrad are such familiar terms that to update them would seem to tear history up by its roots. In any case, since the 1939-45 war was very largely perceived by a majority of Europeans (not only National-Socialist Germany) as the confrontation with Communism (as the strength of the European volunteer movement showed), such a change in nomenclature would at a stroke wipe from sight the very reasons for which these battles took place.

To the English or American reader this preoccupation may seem pointless: it is no coincidence that neither country has suffered the humiliating loss of territory or subjection to alien rule which has been such a feature of 20th Century Eastern Europe. It is impossible to understand the bitterness of the 1939-45 conflict without empathising with the participants, for whom such namings and re-namings reflected the very essence of their struggle for national self-assertion, an ethnic identity, even existence itself. Whether we are living through a period after the 'end of history' or merely an interlude in the cycle remains to be seen.

APPENDIX G

Estonian Pronunciation Guide

Characteristics of Estonian
1. The stress is always on the first syllable of a word, except in some foreign names and loan words.
2. Gradation of vowels and consonants, involving three different lengths: short, long and very long.
3. There is no grammatical gender.
4. There are no articles, definite or indefinite.
5. Multiplicity of cases for declension of nouns and adjectives.

Alphabet[15]

a, b, (c), (c), e, d, (f), g, h, i, j, k, l, m, n, o, p, (q), r, s, t, (s), (z), (z), u, v, (w), o, a, o, u, (x), (y)

- Letters have only one phonetic value. There are very few instances where accepted spelling and pronunciation differ.
- Long and very long vowels are marked with a double letter (aa, ee, ii, etc.).
- Long consonants are marked with a double letter (kk, ll, mm) **only** if they occur between two short vowels or at the end of a word; next to another consonant it will be marked with a single letter.

There are eight vowels in Estonian:

a	as in love
aa	laugh
e	net
ee	(does not occur in English)
i	as in bit
ii	read, reed
o	knot
oo	lord
õ	as the first element in the English diphthong ou
õõ	cold, sober
u	cushion
uu	moon
ä	hat
ää	
aa	
ö	produced by lip-rounding with the tongue in position
öö	for producing the sound "e"
ü	lip-rounding, tongue in position for "i"
üü	

---
[15] Letters in brackets occur only in words of foreign origin.

Appendices

Diphthongs

Twenty different combinations occur, two of these only in foreign names. Both elements retain their phonetic values. In long or very long gradations the first element remains short, only the second element becomes long.

Consonants

There is a 1=1 relationship between letter and sound. Some observations: 1) b, d, g, indicating the short gradation, are voiceless in Estonian, i.e. the vocal chords do not vibrate; the same applies to "s" (there is no voiced "s" in Estonian, in English "wise"). 2) When double consonants occur between vowels, both are pronounced, first at the end of the preceding and second at the beginning of the following syllable. (Unlike in English where the value of "n" is the same both in "manor" and "manner".)

Palatalisation

Six consonants are subject to palatalisation: d, t, l, n, r, s. Palatalisation is not marked in spelling. It can occur when the vowel "i" crops up (or in monosyllabic words would crop up if the word were declined) in the syllable that follows. It is produced by moving the tip of the tongue slightly forward and upward (towards the hard palate(')) from its normal position.

Gradation

Gradation - short, long or very long sounds - is significant only in stressed syllables. The vowels vary in length also in unstressed syllables, but there the duration has no phonetic value. (In fact, the unstressed "short" vowels are normally much longer than the vowels in the stressed syllables, but Estonians themselves are unaware of it, unless they are trained phoneticians. Non-Estonian speakers notice it, but mistake it for stress, and may therefore get their pronunciation wrong).

APPENDIX H
Latvian Pronunciation Guide

The Latvian language is related to the majority of European languages. It belongs to the Baltic group of languages which also includes Lithuanian and Old Prussian (now extinct).

Owing to their long association with their Slav neighbours the language of the Balts has more affinities with the Slavonic languages than with others in lexical, morphological and syntactical fields. Nevertheless, many modern Latvian words are directly derived from German and the Scandinavian languages.

The earliest surviving Latvian documents and books date from the sixteenth century, written in Gothic script. In the twentieth century the Latin alphabet was adopted, with changes in some letters. The new alphabet was based on phonetic principles and also introduced diacritical marks (ā, č).

Latvian today is fully capable of expressing the complexities of modern civilisation in all its aspects; it uses the modern media, possesses an expanding literature and maintains institutions of culture and higher learning.

Although Latvian is a modern language, it has retained many archaisms in its structure which were shed by the English language centuries ago. Latvian still uses hundreds of suffixes that form the declensional cases, various verbal and participial forms and new words from existing bases. In this respect Latvian and English represent two different language types: Latvian, with its multitude of affixes, is a syntactic language, whereas English is of the analytical type. Where Latvian has a single word with one or more suffixes, the English equivalent of it will usually be a phrase of two or more separate words.

There are no articles (*a*, *an* and *the*) in the Latvian language. However, the articles can be implied by the endings of adjectives.

Latvian is a highly inflected language. This means that the endings of nouns, pronouns, adjectives and numerals change, depending on whether they are masculine or feminine, how they are used within the sentence etc. Other changes apply to verbs.

The Latvian Alphabet

a ā b c č d dz dž e ē f g ģ h i ī j k ķ l ļ m n ņ o p r ŗ s š t u ū v z ž

The Latvian alphabet uses 22 Roman letters. Thirteen of these are repeated in a modified form in most cases using special additions called diacritical marks. Some indicate the lengthening of vowels, while others indicate palatal consonants. Four letters used in the English language - q, w, x, y - are not used in Latvian at all, and so the actual alphabet consists of 37 letters.

The Latvian standard alphabet is a phonetic alphabet, with each of its letters corresponding to one sound only, except two letter combinations ch, dz, dž, which mark single sounds.

In the following explanations the English sound or approximate English equivalent is underlined and appears in capitals.

Vowels

There is a clear difference between long and short vowels, both in the alphabet and in pronunciation. Each vowel has two quantities - short and long. The length is

Appendices

marked by a bar over the vowel (ā, ē, ī, ū). There are two different ways of pronouncing 'e/ē'.

a	sUn
ā	cAr
e	pEt
ē	AIr
e	bAt
ē	bAd
i	sIt
ī	mEEt
o	WAllet (pronounced really as a diphthong)
ō	Opera (in words of foreign origin)
u	pUt
ū	fOOd

Consonants

b, d, f, g, k, l, m, n, p, t, v, z are pronounced approximately as in English. Several consonants can be soft or palatalised (ļ, ķ, ņ, ģ). The 'j' usually palatalises the preceding consonant: n+j = ņ, l+j = ļ. The soft 'ŗ' is no longer used in modern written Latvian. 'f, h, ch', monophthong 'ō' and diphthong 'oi' are not Latvian sounds and occur only in loan words.

c	caTS
č	CHurch
dz	laDS
dž	GinGer
ģ	Duty
h	as in the Scottish loCH or the German iCH
j	Yes
ķ	Tune (approximate pronunciation as a counterpart to 'ģ')
ļ	softened l as in miLLion
ņ	softened n as in New
r	rolled r
s	Sit
š	SHe
ž	pleaSure

Diphthongs

All Latvian diphthongs, including o and ie, are pronounced as one monosyllabic sound.

ai	fIne
au	hOW
ei	prEY
ie	like a combination of ee+a
ui	like a combination of 'oo' and 'y' (French 'oui')
oi	bOY
iu	extremely rare, like a combination of 'i' and 'oo'

Voiced and Unvoiced Consonants

The voiced consonant is pronounced unvoiced before an unvoiced consonant, and an unvoiced consonant is pronounced voiced before a voiced one, however only in pronunciation and not in spelling.

Latvian p, t, k have no aspiration, like the French sounds.

The letter 'h' is usually pronounced like the German ach-Laut[x] or ich-Laut[c], e.g. šahs [SHaxs] (*chess*), arhitektūra [arcitektOOra] (*architecture*).

In the Soviet Latvia the letter 'ch' was eliminated from the alphabet, but can be still found in books published outside Latvia.

Stress

The stress of the word is generally on the first syllable.

APPENDIX I

Gazetteer

Pre-1945 German Placenames That Now Form Part of Poland

Altdamm	Dąbie
Arnswalde	Choszczno
Arys	Orzysz
Augustwalde	Wielgowo
Barskewitz	Barzykowice
Bonin	unidentified
Büche	Wiechowo
Christinenberg	Wielka Kliniska
Dahlow	unidentified
Freienwalde	Chociwel
Gut Marienfelde	unidentified
Hammerstein	Czarne
Hassendorf	Żółwino
Hinzendorf	Sowno
Hohenkrug	unidentified
Kannenberg	unidentified
Karlsbach	unidentified
Karolinenhorst	unidentified
Küstrin	Kostrzyn
Lake Damm	Jezioro Dąbie
Lake Ihna	Jezioro Ińsko
Lake Madü	Jezioro Miedwie
Lüttgenhagen	Tarnowko
Marienfließ	unidentified
Marienwerder	unidentified
Massow	Maszewo
Oberhof	Pucice
Reichenbach	unidentified
River Faule Ihna	River Mała Ina
River Ihna	River Ina
River Oder	Odra
Rosengarten	unidentified
Saarow	Żarowo
Schlagenthin	Sławęcin
Schöneberg	Krąpiel
Schönwerder	unidentified
Stargard	Stargard Szczecinski
Stettin	Szczecin
Stutthof	unidentified
Tornow	Tarnowo
Voßberg	unidentified

Placenames with German Equivalents

Estonia

Narva-Jõesuu	Hungerburg
Peipsi Järvi	Peipussee (Lake Peipus)
Ema Jaõgi	Embach (River Em)
Pärnu	Pernau
Rakvere	Wesenberg
Tallinn	Reval
Tartu	Dorpat

Latvia

River Apše	River Apda
Auce	Autz
Jēkabpils	Jakobstadt
Baldone	Baldohn
Daugavpils	Dünaburg
Dobele	Dobeln
Gramzda	Gramsden
Jelgava	Mitau
Liepāja	Libau
Priekule	Preekuln
River Daugava	River Düna
Tukums	Tuckum
Vaiņode	Wainoden

Russian Placenames Changed Since 1945

Leningrad	Sankt-Pyetyerburg
Oraniembaum	Lomonosov
Yamburg	Kingisyepp

Training Grounds

Beneschau	Benešov (Czech Rep)
Hammerstein	Czarne (Poland)
Heidelager	Dębica (Poland)
Hradischko	Hradišťko (Czech Rep)
Sennheim	Cernay (France)

APPENDIX J

Glossary

Abteilung *Detachment* Unit between a Regiment and a Company in those German units which did not use the term Bataillon (Battalion). The difference between an Abteilung and a Bataillon being in their command responsibilities, although in simple terms both refer to a collection of Companies (Kompanien).

Alarmkompanie *Emergency Company* Ad-hoc unit created from non-combat troops, e.g. service troops, to supplement trained infantry.

Allgemeine-SS *General-SS* This was the part-time force which constituted the original SS. Before the take-over of power, it was important in that it had units based all over Germany and allowed the NSDAP to form links with the whole of the German Reich. After 1933 and especially during the War, however, it decreased in importance in favour of the Waffen-SS and organisations controlled by the SS such as the SD, Rusha, Gestapo, Totenkopf units etc.

Aufklärungs *Reconnaissance*

Ausbildungs *Training*

Bewährungskompanie *Probationary Company* A type of unit peculiar to the SS, composed of officers under suspended sentence of court martial. Such individuals, with their ranks and decorations removed, were given the choice of military prison or a chance to 'prove themselves' on the battlefield. These units fostered such a high *ésprit de corps* that many 'rehabilitated' offers chose to stay rather than rejoin their original unit.

Ersatz *Replacement*

Fallschirmjäger *Parachutist*

Feldersatz *Field Replacement*

Feldgendarmerie The German Military Police, often referred to as "chained dogs" (*kettenhunde*) due to their wearing a gorget and chain around their necks when on duty.

Fla *Flugabwehr* Anti-aircraft.

Flak *Flugabwehrkanone* Anti-aircraft gun.

Gauleiter Nazi Party Regional Leader

Hilfswillige (Hiwi) A volunteer used as an auxiliary e.g. as a driver, cook, tailor etc. to conserve German manpower, usually a Russian, Ukrainian, Georgian or other Eastern national.

HIPO *Hilfs-Polizei* Auxiliary Police recruited from local populations.

Infanteriegeschütz *Infantry Gun* A close-support light field gun manned by infantry personnel under the control of the regimental commander.

Kampfgruppe *Battle Group* A feature of the German Army: *ad hoc* combined-arm formations of sub-divisional size rapidly adapted to the tactical situation, very influential with regard to all later military thinking (adopted by British as Brigade Group etc., by US Army as Regimental Combat Teams, Combat Commands etc.). Later in the War, used for remnants of decimated formations.

Katyusha Russian nickname for lorry-mounted salvo rocket launcher; named after a contemporary popular song; known to the Germans as a 'Stalin Organ'.

Knight's Cross of the Iron Cross *Ritterkreuz zum Eisernen Kreuz* The highest award version of the Iron Cross, worn around the neck. Subsequent awards were denoted by the wearing of

Appendices

Oakleaves; Oakleaves and Swords; Oakleaves, Swords and Diamonds; and finally, awarded only once, Golden Oakleaves, Swords and Diamonds.

Kreisleiter Nazi Party District Leader

Kriegsmarine *German Navy*

NSDAP (National-Sozialistische Deutsche Arbeiter-Partei) *National-Socialist German Workers Party* Nazi Party

NSKK (Nazionalsozialistisches Kraftfahrkorps) *National Socialist Motor Corps* Originally Party Branch dedicated to the enhancement of mechanical proficiency and "motor-mindedness" among the German people, later in effect an auxiliary branch to the Wehrmacht indispensable to the war effort; in view of manpower shortages it recruited extensively among sympathetic elements in occupied Europe

OKW (Oberkommando der Wehrmacht) *High Command of the German Armed Forces* Command organisation set up by Hitler to oversee the notoriously independently-minded services - Heer (Army), Kriegsmarine (Navy) and Luftwaffe (Air Force) - respectively controlled by the OKH, OKM and OKL. - enabling Hitler, through Keitel and Jodl, to bypass the General Staff etc. Later, the OKH was left to run the Eastern Front whilst the OKW took responsibility for the other theatres

Pak *Panzerabwehrkanone* Anti-tank gun.

Panther *Panzerkampfwagen V* Heavy tank with sloping armour, produced in response to the success of the Russian T-34 and reproducing some of its better features.

Panzerfaust Shaped-charge (hollow-charge) anti-tank grenade projector useful only at close range (progressively extended from 30 to 150 m).

Panzerjäger *Anti-Tank*

Panzerschreck Shaped-charge (hollow charge) anti-tank rocket launcher developed from captured US bazooka; range greater than the Panzerfaust, though penetration inferior.

Reichsdeutsche German National

Reichsführer-SS (RF-SS) *National Leader of the SS* Heinrich Himmler

Sherman Tank of American origin equipped with a turret-mounted 75mm gun. Extensively supplied to the Russian forces.

SS-Junkerschule *SS Cadet School*

Stalin Russian heavy tank, developed from the KV vehicle, with better performance and able to carry a heavier (122mm) gun. Used in special heavy tank detachments to counter German heavy tanks.

Sturmgeschütz *Assault Gun* Armoured self-propelled 75mm gun operated by the Artillery as an infantry support weapon - a turretless equivalent of the British Infantry Tank. During the Russian campaign, found to be one of the few weapons capable of knocking out heavy tanks (e.g. T-34). Progressively incorporated in Infantry and Panzergrenadier Divisions and ultimately replacing tanks in Panzer Divisions; supplemented by heavier calibre (106-160mm) howitzers in primary role.

Tiger *Panzerkampfwagen VI* First German Heavy tank developed to counter the T-34. Although mounting an 88mm gun, heavy armour and wide tracks, its conventional design and poor mobility meant that it did not perform as well as the Panther..

Volksdeutsche Ethnic Germans, members of the German ethnic minorities from eastern and south-eastern Europe.

zbV *For Special Purposes*

Bibliography

C Beadle and T Hartmann The Waffen-SS: Its Divisional Insignia (1971) Key Publications, UK

R J Bender Uniforms, Organization and History of the Waffen-SS Vol.3 (1972) Bender Publishing San Jose USA

Allen Brandt The Last Knight of Flanders. Remy Schrijnen and his SS-Legion "Flandern"/Sturmbrigade "Langemarck" Comrades on the Eastern Front (1998) Schiffer Publishing, USA

P Buss and A Mollo Hitler's Germanic Legions (1978) MacDonalds and Janes UK

Heinz Ertel and Richard Schulze-Kossens Europäische Freiwillige im Bild (1986) Munin-Verlag, Germany

Eric Haaest Frontsvin, Frostknuder, Forraneder (1975) 3 Volumes, Bogans Forlag, Denmark

Dr K-G Klietmann Die Waffen-SS Eine Dokumentation (1965): Verlag Der Freiwillige, Germany

E G Kraetschmer, Die Ritterkreuztrager der Waffen-SS (1982): Verlag K W Schütz, Germany

Richard Landwehr Freikorps Danmark (1990) **Siegrunen #50**

Richard Landwehr Lions of Flanders (1996) Shelf Books, UK

Richard Landwehr Narva 1944. The Waffen-SS and the Battle for Europe (1981) Bibliophile Legion Books, Silver Spring, USA

R Landwehr, C Caballero and E Norling La Estirpe de Thor (1993:) García Hispán, Spain

David Littlejohn Foreign Legions of the Third Reich Vol.1. (1979) Bender Publishing, San Jose, USA

Jean Mabire Berlin in Todeskampf 1945, (1977) Verlag K.W. Schütz, Germany

Jean Mabire La Division Nordland (1982) Fayard, France

Hans Werner Neulen Europas verratenen Söhne (1980) Universitas, Germany

Hans Werner Neulen An deutscher Seite, (1985) Universitas, Germany

S H Newton Retreat from Leningrad. Army Group North 1944/1945 (1995) Schiffer Publishing, USA

H T Nielsen SS-Oberscharfuehrer der Reserve Alfred Jonstrup **Siegrunen #57**

H T Nielsen SS-Rottenfuehrer Heinrich Husen **Siegrunen #5?**

H T Nielsen SS-Unterscharfuehrer Holger Thor Nielsen **Siegrunen #58**

H T Nielsen SS-Obersturmbannfuehrer Ernst Christian Hartvig Viffert **Siegrunen #59**

H T Nielsen The Danish Flag Collarpatch **Siegrunen #60**

H T Nielsen SS-Obersturmfuehrer Tage Petersen **Siegrunen #60**

H T Nielsen SS-Unterscharfuehrer Jens Christian Gran **Siegrunen #60**

S Erik Norling, Viento del Norte; La División SS *Nordland*, 1943-1945 (1990) Garcia Hispan,. Spain

Nikolaus von Preradovich Die General der Waffen-SS (1985) Kurt Vowinckel Verlag, Germany

Nikolaus von Preradovich Österreichs Höhere SS-Führer (1987) Kurt Vowinckel Verlag, Germany

Richard Schulze-Kossens The Junkerschools, Officer Training In The Waffen-SS (1987)Munin-Verlag, 2nd Ed., Germany

Felix Steiner <u>Die Freiwilligen; Der Waffen-SS, Idee und Opfergang</u> (1973) Verlag K.W. Schütz, 5th Ed, Germany

Wilhelm Tieke <u>Im Lufttransport An Brennpunkte der Ostfront</u> (1971) Munin-Verlag, Germany

Wilhelm Tieke <u>Tragödie um die Treue</u> (1978) 3rd Ed, Munin-Verlag, Germany

Wilhelm Tieke <u>Das Ende Zwischen Oder And Elbe</u> (1981) Motorbuch Verlag, Germany

Wilhelm Tieke <u>Nachträge zu den Truppengeschichten</u> (1987) Tieke, Germany

Periodicals consulted included many issues of <u>Der Freiwillige</u> 1959-1995 and <u>Siegrunen</u> 1976-1996.

Most of the photos and much additional material in this book comes from the extensive archives on the Danish Waffen-SS volunteers belonging to H T Nielsen, the co-author of this work.

Publisher's Acknowledgements

Mr David Adams, of Lindley, Adams & Co Accountants, Crown Street, Halifax

Mr Anthony H Ball, Mr Chris Day and Mr Richard Hepponstall for their advice and support;

Miss Kizzy Hanson for tidying up the original manuscript;

Mr Geoff Ingham of Barclays Bank, Halifax;

Mrs D A Lewthwaite for her unending support and generosity;

Mr Pram Mistry;

Dr Peter Rowley-Conwy for assistance with Danish spellings;

Mrs Rūta Teteris for devising the Latvian language guide;

Mr Alec Toomsalu for devising the Estonian language guide;

Piero, Michele and the staff of the Candia Café, 113 Legrams Lane, Bradford;

Mr Alex Warden and the staff of Trafford Press, Manchester;

Miss Cheryll Wood - Shelf Books organiser.

INDEX

—A—

Albrecht, SS-*Hauptscharführer*, 124
Aronious, SS-*Untersturmführer*, 71
Austria, 147, 154
    Feldbach, 53
    Klagenfurt, 135
    Vienna, 80, 135, 136, 137

—B—

Bachmann, SS-*Untersturmführer*, 153
Bachmeier, SS-*Hauptsturmführer*, 111
Bergfeldt, SS-*Sturmbannführer* Albert, 120, 125, 130, 149, 156
Berthelsen, SS-*Untersturmführer*, 90
Bertramsen, SS-*Untersturmführer* Kaj A H, 62, 70, 73
Birkedahl-Hansen, SS-*Obersturmführer*, 130, 142, 153
Bockelberg, SS-*Obersturmbannführer*, 109
Borum, SS-*Rottenführer*, 83
Broberg, SS-*Obersturmführer* Poul Victor, 50
Brørup, SS-*Untersturmführer* Erik, 13, 15
Bünte, SS-*Untersturmführer* F, 13
Busse, *General*, 122

—C—

Christensen, SS-*Hauptscharführer*, 118
Christensen, SS-*Untersturmführer*, 152
Christophersen, SS-*Unterscharführer* Egon, 90, 91, 93
Clausen, SS-*Untersturmführer* Olav, 20
Collani, SS-*Obersturmbannführer* Hans, 87, 111
Croatia, 9, 12, 44, 45, 46, 47, 50, 51, 52, 54, 55, 59, 61, 62, 63, 135
    Bosanski Novi, 43
    Glina, 43, 45
    Hrastovica, 45
    Karlovac, 43, 63
    Ogulin, 43
    Petrinja, 43, 45, 50, 51, 52, 54, 55, 57, 63
    Samobor, 43, 63
    Sisak, 43
    Zagreb, 43
Czechoslovakia
    Bohemia, 63
    Prague, 9

—D—

Dahl, SS-*Unterscharführer* Aage, 39, 41, 42, 81, 82, 83, 84
Dall, SS-*Obersturmführer* Christian, 20, 135
Darm, SS-*Untersturmführer*, 77
Degrelle, SS-*Standartenführer* Léon, 117, 144
Denmark, 7, 8, 11, 12, 16, 19, 20, 44, 45, 47, 49, 53, 62, 73, 92, 134, 135, 153
    Copenhagen, 20, 47, 62, 113
    Odense, 48
Dirksen, SS-*Untersturmführer*, 149, 153

—E—

Eggers, SS-*Untersturmführer* Freiherr, 13
Elfsen, SS-*Untersturmführer*, 110
Erichsen, SS-*Untersturmführer* Georg, 20
Estonia, 18, 64, 77, 89, 100, 107, 110, 117, 137
    Auga, 78
    Auvere, 107
    Hundinurga, 107, 108, 109, 110, 111
    Kirikuküla, 109
    Kohtla-Järve, 97, 118
    Kudruküla, 78
    Lembitu, 107
    Lipsu, 103
    Mereküla, 86
    Narva, 53, 68, 69, 77, 78, 87, 89, 90, 95, 96, 97, 98, 99, 100, 101, 102, 104, 108, 109, 111, 117, 137
    Dolgaya Niva, 87, 89, 90, 91
    Hermannsburg, 77, 96
    Ivangorod, 77, 78
    Kreenholm, 87, 89
    Lilienbach, 87
    Natalin, 91
    Narva-Jõesuu (Hungerburg), 64, 65, 76, 77, 78, 102, 104
    Padoga, 76
    Pärnu, 118, 119
    Rakvere, 108, 118
    Repniku, 104
    Riigi, 78, 102, 103
    River Em, 117
    River Narva, 64, 76, 77, 78, 79, 87, 89, 101, 102, 103, 105, 118
    Saksamaa, 104
    Siivertsi, 78, 79
    Sillamäe, 118
    Soldino, 104
    Sooküla, 107

Index

Tallinn, 78, 89, 119
Tartu, 117
Tirtsu, 107, 108, 110
Usküla, 91
Vaivara, 102, 104, 108
Vanaküla, 103, 104
Vepsküla, 79

—F—

Feilberg, *SS-Untersturmführer* Kaj Gustav, 135
Fenger, *SS-Untersturmführer* E, 13
Finland, 63, 64, 65, 69, 76, 78, 86, 90, 102, 105, 117
Fischer, *SS-Sturmbannführer*, 45, 77
Frederiksen, *SS-Obersturmführer* Johannes, 23, 26, 31, 100
Frühauf, *SS-Hauptsturmführer*, 105

—G—

Gerls, *SS-Untersturmführer*, 13
German Army, 68, 86, 111
  Armies
    3 Panzer-Armee, 147
    11 Panzer-Armee, 138, 141, 147
    18 Armee, 63, 64, 66, 101
  Army Groups
    Army Group Centre, 101, 117
    Army Group North, 76, 101, 117, 121, 122
  Battalions
    Armee-Abteilung *Narwa*, 101, 102, 104, 117, 118, 119
    Armee-Abteilung *Steiner*, 153
    Aufklärungs-Abteilung 115, 144
    Panzer-Lehr-Abteilung, 9
    Schwere Panzer-Abteilung 502, 78
  Corps
    I Armeekorps, 122
    II Armeekorps, 118
  Divisions
    4 Panzer-Division, 124
    11 Infanterie-Division, 102, 105, 111, 120, 121, 123
    14 Panzer-Division, 120, 130
    30 Infanterie-Division, 123, 124, 125
    225 Infanterie-Division, 120, 121
    281 Infanterie-Division, 138
    Division zbV 300, 118, 119
  Establishments
    Panzertruppenschule *Putlos*, 9
    Panzertruppenschule *Wünsdorf*, 9
Germany, 11, 89, 119, 122, 131, 138, 145, 150, 155
  Altdamm, 145, 146
  Alt-Künkendorf, 147
  Altlandsberg, 149
  Arnswalde, 139, 140, 141

Arys, 9
Augustwalde, 145
Bad Freienwalde, 147
Barskewitz, 142
Bavaria, 9
Bayreuth, 11
Berlin, 16, 147, 149, 150, 151, 152, 153, 154, 156, 158
  Anhalt Railway Station, 153
  Belle-Alliance-Platz, 153
  Berlin Zoo, 153
  Cottbuses Tor, 153
  Friedrichstraße, 153
  Führer Bunker, 152
  Hallescher Platz, 153
  Jungfernheide, 152
  Karlshorst, 150
  Kochstraße, 153
  Köllnische Heide, 151
  Landwehr Canal, 151
  Neukölln, 150, 151, 152
  Niederschöneweide, 151
  Prinz-Albrecht-Straße, 154
  Puttkamerstraße, 153
  Reichs Chancellery, 152
  Reichsbank, 153
  Teltow Canal, 152
  Tiergarten, 150, 153
  Treptow Park, 151
  Weidendamm Bridge, 154
Bonin, 140
Büche, 142
Buchholz, 149, 150
Buckow, 148
Christinenberg, 145
Daarz, 144
Dahlow, 142
Dahlwitz, 150
Dömitz, 154
East Prussia, 122
Eberswalde, 149
Erlangen, 9
Falkenberg, 143
Finow Canal, 153
Freienwalde, 142, 143
Friederichsdorf, 145
Garzau, 148
Gielsdorf, 148, 149
Groß Starlitz Lake, 143
Grunewald, 150
Gut Marienfelde, 140
Hannover, 93
Hassendorf, 138
Hermersdorf, 148
Herzfelde, 150
Highway 104, 145
Highway 158, 142

Hinzendorf, 144
Hohenkrug, 145, 146
Hohenlandin, 147
Hohenstein, 148
Hoppegarten, 150
Kannenberg, 143
Karlsbach, 144
Karolinenhorst, 144
Ketzin, 154
Kulmbach, 11
   Schloß Plassenburg, 11
Küstrin, 147
Lake Damm, 145
Lake Ihna, 139
Lake Madü, 138, 139
Lake Müggel, 150
Lange-Berge, 141
Lübow, 144
Ludwigslust, 154
Lüttgenhagen, 145
Mahlsdorf, 149
Marienbad, 48
Marienfließ, 142
Marienwerder, 140
Massow, 144
Mulkenthin, 144
Neuenhagen, 150
Nieder-Finow, 149
Nöblin, 143
Nürnberg, 8, 9
Oberhof, 145
Oberschöneweide, 150
Pichelsdorf, 152
Plötzensee, 152
Pomerania, 146, 147
Reichenbach, 139
Resehl, 144
River Faule Ihna, 141
River Ihna, 138, 139, 141, 144
River Oder, 145, 146, 147
River Spree, 150, 151, 152, 153
Rosengarten, 146
Rosenow, 144
Saarow, 144
Schlagenthin, 139
Schöneberg, 141
Schönwerder, 140, 141
Schwabach, 8
Schwedt, 147
Schwerin, 149
Seefeld, 144
Sommersdorf, 147
Stargard, 140, 141, 142, 143
Steinhöfel, 143
Stettin, 138, 141, 144, 146
Stolzenfelde, 140
Stör Canal, 149

Strausberg, 148, 149
Streesen, 141
Stutthof, 146
Thuringia, 9
Tornow, 141
Trampke, 142
Upper Franconia, 7, 11
Voßberg, 143
Warnemünde, 153
Wattin, 147
Wittenfelde, 143
Wussow, 147
Gordon, *SS-Untersturmführer*, 141
Groß, *SS-Obersturmbannführer*, 141
Gürz, *SS-Hauptsturmführer* Martin, 121
Gyldenkrone, *SS-Untersturmführer* Emil Freiherr, 13

—H—

Hämel, *SS-Hauptsturmführer* Heinz, 13, 18, 45, 70, 90, 91, 94, 108, 157
Hansen, *SS-Hauptsturmführer* K I, 11, 14
Hansen, *SS-Rottenführer* Helge, 80
Hansen, *SS-Untersturmführer* Robert, 61, 74
Hartmann-Lauterbacher, *Gauleiter*, 93
Hazal, *SS-Untersturmführer*, 13
Hecht, *SS-Untersturmführer*, 13, 15
Hein, *SS-Obersturmführer*, 13, 25, 68
Hektor, *SS-Oberscharführer* Albert, 113
Helmers, *SS-Obersturmführer* Johannes, 134
Hennecke, *SS-Hauptsturmführer* Heinz, 13, 68, 75
Herlov-Nielsen, *SS-Untersturmführer*, 70
Hermann, *SS-Sturmscharführer*, 152
Himmler, *Reichsführer-SS und Chef der Deutschen Polizei* Heinrich, 7
HIPO, 45
Hitler Youth, 148
Hitler, Adolf, 7, 66, 117, 122, 153
Hoel, *SS-Hauptsturmführer*, 69
Holtkamp, *SS-Hauptsturmführer*, 69
Huescke, *SS-Unterscharführer*, 83
Hungary
   Budapest, 89
Hvenekilde, *SS-Oberscharführer*, 65

—I—

Ihle, *SS-Unterscharführer* Fritz, 53, 136
Illum, *SS-Oberscharführer*, 152
Italian Army, 43

—J—

Jacobsen, *SS-Sturmmann* Erik, 81
Jensen, *SS-Oberscharführer* Albert, 113, 114, 158
Jensen, *SS-Untersturmführer* H P, 13

Index

Jessen, *SS-Untersturmführer*, 112
Johannsen, *SS-Unterscharführer* Jørgen, 72
Jonstrup, *SS-Unterscharführer* Alfred, 60, 84, 127, 128, 129, 132, 133
Jörchel, *SS-Obersturmbannführer* Wolfgang, 87
Jørgensen, *SS-Rottenführer*, 109
Jørgensen, *SS-Untersturmführer*, 13

—K—

Kanstrup, *SS-Rottenführer* Arne, 40, 44, 46
Kappus, *SS-Sturmbannführer*, 105
Karl, *SS-Obersturmbannführer* Friedrich, 89
Kausch, *SS-Obersturmbannführer* Paul-Albert, 9, 111, 151
Kleinheisterkamp, *SS-Obergruppenführer und Generalleutnant der Waffen-SS* Matthias, 101
Klotz, *SS-Obersturmbannführer* Rudolf, 147, 148, 149, 156
Koeppen, *SS-Untersturmführer* Peter, 20
Kogelgruber, *SS-Hauptsturmführer*, 13
Koopman, *SS-Untersturmführer*, 91
Körbel, *SS-Obersturmbannführer*, 152
Krebs, *General*, 154
Kreutel, *SS-Oberscharführer* Oskar, 75
Kriegsmarine, 86, 105
Krügel, *SS-Obersturmbannführer* Albrecht, 89, 92, 121, 125, 126, 129, 139, 140, 146
Krukenberg, *SS-Brigadeführer und Generalmajor der Waffen-SS* Dr Gustav, 152, 153
Kruse, *SS-Untersturmführer*, 146
Kryssing, *SS-Brigadeführer und Generalmajor der Waffen-SS* Christian Poul, 64, 69, 74, 78, 86
Kure, *SS-Untersturmführer* Ole Peter, 13, 17, 23, 26

—L—

Landmesser, *SS-Untersturmführer*, 13
Lang, *SS-Sturmbannführer* Franz, 9
Langendorf, *SS-Obersturmführer* Georg, 93
Largen, *SS-Untersturmführer* V E, 13
Larsen, *SS-Rottenführer* Egon, 137, 153
Larsen, *SS-Sturmmann* Svend, 158
Larsen, *SS-Untersturmführer* H, 13
Lärum, *SS-Hauptsturmführer* Erik, 70, 73, 74, 90, 108, 109
Latvia, 117, 119, 138
  Annenhof, 123
  Asenbergi, 121
  Auce, 127
  Baldone, 120
  Cempulli, 120
  Daugavpils, 117
  Dekmeri, 121
  Dobele, 121
  Goldnieki, 124
  Gramzda, 125, 126
  Grudulis, 123, 126
  Gulbji, 119
  Jēkabpils, 101
  Jelgava, 121
  Kalēti, 123
  Katlapaji, 121
  Kelputi, 125, 126
  Kirkstal, 123
  Klein-Trekni, 123
  Kurland (Kurzeme), 20, 75, 121, 122, 123, 125, 129, 130, 131
  Lidakas, 119, 120
  Liepāja, 123, 124, 138
  Maki, 124
  Ozoli, 123
  Priekule, 123, 124, 126, 130, 138
  Purmsāti, 123, 124, 125, 126, 127, 130
  Riga, 19, 119, 121, 122
  River Apše, 123
  River Daugava, 119, 122
  River Kekāva, 119, 120
  Susta, 124
  Tigurgas, 119
  Trekni, 123, 124, 125, 126
  Trusi-Trekni, 123
  Tukums, 121
  Vaiņode, 123
  Vaici, 120
Laursen, *SS-Unterscharführer*, 130
Lercke, *SS-Obersturmführer* Grev, 82
Lindemann, *Generaloberst*, 63
Lithuania
  Skuodas, 123, 126
Lotze, *SS-Obersturmführer* Dr Konrad, 13, 19
Luftwaffe, 64, 66, 68, 149
  9 Fallschirmjäger-Division, 148
  9 Feld-Division, 63, 64, 66
  10 Feld-Division, 63, 64, 66
  13 Feld-Division, 118
  Fallschirmjäger-Regiment *Schacht*, 143, 145
  III Feldkorps, 63
Lührs, *SS-Hauptsturmführer* Hermann, 152
Lund, *SS-Untersturmführer* Ove, 158

—M—

Madsen, *SS-Untersturmführer* Leo Anton, 73, 90, 104, 110, 140
Martinsen, *SS-Obersturmbannführer* Knud Borge, 11, 12, 13, 14, 21, 22, 24, 27, 40, 45, 47, 62
Meggl, *SS-Hauptsturmführer*, 105
Meier, *Kreisleiter*, 93
Meier, *SS-Hauptsturmführer*, 108
Mellenthin, *SS-Unterscharführer*, 107
Meyer, *SS-Obersturmführer*, 13, 54
Model, *Generalfeldmarschall* Walter, 66, 76

Mohr, Danish Ambassador, 11, 12, 31, 32, 33
Moira, Troopship, 138
Mortensen, *SS-Rottenführer* Andreas, 60
Mühlenkamp, *SS-Obersturmbannführer* Johannes-Rudolf, 9
Mussolini, Benito, 43

—N—

Neergard-Jacobsen, *SS-Sturmbannführer*, 11, 13, 15, 21, 25, 30, 38, 45, 54, 70, 77
Nielsen, *SS-Rottenführer* Jens Peter, 84, 85
Nielsen, *SS-Sturmmann* Carl, 48
Nielsen, *SS-Unterscharführer* Holger Thor, 38, 48, 49, 53
Nielsen, *SS-Unterscharführer* Svend, 80, 120
Nielsen, *SS-Unterscharführer* Vagn Thor, 80, 97
Noach, *SS-Oberscharführer*, 124
Norreen, *SS-Obersturmführer* Octavious Righardt Holger, 44, 45, 46, 47
Norway, 7
Nugiseks, *Waffen-Unterscharführer* Harald, 79

—O—

Olesen, *SS-Unterscharführer* Kaj, 114, 160
Olsen, *SS-Mann* J, 83, 84

—P—

Pehrsson, *SS-Obersturmführer*, 125
Petersen, *SS-Obersturmführer* Jens Wilhelm, 13, 151
Petersen, *SS-Unterscharführer*, 19
Poland
    Dębica, 7
Pösch, *SS-Oberscharführer*, 143
Positions
    Grenadier Hill, 102, 105, 109, 110, 111, 118
    Hill 17.1, 123
    Hill 28.3, 125, 126
    Hill 39.1, 123
    Hill 69.9, 105, 108, 109, 118
    Hill 84, 143
    Horse Head Hill, 123
    Marienburg Line, 101
    Orphanage Hill, 102, 105, 107, 108, 109, 110
    Outpost *Fir Hedge*, 89
    Outpost *Sunshine*, 89, 90, 91, 101
    Panther Positions, 65
    Tannenberg Positions, 78, 101, 102, 103, 104, 105, 107, 108, 109, 110, 111, 117, 118
Poulsen, *SS-Obersturmführer* Egil, 13, 16, 17, 25, 50

—R—

Rantzau-Engelhardt, *SS-Obersturmbannführer* P, 64, 71, 86, 118, 119
Rasmussen, *SS-Hauptsturmführer* Ellef Henry, 145, 149, 154
Rasmussen, *SS-Untersturmführer* Ellef, 157
Red Army, 65, 66, 68, 70, 76, 77, 79, 86, 87, 90, 101, 102, 103, 104, 105, 107, 109, 110, 111, 117, 118, 119, 120, 121, 122, 123, 124, 125, 126, 127, 129, 130, 138, 139, 140, 141, 142, 143, 144, 145, 147, 148, 149, 150, 151, 152, 153, 154
    2nd Baltic Front, 65, 101
    2nd Storm Army, 63, 66
    8th Army, 76
Remer, *Generalmajor*, 139
Riedler, *SS-Untersturmführer*, 25
Riedweg, *SS-Obersturmbannführer* Dr Franz, 108
Roensch, *SS-Hauptsturmführer*, 71
Rossmann, *SS-Hauptsturmführer* Willi, 14, 81, 125
Rott, *SS-Obersturmführer*, 13
Rühle von Lilienstern, *SS-Hauptsturmführer* Hans-Joachim, 68

—S—

Saalbach, *SS-Sturmbannführer* Rudolf, 20, 68, 117, 119, 153, 154
Salskov, *SS-Untersturmführer* Jørgen, 13, 32, 50
Schacht, *Major*, 145
Schäfer, *SS-Obersturmführer*, 13
Scheibe, *SS-Sturmbannführer*, 109
Schmidichen, *SS-Untersturmführer*, 69
Scholles, *SS-Unterscharführer*, 151
Schoofs, *SS-Obersturmführer*, 143
Schörner, *Generaloberst*, 117, 122
Schramm, *SS-Obersturmführer*, 13
Schrijnen, *SS-Sturmmann* Remi, 110
Schröder, *SS-Untersturmführer*, 13
Schulz-Streeck, *Hauptmann* Dr Karl-Heinz, 71
Schwabenburg, *SS-Hauptscharführer*, 118, 124, 125
Seebach, *SS-Obersturmführer* Walter, 13, 17, 25, 27, 30, 42, 56, 57, 76
Sidon, *SS-Obersturmführer* Fritz, 68, 157
Sommer, *SS-Unterscharführer* Preben, 114, 160
Sørensen, *SS-Sturmbannführer* Per, 13, 16, 24, 68, 125, 127, 130, 139, 140, 141, 142, 143, 144, 145, 147, 148, 149, 150, 151, 152, 157
Spahn, *SS-Untersturmführer* Robert, 75
Spleth, *SS-Untersturmführer*, 101
Sporck, *SS-Rottenführer* Kasper, 68, 78
SS
    Establishments
        Beneschau Training Ground, 9, 63
        Dresden Engineer Training Ground, 8

Index

Grafenwöhr Training Ground, 7, 8, 11, 12, 21, 28, 31, 33, 34, 42, 47, 100
Hammerstein Training Ground, 138
Heidelager Training Ground, 7
Hradischko Training Ground, 8, 9
Nürnberg Training Ground, 8
Sennheim Training Ground, 9
SS-Junkerschule *Bad Tölz*, 14, 20, 134, 135, 137
Germanische-SS
   Schalburg-Korps, 12, 16, 47
   Vagtbataillon Sjaelland, 16
Waffen-SS, 7, 8, 9, 11, 12, 43, 66, 70, 71, 86, 89, 111, 118, 139, 140, 143, 144, 145, 150, 151, 155
   Battalions
      I/5 SS-Frw.Stu.Bde *Wallonien*, 117
      I/SS-Pz.Gren.Rgt.23 *Norge*, 8, 66, 70, 89
      I/SS-Pz.Gren.Rgt.24 *Danmark*, 16, 19, 40, 43, 45, 46, 47, 52, 62, 65, 66, 68, 71, 77, 87, 89, 147, 154, 157
      I/SS-Pz.Gren.Rgt.48 *General Seyffardt*, 68
      I/SS-Pz.Gren.Rgt.49 *De Ruyter*, 102
      I/SS-Rgt. *Nordland*, 8
      I/SS-Rgt.66, 140
      I/Waf.Gren.Rgt.d.SS 47, 108
      II/SS-Art.Rgt.11, 124, 126
      II/SS-Pz.Gren.Rgt.23 *Norge*, 8, 89, 105, 109, 123, 124, 130, 139
      II/SS-Pz.Gren.Rgt.24 *Danmark*, 16, 18, 45, 66, 69, 71, 72, 75, 76, 77, 80, 81, 85, 87, 89, 90, 91, 94, 107, 108, 113, 114, 120, 121, 123, 125, 130, 139, 140, 141, 142, 143, 144, 145, 146, 147, 148, 149, 152, 154, 156, 157, 158
      II/SS-Pz.Gren.Rgt.48 *General Seyffardt*, 68
      II/SS-Pz.Gren.Rgt.49 *De Ruyter*, 102, 105, 123
      II/SS-Rgt. *Nordland*, 8
      III/SS-Art.Rgt.11, 70
      III/SS-Pz.Gren.Rgt.23 *Norge*, 8, 63, 77, 105, 107, 121, 123, 124
      III/SS-Pz.Gren.Rgt.24 *Danmark*, 15, 38, 45, 47, 54, 55, 65, 69, 70, 71, 77, 87, 105, 107, 108, 109, 110, 120, 121, 123, 124, 125, 127, 130, 140, 141, 142, 144, 145, 146, 147, 148, 149, 152, 156
      III/SS-Pz.Gren.Rgt.49 *De Ruyter*, 123
      III/SS-Rgt.9 *Germania*, 43
      Schwere SS-Panzer-Abteilung 503, 137, 153
      SS-Ersatzbataillon Germania, 53
      SS-Feldersatz-Bataillon 11, 9, 127
      SS-Fla-Abteilung 11, 9, 145, 146
      SS-Kampfbataillon *Charlemagne*, 152
      SS-Nachrichten-Abteilung 11, 8
      SS-Panzer-Abteilung 11 *Hermann von Salza*, 8, 9, 17, 43, 46, 63, 65, 68, 69, 82, 87, 103, 110, 111, 121, 143
      SS-Panzer-Aufklärungs-Abteilung 11, 8, 20, 46, 53, 63, 66, 68, 69, 78, 86, 117, 119, 153
      SS-Panzerjäger-Abteilung 11, 8, 66, 70, 71, 138, 140
      SS-Pionier-Bataillon 11, 8, 66, 70, 87, 103, 145, 148, 151
      SS-Pionier-Bataillon 54, 78, 87, 123, 127, 143
      SS-Skijäger-Bataillon *Norge*, 90
      SS-Wirtschaft-Bataillon 11, 8, 127
   Brigades
      4 SS-Freiwilligen-Panzergrenadier-Brigade *Nederland*, 7, 9, 64, 65, 66, 68, 69, 71, 77, 78, 87, 102, 104, 105, 107, 109, 111, 117, 118, 119, 122, 123
      5 SS-Freiwilligen-Sturmbrigade *Wallonien*, 117
      6 SS-Freiwilligen-Sturmbrigade *Langemarck*, 102, 105, 107, 108, 110
      SS-Infanterie-Brigade 1 (mot), 11
      SS-Infanterie-Brigade 2 (mot), 8
   Companies
      1/SS-Pi.Btl.11, 66, 89
      1/SS-Pz.Abt.11 *Hermann von Salza*, 87
      1/SS-Pz.Gren.Rgt.24 *Danmark*, 19, 34, 40, 45, 47, 100
      2/SS-Pi.Btl.11, 66
      2/SS-Pz.Gren.Rgt.24 *Danmark*, 34, 53, 136
      3/SS-Felders.Btl.11, 127
      3/SS-Pz.Aufkl.Abt.11, 125
      3/SS-Pz.Gren.Rgt.24 *Danmark*, 35, 68
      4/SS-Pz.Gren.Rgt.24 *Danmark*, 35, 45
      5/SS-Art.Abt.11, 86
      5/SS-Pz.Aufkl.Abt.11, 78
      5/SS-Pz.Gren.Rgt.24 *Danmark*, 16, 17, 19, 35, 45, 50, 76, 108, 125, 126, 127, 139, 143, 144, 149
      6/SS-Pz.Gren.Rgt.24 *Danmark*, 36, 48, 73, 80, 108, 118, 120, 121, 125, 126, 130, 139, 140, 143, 145, 149, 156
      7/SS-Pz.Gren.Rgt.23 *Norge*, 69, 108, 110, 111
      7/SS-Pz.Gren.Rgt.24 *Danmark*, 37, 38, 45, 48, 49, 53, 61, 70, 73, 74, 89, 90, 91, 93, 100, 102, 104, 108, 110, 113, 125, 126, 130, 139, 140, 143, 144, 145, 149
      8/SS-Pz.Gren.Rgt.24 *Danmark*, 17, 66, 75, 108, 109, 114, 126, 130, 139, 145, 146, 148, 149, 150, 153, 157
      9/SS-Pz.Gren.Rgt.23 *Norge*, 111
      9/SS-Pz.Gren.Rgt.24 *Danmark*, 13, 54, 70, 77, 87, 91, 107, 108, 142, 157
      10/SS-Pz.Gren.Rgt.23 *Norge*, 124, 141

10/SS-Pz.Gren.Rgt.24 *Danmark*, 45, 77, 107, 111, 124, 126, 134, 142, 146
11/SS-Pz.Gren.Rgt.23 *Norge*, 79
11/SS-Pz.Gren.Rgt.24 *Danmark*, 39, 73, 81, 104, 105, 107, 109, 110, 111, 120, 121, 124, 126, 130, 146
12/SS-Pz.Gren.Rgt.24 *Danmark*, 82, 109, 126
13/SS-Pz.Gren.Rgt.23 *Norge*, 8, 20, 135
13/SS-Pz.Gren.Rgt.24 *Danmark*, 105, 108, 109, 118, 120, 124, 130, 151, 153
14 (Flak)/SS-Pz.Gren.Rgt.23 *Norge*, 8
14 (Flak)/SS-Pz.Gren.Rgt.24 *Danmark*, 118, 120, 126, 151
15/SS-Pz.Gren.Rgt.23 *Norge*, 8
15/SS-Pz.Gren.Rgt.24 *Danmark*, 148
16 (Pi)/SS-Pz.Gren.Rgt.24 *Danmark*, 8, 63, 65, 69, 71, 76, 79, 100, 140, 148, 149, 150, 152
Alarmkompanie/SS-Pz.Gren.Rgt.24 *Danmark*, 125, 126, 127
Ersatzkompanie/SS-Pz.Gren.Rgt.24 *Danmark*, 148
SS-Bewährungskompanie 103, 111
SS-Vielfach-Werfer-Batterie 521, 107
Corps
    III (Germanische) SS-Panzerkorps, 7, 8, 9, 11, 12, 21, 45, 63, 64, 65, 66, 68, 69, 71, 74, 76, 77, 78, 79, 86, 89, 101, 102, 104, 105, 107, 109, 110, 111, 112, 117, 118, 119, 121, 122, 123, 124, 129, 130, 131, 135, 136, 137, 138, 139, 140, 141, 146, 147, 148, 154
    IV SS-Panzerkorps, 7
    VI Waffen-Armeekorps der SS (*Lettisches*), 129
Divisions
    1 SS-Panzer-Division *Leibstandarte SS Adolf Hitler*, 111
    4 SS-Polizei-Panzergrenadier-Division, 64, 138
    5 SS-Panzer-Division *Wiking*, 7, 8, 9, 11, 20, 43, 48, 53, 64, 70, 74, 80, 89, 134, 147, 154, 157
    6 SS-Gebirgs-Division *Nord*, 90
    10 SS-Panzer-Division *Frundsberg*, 138, 139, 145
    11 SS-Freiwilligen-Panzergrenadier-Division *Nordland*, 7, 8, 9, 11, 17, 18, 43, 53, 56, 64, 65, 66, 68, 69, 70, 71, 76, 77, 78, 87, 89, 104, 107, 108, 109, 110, 111, 112, 117, 118, 119, 120, 122, 123, 124, 125, 127, 129, 130, 138, 139, 140, 141, 142, 143, 144, 145, 147, 148, 149, 150, 151, 152, 153, 154, 158
    20 Waffen-Grenadier-Division der SS (*estnische Nr 1*), 78, 79, 102, 105, 108, 111, 119
    23 SS-Freiwilligen-Panzergrenadier-Division *Nederland*, 130, 138, 141, 142, 143, 144, 145
    27 SS-Freiwilligen-Grenadier-Division *Langemarck*, 138, 140, 141, 145
    28 SS-Freiwilligen-Grenadier-Division *Wallonien*, 138, 141, 142, 144, 145, 146
    33 SS-Freiwilligen-Grenadier-Division *Charlemagne*, 152
    38 SS-Panzergrenadier-Division *Nibelungen*, 135
    Führer-Begleit-Division, 138, 139
    Führer-Grenadier Division, 138
    SS-Division *Totenkopf*, 7, 64
Kampfgruppen
    Panzergruppe *Saalbach*, 117
    SS-Kampfgruppe *Aigner*, 123
    SS-Kampfgruppe *Bachmann*, 153
    SS-Kampfgruppe *Kausch*, 103
    SS-Kampfgruppe *Küste*, 64, 69, 71, 77, 78, 86
    SS-Kampfgruppe *Langemarck*, 138
    SS-Kampfgruppe *Sørensen*, 126, 127
    SS-Kampfgruppe *Wagner*, 117
    SS-Kampfgruppe *Wallonien*, 138, 141
Legions
    Dutch, 8
    Flemish, 8
    Freikorps Danmark, 7, 8, 11, 12, 14, 15, 16, 17, 18, 19, 21, 22, 23, 24, 31, 33, 38, 48, 52, 59, 60, 64, 68, 73, 74, 80, 85, 90, 100, 113, 114, 121, 127, 130, 133, 152, 158
    Legion Norwegen, 7, 8
Operations
    Operation *Lützow*, 64
    Operation *Stinkfisch*, 89
    Operation Thunder, 121
    Operation Tree Bough, 117
Regiments
    SS-Artillerie-Regiment 11, 8, 65, 66, 69, 70, 71, 89, 90, 127
    SS-Grenadier-Regiment 1 *Danmark*, 8, 11, 43
    SS-Grenadier-Regiment 2 *Norge*, 8, 43
    SS-Panzergrenadier Regiment Schill, 156
    SS-Panzergrenadier-Regiment 23 *Norge*, 43, 63, 64, 65, 66, 69, 70, 71, 77, 78, 79, 86, 87, 104, 105, 121, 124, 125, 139, 144, 148, 151, 152, 153
    SS-Panzergrenadier-Regiment 24 *Danmark*, 8, 9, 11, 12, 13, 14, 15, 16, 25, 28, 31, 32, 33, 38, 43, 45, 48, 55, 63, 64, 65, 71, 77, 78, 83, 84, 87, 90, 97,

Index

100, 101, 102, 103, 104, 105, 107, 112, 118, 119, 121, 124, 125, 126, 127, 130, 133, 138, 139, 140, 141, 142, 146, 147, 148, 149, 150, 151, 152, 153, 154, 156, 157, 158, 159
SS-Panzergrenadier-Regiment 48 *General Seyffardt*, 9, 71, 76, 87, 102, 103, 104
SS-Panzergrenadier-Regiment 49 *De Ruyter*, 9, 87, 103, 104, 105, 111, 119
SS-Panzergrenadier-Regiment 9 *Germania*, 7
SS-Panzer-Regiment 11 *Hermann von Salza*, 143, 147, 151
SS-Polizei Regiment 14, 43
SS-Regiment Deutschland, 157
SS-Regiment *Nordland*, 7, 8, 11
Steiner, *SS-Obergruppenführer und General der Waffen-SS* Felix, 8, 9, 11, 21, 22, 24, 28, 29, 30, 31, 32, 55, 56, 57, 58, 65, 76, 77, 109, 111, 119, 138, 141, 147, 149
Stenger, *SS-Obersturmführer*, 13, 25, 27
Stoffers, *SS-Obersturmbannführer* Arnold, 86
Strupp, *SS-Rottenführer* Walter, 81
Szwerinski, *SS-Untersturmführer*, 13

—T—

Tebring, *SS-Sturmmann* Kurt, 82
Ternedde, *SS-Sturmbannführer* Rudolf, 13, 17, 40, 92, 121, 124, 127, 140, 146, 147, 148, 149, 150, 152, 153, 154, 156
Thorgils, *SS-Obersturmführer* Knud, 13, 31, 32
Thorius, *SS-Obersturmführer*, 13, 25, 82
Thorkildsen, *SS-Obersturmführer*, 112, 142, 146
Tito, 9, 43, 45
Trautwein, *SS-Hauptsturmführer*, 104, 105, 107, 110

—U—

Unrein, *General* Martin, 138, 141
USSR, 11
  Alyexyeyevka, 71
  Babruisk, 11, 14, 73
  Byegunitsy, 69
  Dolgaya Niva, 64, 66
  Dyatlitsy, 66, 68
  Globitsy, 64
  Gomontovo, 69
  Gorbovitsy, 64, 65, 69
  Gubanitsy, 68, 69
  Gurlovo, 70, 71
  Kapylosha, 68
  Kastivskoye, 65
  Keikino, 69, 71
  Khulduzy, 68
  Kirovo, 64, 69
  Klopitsy, 63, 64, 68
  Komarovka, 77
  Koporye, 65, 69
  Kotly, 64
  Kronstadt, 65
  Kyernovo, 64
  Kyerstovo, 69, 70
  Lake Ilmen, 63
  Lake Peipus, 76, 118
  Lamokha, 69
  Leningrad, 46, 63, 65, 68
  Litisno, 70
  Lopukhinka, 64, 66
  Opolye, 70, 71
  Oranienbaum, 46, 63, 64, 65, 66, 68, 77, 86, 87
  Ostrov, 69
  Padoga, 71, 76
  Peterhof, 63
  Pskov, 101
  Pyetrovichy, 65
  Rachino, 69, 70
  River Luga, 66, 69, 71, 76, 77, 78
  Ropsha, 65
  Syergovitsy, 70
  Vitino, 66, 68
  Volosovo, 63
  Voronino, 64, 65
  Vyelikino, 69
  Yamburg, 18, 65, 69, 70, 71, 76, 77
  Yukhkoma, 71
  Zaozyorye, 65, 69

—V—

Vandborg, *SS-Oberscharführer*, 146
Volkssturm, 152
Vollmer, *SS-Sturmbannführer*, 7
von Bock und Pollach, *SS-Obersturmbannführer*, 129
von Eggers, *SS-Untersturmführer* Christian Ulrich Ditlev, 75
von Küchler, *Generalfeldmarschall*, 66
von Manteuffel, *General der Panzertruppen* Hasso, 147
von Schalburg, *SS-Obersturmbannführer* C F, 127, 133
von Scholz, *SS-Brigadeführer und Generalmajor der Waffen-SS* Fritz, 8, 18, 56, 69, 70, 72, 94, 108, 109
von Westphalen, *SS-Obersturmbannführer* Hermenegild Graf, 8, 11, 13, 25, 27, 30, 31, 32, 38, 45, 56, 59, 65, 89

—W—

Wagner, *SS-Brigadeführer und Generalmajor der Waffen-SS*, 144

Walther, *SS-Hauptsturmführer* K, 13
Weber, *SS-Standartenoberjunker* Fritz, 137
Wehrmacht, 7, 147
Westergaard, *SS-Unterscharführer* Erik, 19
Wichart, *SS-Hauptsturmführer*, 77
Wichmann, *SS-Hauptsturmführer*, 68
Wild, *SS-Oberscharführer* Philipp, 87
Witten, *SS-Sturmbannführer*, 126, 127
Wojahn, *SS-Hauptsturmführer* Otto, 93
Wolf, *SS-Obersturmführer*, 13
Worsoe Larsen, *SS-Obersturmführer* Bent, 13, 18, 25, 39, 77

—Y—

Yugoslavia, 53

—Z—

Zhukov, Marshal, 147
Ziegler, *SS-Brigadeführer und Generalmajor der Waffen-SS* Joachim, 9, 109, 132, 149, 150, 151, 152, 154